LOUISA C⁻
farm—a co-c
Geoff—in the   ιιs
founding in 2   ..as brought
hundreds of sou   ..ιn seeking guidance
and deep healing. ᴜince childhood, Louisa's aim
has been to help bring peace to the earth. From a very young age
she would sing, seemingly bursting from her soul, 'Make me a
channel of your peace!' Louisa is the author of *A Memory Returned*
(2013, under her pen name Anna Delves), which was written after
the death of her eldest son. She has also written *From Chrysalis
to Butterfly* (2008, also under Anna Delves), which gives the
background to her present work with the retreat. Louisa loves to
walk in the beautiful countryside of the Cotswolds with her dog,
always in close communion with Source. She farms sheep, creating
a level of communication that enables a harmonious relationship
between animal and human being. Louisa has two other children
and several grandchildren.

THE ALPHA
AND THE OMEGA

*How the balance on earth was lost
and is now being restored*

LOUISA CRISP

CLAIRVIEW

Clairview Books Ltd.,
Russet, Sandy Lane,
West Hoathly,
W. Sussex RH19 4QQ

www.clairviewbooks.com

Published by Clairview Books 2023

Colour image on p. 108 by Jennifer Davis
Diagrams by Louisa Crisp
Edited by Sharon Cawood

A CIP catalogue record for this book is available from the British Library

ISBN 978 1 912992 48 5

Cover by Morgan Creative. Photograph by Marc Zimmer
Typeset by Symbiosys Technologies, Visakhapatnam, India
Printed and bound by 4Edge Ltd, Essex

I didn't choose to write this book. It happened through me.

Contents

Acknowledgements

This book could not have been put together without the permission of hundreds of souls coming to the retreat over the last 17 years and bravely unearthing their connection to the time of Jesus. There are also those who have unearthed the pre-Split era and have taught me much as they did so.

While I have decided not to put personal names to paper, most, but not all of you, know who you are and my deepest thanks go to you for everything you have contributed to the book and to my life's journey. We are an unspoken team, who have come together to do this work, having agreed to do so at some level. Now we can hand over our findings and ask that the highest good will come from what we have done.

No doubt more souls will come forward in the future and will help to build a revised edition in due course. But, for now, it seems there is enough here for the universe to put to good use. It feels very timely…

Introduction

Jesus said: 'I am the alpha and the omega, the beginning and the end.'

What I have tried to convey to everyone who reads this book are insights which I originally thought were far too complicated to ever consider putting down on paper. In fact, for many years I thought a brief explanation of the cosmic field as an afterthought in what is now the second part of this book would not go amiss! However, the universal mind knew otherwise. During writing, it has slowly become clear to me why the following two parts of history should be put together in one book. To my enormous surprise, I discovered they tie in! All the help I need has come at the right time, and the right words have been provided to help convey this difficult topic in written form.

The information given in these pages has mostly been awoken in me over time as a result of my contact with all those souls who visit the retreat, and a little has come from general interaction in daily life with friends and family. Guests who come to the retreat are drawn because it feels like the right place for them to heal and it feels like I am the right person to help them. As we sit together over a period of time, they trust me and I trust them and we form a union between us that allows a deep exchange of information. I am able to see what people need to heal in that moment and show them how to go about it. The healing they receive is very profound. Whether they can accept it or not is another matter, although over the years I have become better at putting it across, so happily more and more people 'get' it.

As you read this book, you will see that I regularly refer to the three S's: Swamped, Sun and 'watching' Source. You will understand what these and other terms mean as you begin to engage with the text, but for ease of understanding in the first instance, I have compiled a Glossary which you will find at the back of the book.

Understanding of the Swamped experience came to me very slowly to start with. However, Swamped experience souls just kept on coming to see me and my knowledge began to broaden. After a few months, a batch of Sun experience souls began to arrive. They turned up one after another until I could not ignore the messages they were bringing me. Those who knew me in those early days have watched my understanding grow from next to nothing to what I have written here, with amazement. So have I!

You may find that the first part of the book is beyond you at this time. The two parts of the book can stand alone so if what I have conveyed in the second half is more to your taste, then I suggest skipping the first part and enjoying the second. You can always go back to the first at a later time if you wish.

Note that any names referenced in stories throughout the book have been changed to protect the individuals.

**

I once said to my deceased son: 'Why me? Why should such knowledge as this be given to such an ordinary person as me?' He replied so simply: 'Ordinary is good.'

I now realise that because I had absolutely no prior knowledge on the subject of the cosmos, no scientific background and no desire to even dig into it, I was the perfect empty vessel for the universe to utilise. A high-flying academic visited me in 2020 and after I had explained some cosmic things to her, she looked studiously at me and exclaimed: 'How could you possibly know all these things? I am a scientist and I know a great deal about this, but you, you are no one! How can this be?'

I was not offended; I knew perfectly well what she was saying and agreed with her. But I was also chuffed that she didn't pooh-pooh any of it, in fact she asked me questions! My instinctive approach to her 'learned knowledge' had burst a door open for her. Hopefully, this will be true for many of you too.

Some points to bear in mind as you read this book

The whole of creation comes from Source. How could it not?

Various adventures on the route to conscious oneness have been necessary. They have not taken place in order to destroy, but in order to achieve. You will destroy more than yourself if you do not let go of that which does not serve the highest good.

Be at peace. Know that you are one with the all.

This is the greatest gift to yourself and creation that you can receive.

PART 1

The Alpha—The Beginning of Separation and the Demise of the Lions

1
Is a Joyful Experience on Earth Really Possible?

How do I put into words such mind-blowing events that have been unfolding since the beginning of this cosmic expansion?

What I am going to convey has been consciously coming to me since January 2009. Between 2019 and 2022, understandings have been coming so thick and fast that I have nearly fallen over myself to keep up. But I had a knowing that, after the recent global pandemic, when so much understanding fell into place, I could now attempt what I never thought could be done—a written explanation of all that I know.

The dawning of a joyful way of being is upon us. It is possible for all those who:

> Trust *more* than fear
> Love *more* than hate
> And Believe in the freedom of the soul.
> Conquer these three and the soul will free itself....

We came into this cosmic expansion with a memory based only on fear. As we let go of this fear from every part of our experience, we can exchange our fear base for a joy base. Once we have achieved a joy base, it is in situ forever; it can never be undone.

As there is still so much I don't understand, I can only take you from the point of knowing that this is not the first expansion of our cosmic field; it has happened before.

In a gathering of like-minded people one day, I was trying to explain something to those who were present when I inwardly heard the words, 'This is the eighth expansion.' The words came to my ears faintly and a lot of people were in the room so I was never 100% sure I had heard it correctly. However, many years later, I have had confirmation that this is correct. I now understand more about the previous seven expansions, where and why they ended when they did and that the cosmos is currently expanding further than ever before. The eighth expansion is a more progressed and better version of creation than all the others, but built on the experiences of the others, of course.

I remember a little of the seventh one: we had reached planetary form and had evolved to the nature state at least, though much seemed dark. In the glimpse that I had, I saw trees growing in tangles and choking each other with their roots and branches as each feared the others' existence. The intense state of fear that nature lived in resulted in everything eventually killing the other off, until nothing was left and the whole seventh experiment was over. It then began to contract back to nothingness.

As this experiment played out and approached the brink of nothingness yet again, it, 'we', made a definitive decision: 'If ever we expand again, we have to find another way. We must *never again* do this governed by fear, so horrendous has it been. There must be another way.'

And with that we vanished back into nothingness, with a mere memory of our experience and a spark of resolve left to be reignited, should there ever be a future venture into consciousness.

However, we are a tenacious bunch. Having found being-ness in the first place, rediscovering that nothing-ness was absolutely no fun, we were restless and all we, collectively, wanted to do was try again.

Of course, before long, nothingness or 'no-thing-ness' got fed up with this state, and here we were—experiencing again.

An Aside

There was a moment when I sank into the full experience of nothingness, thinking it would be pure peace and perfect bliss, but it wasn't—it was the very opposite: it was nothing, non-existence, emptiness; it was horrible. I must have called inwardly for help for suddenly I found myself back in being-ness again.

May the words written in this book speak to your heart as you read, for they are truth—the truth as best as I can convey it at this time. At a later date, others will impart this wisdom in a different, perhaps clearer, way, and so evolution rolls on.

2

The Start of the Eighth Expansion—and the Big Bang which Followed

This latest expansion began once again in the core of the memory of nothingness. There was a yearning to exist, a yearning to find a better way through the mires that we had experienced so far. It was not a conscious yearning, and therefore no memories were conscious as we yearned, but that yearning caused the density within nothingness to alter: 50% of it became thinner and thinner and 50% became thicker and thicker. The process continued as the yearning continued and a certain set of emotions were experienced in the collective field. For instance, there was a sense of being unable to control what was going on, which made everything feel vulnerable. It felt lost in the process and a deep terror dawned. The process continued until eventually the thick and the thin elements broke free of one another. The thicker version had become what we now call 'matter' and the thinner version what we call 'energy'.

There was cautious rejoicing in the collective field. Energy (the thinner version) was looking at matter, and matter (the thicker version) was looking at energy, each knowing they were different, and that gave us (the collective) consciousness or a knowing that we existed. It was when this separation occurred that we had our first experience of duality in this expansion of the cosmos. However, it quickly dawned on both matter and energy that the two sides could not live for long without reintegrating with each other, and that this state of separation could only be temporary. This was because energy discovered it could not *experience* without being in matter, and matter discovered it could not *move* without being energised.

The Big Bang

Just as these realisations were becoming conscious, matter, in its frustration around not being able to move, started to crack and crack again, irritating itself with the feeling of contact with another part of itself. The cracks started to open up wider and eventually the whole field of matter exploded into the experience we now call the Big Bang. The parts of matter, as they separated, knocked and banged ruthlessly against each other, forming shapes of differing sizes. In this terrifying and out-of-control manner, they became what we call the planets of today. Meanwhile, energy was helplessly scattered through the process and found itself spinning all over the place. In this way, matter became the first perpetrator of our experience and the victim of its actions was energy, thus beginning the perpetrator/victim pattern that is present throughout the cosmic field today.

This huge and uncontrollable shifting in matter caused the collective energy to experience shock, anger, fear and panic. The enormous *shock* came from the fact that we appeared to be repeating the seventh expansion, when this was not what we had signed up for. We were so *angry*. We did not want to go through another seventh expansion experience. It had been horrific. Why had we allowed ourselves to do this, when we had asked, within ourselves, for something different? Why, oh, why do we have to do this again? The *fear* path that seemingly lay ahead of us was too much for us, so we *panicked* and cried out in the agony of the moment: 'No, no, no, no, noooo!' We were inconsolable. What had happened to the 'other', easier way we had wanted to experience as we approached the close of the seventh expansion?

Judgement

The truth is that, at the end of the seventh expansion, we had judged the suffering and fear we had experienced as *wrong*. We had automatically assumed that in the next expansion we would emerge immediately into 'another' way. And here we were, expanding again with what seemed like the same old fear in the driving seat. Our trust and balance went out of the window in a trice. It seemed like a downhill slope for us from that moment onwards.

What we hadn't realised was that, while we had created fear for ourselves in a different expansion and yes, we could change it, we had to create that change! The only way forward was to expand again in exactly the same mould as we had left off and then allow 'another' way to emerge as we let go of fear and created a space for the 'other way' to flourish.

This judgement or sense that something wasn't quite right has caused us huge problems. The anger that this expansion was not as hoped for and that we were forced to suffer again was intense. As the great splits formed through the dense matter, they creaked and groaned and eventually blew apart, causing the big ball of matter to become several parts. As the emotions only increased from this point, the cracks continued to appear and separate. Large formations of matter bumped and banged against each other, setting off clouds of black dust into the ether and causing all sorts of further break-offs. And so the planets came slowly into being, becoming smaller and smaller in size as they bounced off each other. In their terror, they were slowly pushing each other further and further into space, the gaps between them gradually becoming greater and thus the collisions becoming fewer.

My Own Experience of the Big Bang

One evening, very unexpectedly, I was taken back into a personal memory of the Big Bang. This experience lies deep in all of us and, although we all carry the memory, it is rarely brought to the forefront of our minds. However, on this occasion and at this specific time, the universe clearly wished me to remember it. (I had probably asked to know what the Big Bang was all about at some point in my life, because these things don't happen unless we request them!)

I had gone to bed early one evening as I was feeling spaced out and not quite myself. I found myself sinking into a place where I was surrounded by total chaos. There were stars (planets) shooting about all over the place and I found myself travelling in amongst them. I was lost and frightened and helpless. I knew no one and felt far away from anything familiar. The experience then became much more violent. I became aware that planets were crashing and banging into each other, completely out of control. It was like being in the middle of the most enormous war zone, except there were only planets and crashing noises with explosions everywhere. I was being thrown about helplessly and tossed literally from one explosion to the next.

I was terrified beyond belief. I seemed to have no control of the situation and felt unable to get out. I had had enough. I tossed and turned in my terrorised state and looked for a way out. I had lost touch with my intuition and could not think straight. Where was the exit? I was calling for help.

I can't remember why my partner, Geoff, came in at that moment but I remember saying to him, 'I'm stuck. I can't get out. Help me. Help me!'

I heard his calm voice commanding me, 'Get out of bed. Walk. Walk the floor.'

I got out of bed and started to walk the floor. After 10 minutes, I began to feel more like myself so I got back into bed as I was cold. I was shivering and shell-shocked to say the least. However, I shortly found myself slipping back into the Big Bang experience. I began to panic and shake. I was really scared that I would not come back from this. From what seemed like a huge distance, I heard Geoff command me again, 'Get out of bed again. Walk the floor. Walk up and down. Keep going.'

I got back out of bed and this time I paced the floor until the experience had almost completely gone. This took half an hour or so. When I felt much more like myself than I had the previous time, Geoff allowed me back into bed and it worked. I did not slip back into the experience but held myself in my body, though feeling very, very frightened of what had just happened. The whole experience had been the strongest I had ever had at the time. I lay quite still, in a state of awe. Geoff stayed beside me to keep me from slipping back into the experience. I knew if he hadn't been there, I might have ended up in an institution! But, of course, the universe had made sure he was there when it happened, so that I would be completely safe. When I realised this, I began to calm down and remember how 'looked after' I really was.

I have rarely spoken with anyone about this experience but now feel it is time to share it. There is a danger in sharing it, in that it needs to be heard correctly and safely, so I have asked for this for anyone who reads it.

Going back to a wider perspective, we all carry this memory in our hearts somewhere. We will each need to release these deep collective emotions from our system at some stage of our evolutionary process. However, for most of us it is enough to know it took place and to log that, at some stage, we will need to face it.

I don't know how many millions or billions of years it took for the effects of the Big Bang to calm down. I'm sure scientists could put an estimate on it but it is immaterial to me. The fact is that it did calm down as the distances between the masses became larger. Eventually, it settled enough for us to remember our intention to reintegrate matter and energy. But how, how might this process begin?

3
Our First Experiment

The collective experience thought up a plan. It was decided to allow energy to enter into a few of the billions of planets that had formed out of the Big Bang experience. It was felt that if we integrated with a few as we continued expanding, with the intention of holding onto consciousness, we might be able to make it happen safely.

So, energy started to integrate with the various planets that it came across. We (the collective) felt excited by the prospect of reuniting, and the energy rushed about its business with enthusiasm, while matter eagerly received the energy.

Approximately halfway through the integration process, there was a sudden realisation by the leading edge of the energy that far too much energy was rushing into each chosen planet and that there was a huge danger that the imbalance between matter and energy would destroy the very matter it wished to mix with. A call from the leading edge went out to the energy that was following it: 'Danger! We need to withdraw. This will not work. We might destroy ourselves and the matter we are mixing with. We must withdraw immediately!'

The incoming energy put on its brakes and started to reverse. It felt huge fear that it might have already injured or destroyed a part of itself, and that this might in turn overset the whole of the cosmic experience. As quickly as it had rushed into being, it began to rush back out. The energy that had entered last was of course the first to come out.

As the energy released from its incarnated state, it brushed itself off and looked around (I will label this energy that which had a 'Sun experience'). As it looked around, Sun energy became aware that it felt different to the rest of the energy. There was plenty of energy around but the experience it had just been through made it feel separate to the rest of that energy. The energy that had not experienced incarnation seemed to have retained a purity that made the newly formed Sun energy feel tainted.

Feeling different or tainted triggered a whole set of emotions within the Sun energy. It completely forgot that it had been part of the collective that had agreed to enter these planets. It therefore allowed itself to feel resentful towards the rest of the energy and to blame it for its current state of impurity. In its denial of the truth, it felt misunderstood, betrayed and blamed for what had occurred. It knew deep within that it had only tried to do its very best to integrate with matter but felt it had failed in some way and this brought shame.

It is important to note at this time that the rest of the 'watching' energy did not feel any of these things. It was in fact very grateful for the experiment we call Sun because it taught us that if we take too much energy into too small an amount of matter, the chances are that the matter will overheat and a burnout could destroy it. This has probably already happened in some planets that were entered at that time, while, as we see daily, other planets are still burning out.

4
Our Second Experiment

Having recovered and learned from the first experiment, the collective took stock and formed a second plan.

It seemed like a good idea to allot a further amount of energy and allow this restricted amount to enter a different set of planets and see if a reintegration could take place safely, without putting matter at such risk. Most of the energy selected was from that which had watched the Sun experience from afar, but a small part may have actually been involved in the Sun experience. The question mark/ grey area over this comes from the fact that a very few souls cannot quite decide if they are from either or both the Sun and Swamped experiences. (There is still so much to understand!)

The bulk of the newly selected energy, upon entering the core of this further set of planets, was cautious, mindful of the previous experiment, and therefore made its way from the core at a steady rate. As it progressed, it found itself spreading through the planet, getting thinner and thinner in density as it did so. When it was nearing the surface, the energy suddenly discovered it could travel no further; it had spread itself as thinly as was possible. It desperately wanted to fully integrate but there was no more energy to fulfil the task. At the core, it didn't dare ask the collective for more energy for fear of repeating the first experiment. Therefore, the energy began to return to the core of the planet it had entered. When it reached its destination, it recovered, felt better about itself again and decided to have another go at infiltrating. The attitude was: 'Come on! We can do this!'

Bravely, the energy tried again, but naturally it could only reach exactly the same place as it did before. After several attempts, the energy eventually withdrew from each of these experimental planets, feeling a complete failure. It felt the collective had trusted it with a mission it had not been able to achieve. (I will call this attempt the Swamped experiment because energy was swamped by matter.)

So, the collective experience had conjured two major attempts to integrate matter and energy: the first, the Sun experiment, where there was too much energy for too small an amount of matter; and the second, the Swamped, where there was too much matter for too little energy.

Importantly, any part of creation that has subsequently sprung from the Sun experiment tends to resonate more strongly with that energetic field, and anything that has sprung from the Swamped experience will resonate more strongly with the second experiment. While each are holding this unresolved imbalance, they will at some point have to understand why they are the way they are before they can let go of the experimental field from which it was derived, in order to become fully rebalanced.

Similarly, the 'watching' Source energy that did not experience either the Sun or Swamped experiments will have to understand what it observed during that time in order to rebalance itself and become as pure as it was before any experiments took place.

Of course, the collective mind was then left with a huge dilemma: how should it progress from here?

5

Planet Earth: Our Third Experiment

The collective energy mulled over all it had learned from the two experiments already attempted and came up with a third idea. It was decided to select an equal amount of energy from the Sun experience, the Swamped experience and the Source energy that had not had an incarnated experience but had watched the other two. It was believed that by incarnating the three experiences into a further set of planets in equal measure, they could teach one another, work together and thus be able to hold the balance as they merged with matter. An agreement was set up between them to that effect. (The experiences we have been referring to as Sun, Swamped and watching Source, will for ease now be referred to as the three S's.)

Energy Merges with Matter on Planet Earth

There are plenty of planets in the cosmos which soon became part of this third experiment. They are currently all at differing stages of evolution. One particular planet started to merge much faster than all the others. This planet tried to integrate matter with energy so fast that it lost its balance. It is not a completely lost planet, but it may take a long time to reverse its rushed actions and get back on track. However, the other planets from the third experiment have subsequently been able to learn from this mistake.

As the three S's unified in their intention to work together, teach each other and hold the balance as they entered our planet, they forgot to respect 'earth matter' as another part of themselves and as a living, breathing part of the whole experiment. They treated the earth as something that didn't have feelings or importance. As they drew closer to earth, the three S's were already mixing together and failed to ask permission or acquire a respectful agreement to enter the matter. They simply barged in as if they had a divine right to do so.

From earth's point of view, it had the following effect: earth, alongside all other planets, had been slowly recovering from the effects of the Big Bang. This had taken billions of years. As the three S's made their way towards earth, it was feeling comparatively safe and calm and was reaching out to know itself in its own right. The fires that had been raging out on the surface since the Big Bang were nearly embers and one could say that our planet was in a relative state of peace. Earth was not expecting what was about to happen.

There was a sudden change. Seemingly out of the blue, an impact was felt in the centre of earth that felt of different origin to itself. It was not pleasant and nor was it welcome. There had been no warning! The impact drove earth into a collective feeling of uncertainty, alarm and fear. As the energy penetrated deeper, earth felt invaded, then consumed and finally totally overwhelmed.

As the invasion became total, earth felt lost. A deep sadness became trapped in the whole of the planet. Why had it not been allowed to rest and recuperate? What had it done to deserve such trauma to invade its whole being? Earth seemed helpless to stop this abrupt invasion and felt it was outside of its control.

As the energy became integrated on earth once more, it caused the inner fires that had been smouldering to reignite. Earth had no conscious memory that a part of itself had left itself at the beginning of the cosmic expansion. Therefore, when the same life force was returning to itself it had no sense of recognition. The three spinning S's that landed therefore appeared to be the enemy. Moreover, the collective mind had not foreseen that the Sun and Swamped experiences would remember their previous planetary experience as they became incarnated once more and, in their fear of failing again, would react adversely.

So the agreement that had started out as what seemed like a very good idea in spirit became more and more difficult to uphold as matter and energy were integrating. Not only did the earth have a negative reaction to the incoming energy but the three S's reacted badly to one other too.

The Swamped experience remembered what it had believed to be a 'failed' episode and immediately decided that it must warn and teach the rest of the energy so that it could succeed this time around. It hurriedly rushed forward on its journey as if there was no time to lose, calling: 'Come on, come on! We must get a full head of steam going and make it to the surface this time!' Swamped responded unanimously.

Meanwhile, the Sun experience remembered its own previous sojourn and declared this time that energy must hold back and not rush. It desperately tried to warn the other two S's of its own previous belief that it had the potential to destroy the planet. Therefore, Sun experience tried unanimously to force a tentative and controlled journey through our earth.

The accompanying watching Source energy looked at these two differing experiences that were oozing fear and distrust of each other. It took the middle road and decided that it was the only intelligence that could come through this with any sort of success at all, and that it would therefore have to hold the balance between Sun and Swamped. However, watching Source failed to convince the Sun and Swamped experiences to stop reacting to their fear and work together. Meanwhile, Sun and Swamped had both concluded that watching Source had no previous experience of the incarnated state, therefore it was ignorant and naive and should not be listened to.

So, as the differences emerged between the three S's, they began to *judge* each other as 'wrong'. This judgement caused *resentment* between them. They all began to *fear* that this third attempt at merging matter with energy would yet again not work. They redoubled their efforts to put their points across and became very *angry* with each other when they did not listen. So, these four states (judgement, resentment, fear and anger) caused the energy that had entered the earth's core to start spinning faster and faster in a clockwise direction, as the differences became more and more intense. Eventually, it became such a speedy swirl that the three S's became lost in each other, unable to stay separate; one could liken it to a Catherine wheel. The entire process became *overwhelming* for all.

As the overwhelmed swirl of emotions spun out of control, random energy that was hanging on at the periphery started to let go and break free, in an attempt to survive and escape the terrifying situation. It spun wildly in all directions through matter, slowing as it travelled further and further away from the swirl. Eventually, it slowed enough to look back at the scene it had left and was horrified. This state of spinning confusion was no place to be returning to! So this energy that had broken free became 'pioneering', deciding: 'Better to march on into what seems like oblivion than to go back into that terrorising swirl.'

And so the mixed-up energy of the Sun, Swamped and watching Source experiences continued its journey to the surface of the earth, and other spinning energy, aware of the pioneer's progress, gradually let go of the swirl and followed in its tracks.

***

It is important to note, at this stage, that the key emotions in the collective experience as we entered earth are the same key emotions that play out in our current individual experience. The patterning that took place in those early years of evolution has not left us, but continues to replay itself, over and over again. This judgement of something being wrong causes separation when we believe we are right, when the truth is that there is no right and wrong. Our original conception of being wrong as we began this eighth expansion was not wrong; it was the only way we could move forward to then create something different. So it follows that every perception we judge to be wrong is a step into separation; however, when we know everything to be a part of the whole, it is a step into unity.

Helpful Hints for Healing the Moment We Entered the Planet

—Thank each other for their part in our collective evolution.
—Accept each other as equal.
—Respect the role others played in our progress.
—Know that we are succeeding as never before.
—Acknowledge that we are all Source.

Then the judgement, resentment, anger, fear and feeling overwhelmed that began as we entered planet earth will drop away.

6

A Mishap

The three S's made steady progress from the core of earth towards what we now call the surface. They could increasingly sense the lessening of earth's intense density and the growing proximity of another realm beyond. As the Swamped energy got close to the point it had reached on the previous planet, a déjà vu memory returned to its consciousness: 'Haven't we been here before? Isn't this where we got stuck last time?'

It began to panic and feel that it must race onwards ever faster and, above all, reach the earth's crust for complete integration with the planet this time around. Without consulting the Sun and watching Source experiences, it broke ranks and took off for the surface of earth. It must be said that the intention of the Swamped experience at this point came only from a complete desire to do the right thing. The fact that it did not consult with Sun and watching Source was an innocent mistake and they were therefore taken completely by surprise. As Sun and watching Source had no previous resonance with the Swamped experience, they had no expectation of the impact that would occur when Swamped energy reached that fateful place. The Sun and watching Source (comprising two thirds of the energy that had entered earth) stopped dead in their tracks as they felt the balance shift. Where it stopped was what we might refer to as an inner ring that Swamped energy had accidently created during its first experience in matter. The humongous shock that Sun and watching Source felt as the breach of the agreement occurred was all-consuming, and drove them into panic, fear and extreme anger. How could the Swamped energy let the agreement down like this? They started to call out to the Swamped energy to stop, but nearly one fifth of it had already shot forward towards the earth's crust before the vociferous reasoning from Sun and watching

Source penetrated the Swamped energy field. Experiencing a huge dilemma within itself, the Swamped energy hesitantly slowed down and listened to the pleas. Sun and watching Source were trying to remind it:

> Hey! Don't forget, we agreed to work together, teach each other and hold the balance on this planet. Your charge for the surface is out of control. You are taking us out of balance. Stop! Listen to us. Let's decide together what it is best to do. Don't ruin our mission. Don't go!

Eventually, what was left of Swamped energy, around 80%, came to a halt, feeling uncomfortable and lost. Around 20% of its 'kin' had gone ahead into the distance. Should it follow? Or had it done the right thing to stop and listen to the pleas of others? It wasn't sure but amongst the Sun and watching Source energies, there was a sense of overwhelming relief.

The lost planet, referred to in Chapter 5, came to the rescue. It sent the intelligence that it had suffered the same experience but on its planet the Swamped energy there had *not stopped* at all. It had not listened to or absorbed the pleas of Sun and watching Source. This had therefore scuppered progress greatly, because while two thirds were still left on the inner ring and therefore still holding the greater balance, 33% was now lost to them.

This intelligence helped the 80% of Swamped energy enormously and it managed to trust and hold fast on the inner ring. This meant that only around 7% of the total energy that had entered the planet in the first place was lost to the coalition, while 93% was still holding the balance on the inner ring. This would give earth a far greater chance than the lost planet of pulling back from the brink of failure in the future.

Steadily, the gap between Swamped energy that had shot ahead and that which had stayed behind got wider and wider. Sun, watching Source and the 80% of Swamped that had remained, sat tight on the inner ring inside planet earth where the division had taken place.

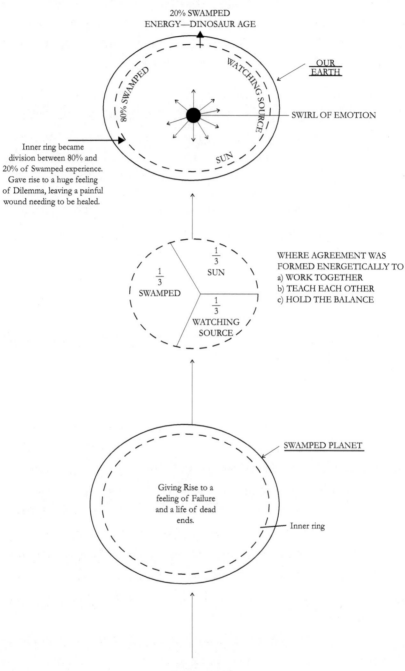

Diagram 1

They were in huge fear that the loss of the 20% of Swamped energy had taken the planet irretrievably out of balance and their primary objective was to hold on to what remained and keep the remaining energy in balance if they could. Their overriding instinct was to stay completely still and wait, focusing only on holding the balance as best they could. What else could they do? So, that is exactly what happened.

Meanwhile, some of the 20% of Swamped energy that had panicked began to reach the surface of the earth. Initially, there was joy. It had made it! It was a success. However, it soon realised that no further energy was following and it seemed to be alone. Swamped energy persuaded itself that it had been right to rush ahead, that it knew best, and set about living what turned out to be a very dark existence on the earth's surface by itself. It did not wish to contemplate that the imbalance it had created within its own sphere was doomed to failure.

Over many millions of years, this part of Swamped energy integrated with surface matter, ignoring its Source connection, eventually evolving into vegetation of sorts, and later into living creatures, mostly of dinosaur nature. The surface of the world was dark and angry and much fighting took place. As there was nothing to balance out the experience, a headstrong and single-minded energetic field evolved. The creatures got bigger and bigger but there was no joy in the perceived success, only fear.

Eventually, the energy became so violent that all that had been created on the earth surface began to kill itself off. This included vegetation, which choked and strangled itself in its tangling roots, and all living creatures that had fought for supremacy, believing as they always had, that this was the only way forward. The situation on earth was dire.

The last of the 20% of Swamped energy that was only now reaching the earth's surface was faced with a bleak and dismal scene. It faltered and eventually gave up the idea that an existence on the surface was desirable or even possible. As the last of the dinosaur experience gave up, it joined the rest of the Swamped energy and together sunk slowly back into the earth, making its way back towards the inner ring, where the rest of the energy was patiently waiting. It had its tails between its legs, so to speak, and it felt it had been a huge failure. No part of earth energy had ever been so gloomy.

***

Meanwhile, the 80% of Swamped energy that had remained behind with watching Source and Sun, was caught in a massive dilemma. It had watched the rest of Swamped energy disappear into the distance many moons before and had never been totally sure if it had done the right thing to stop or if it should have followed its own kin. However, it had decided to wait it out, trusting that a solution to the dilemma would appear. The energy caught in the forefront of the decision to stop was affected the most greatly, it being the most aware of the division that had formed. It also felt the most responsible for the decision and became lost in self-pity.

When the dinosaur experience finally returned to the inner ring where the rest of the energy had been left holding the balance, it was greeted with real anger:

> Why did you rush forward? You promised to work together with us on this mission. You might have ruined everything; in fact, you nearly did. We had all agreed to hold the balance. You broke that agreement. We have had to hold the balance while you were gone. We cannot trust you again.

The dinosaur energy was already feeling very bad about what it had done and this reception from the rest of the energy rubbed salt into a very raw wound. Its initial rush for the surface had come from an overwhelming desire *not* to fail on this planet, but its actions were born of its own intense fear and an egoic notion that it knew best, so it ended up putting our planet at huge risk. Upon its return, it sunk into a deep gloom, becoming the most damaged and darkest energy on the planet. It was angry to have been judged in this way; it knew it had done what it thought was best for everything at the time and felt it was now being judged like a criminal that could never be forgiven. The fury in it was aroused to the extreme.

The 93% of the energy on the inner ring jumped into action and took control. It put the dinosaur energy under a form of lock and key, telling it that it could not risk an event like that ever happening again. Then, as all the energy that had first entered earth was now reunited, it recommenced the journey towards the surface once more, feeling balanced and safe enough to do so.

In time, the reunited energy exploded onto the surface of earth, feeling the freedom of the lack of density as it did so. It was aware it had fully infiltrated earth but the damage it had sustained was very great and would cause earth many problems in the future. The details of what followed on earth are written in my book entitled *A Memory Returned* and it is not my intention to repeat it here.

The healing of this mishap can only happen as enough of us let go of the shock, anger, fear and panic that we sustained at the time. Those emotions are currently being played out on earth in both large and small ways. Every time a 'ruler' that resonates with the dinosaur age feels under enough threat, there is a danger that they will increase control in their own country or invade another sovereign nation to make themselves 'right' and feel safe. They then impose themselves on those around them to bring this about. The same goes for us as individuals when we feel threatened in some way. We reach out to others, telling our story to make ourselves right and therefore feel safer. In actual fact, in all these cases, we are spreading the shock, panic, fear and anger that are rooted in the above event. Until we let go of these emotions at this level, we are likely to continue this pattern. When we decide to release the pattern and forgive the perpetrators, sending forgiveness and unconditional love to rulers and individuals alike, we alter the course of our earth in a powerful way.

***

A lady who I shall refer to as Meg shares her experience.

Meg first came to see me well over a decade before I understood the above. As I tuned into her, I could feel an old experience where she, in energetic form, had emerged onto the earth's surface and all she was aware of was darkness and a massive expanse of black water. It was bleak, eerie, windless and nothing seemed to be alive. She was overwhelmed and very fearful.

As I had never seen this experience in anyone else I had tuned into over the years, I had often wondered what it was we had witnessed. Meg and I stayed in touch, unravelling much of her past lives and discussing Swamped energy but never referring back to that eerie experience. One day, Meg told me she felt as if there was nothing left in her life, nothing was flourishing, and it felt as if all doors in life had been closed to her. She felt she did not belong anywhere, and was in a constant dilemma, unable to make any decisions. She was, in her words, 'done'.

First of all, I thought she meant she was going to take her own life but she assured me quickly that this was not the case; she just couldn't understand why she felt herself to be in such a dead place and so on. I recalled the vision I had had all those years ago and suddenly understood she was now showing me this very same place. Together, we worked out that she had been one of the last of the Swamped energy who had hesitated but finally crossed over the 'division' into what we now refer to as the dinosaur age. She described feeling guilt and shame as she realised that no other energy was following her. The rest of her kind had stopped and she was left trotting after the initial 20%, convincing herself that she had no choice but to carry on and that there was no way back. She felt the separation very keenly. She limped on, finally reaching the surface of earth and experiencing it as we had been shown so many years before. She now felt certain that she must have been amongst the last of the separated Swamped energy to reach the surface, just as the dinosaur age ended, and had decided to sink back into the earth.

Her bleak and eerie experience was at last understood. Meg had spent a huge part of this life feeling the following:

- Her life was one huge dilemma.
- She was a failure at everything she tried.
- She never flourished.
- She found it hard to make decisions.
- She lived a feeling of separation from the whole—living life on the outside and wishing she could be part of a group.
- She had so often felt hopeless and helpless: what's the point?

Once Meg understood why she had felt this way, linking it to the end of the dinosaur experience, she took action. She asked forgiveness for not listening to Sun and watching Source energy as they pleaded for Swamped energy to stop, and for then crossing the gap, breaking the agreement. She now knew her energy should never have followed the path of the leading Swamped energy. She asked forgiveness for the part she played in forming what later became a huge wound or division within the Swamped experience.

Having received forgiveness, Meg imagined herself journeying back over the wound/division and rejoining the 80% of her kin which had not crossed over. She let go of all the states of mind listed above, knowing she need not experience them anymore. She found herself in the middle of the 80%, being welcomed and loved. Suddenly, she felt herself holding her hands out to the remaining 20% of Swamped energy, inviting them to join her and the rest of their kind. For Meg, a wound will never exist again for she has healed her part of it forever. What's more, she has opened a door for others to follow.

A second soul, upon understanding his connection to the dinosaur experience, was only able to let the anger within him dissipate after he realised the original rush to the surface of earth was done with only good intention. He was then immediately reminded of a well-known song, sung by the blues band The Animals in 1965:

'I'm just a soul whose intentions are good,
Oh Lord, please don't let me be misunderstood.'

How sad that we so totally misunderstood the action of the 20% Swamped energy at the time and did not greet it with understanding and love on its return to the inner ring.

7

A Few Beautiful Memories from the Pre-Split Era

As I was walking the dogs one afternoon, I realised a deep old memory was trying to attract my attention. I was astonished as I had never been contacted in this way before. However, the memory wanted to remind me of something so I stopped and listened! The following memory was drawn from the mountains around the site at Machu Picchu in Peru.

The mountains were remembering music as it had been before the Split (which is fully explained in the following chapter; see also the Glossary). The incarnated world would become very still. In that stillness, etheric essences would come to the fore, each carrying a different vibration, and this was the *music* earth could resonate with if it so chose. Music, as we know it now, is our attempt to recreate what we 'tuned' into long ago. Our current instruments and tunes are the physical manifestation of our longing for that music or connection with etheric essences that we knew before the Split.

In the stillness, when the incarnated experienced the etheric essences, they were as little pieces of shiny light, like a swirl of circling glitter. This is why we put glitter on our Christmas card angels now. The memory is not quite lost.

I have asked to hear this wonderful music again but so far I never have. However, the memory haunts me as it was unlike anything I had ever heard before, so beautiful it was, beyond description.

***

Another memory I had was of a ripe fruit purposefully falling off a tree in front of me as I passed by. The tree had known I was in need of sustenance. It wasn't that the fruit felt its individual state but the tree's inner knowing allowed it to drop the fruit exactly when and where I needed it.

***

Animals, when they had finished with their bodies, would naturally drop dead in front of another animal, offering that body as sustenance to another. It was an understanding in the oneness of everything at the time.

***

There was a time when I was walking through woodland and the trunks of the trees showed me how they had evolved as such in their longing to become more than grass. The woodland seemed to me to be, in that moment, a lawn of trees (more substantial than grass), and it was as if I was walking in the base of the lawn. I could feel the pre-Split energy. The trees had the same idea of growing beyond the surface as grass but in as substantial a way as they could, in an effort to survive longer.

***

A few beings today have a memory of the pre-Split era and remember it as a oneness that they long to experience again. The individual 'fight' for existence is not present there and this memory brings a peace that they know in their hearts but cannot seem to bring back into being. Some have labelled it Atlantis, or Lemuria, a lost continent or even another planet. This is because they have not yet understood the Split and are trying to put a name to what they are remembering. The truth is that nothing was lost—we remain on the same planet, but our experience here is now individual so, while we perceived ourselves to be somewhere else as the Split occurred, we were actually in exactly the same place.

8
The Split on Earth

Did you know that every last second of every minute of every day of every single life you have ever lived is a reproduction of your experience at the Split?

The Split, or as it is more commonly known, the Fall, was a very important moment on this planet and occurred possibly millions of years after the first energy had merged with earth. It occurred at a time when vegetation and countless varieties of animals were well established on the earth surface. At this point, we had begun remembering again that our original remit, before this expansion of the cosmos, was to find 'another' way to exist other than through fear. As this yearning grew deeper, it finally caused a split on the surface of this planet which resulted in everything on the surface becoming individually conscious as opposed to having a unified consciousness. Scientists refer to it as the moment one of the largest tectonic plate shifts earth has ever experienced, took place.

It took me around 14 years to realise that everything that has happened since is a reproduction of the Split, to the extent that I do now. I suppose it became fully clear when I finally let go of the last piece of my own jigsaw. At this point, I stopped doubting and would present those who I was talking with this challenging fact, enabling their releasing process to go even faster.

Before the Split occurred, there was no 'perceived' hard crust between the outer surface and the inner earth. It was only as individual consciousness became our reality that we created an earth that we believed to have a hard crust around its surface. This was brought into belief systems by both inner earth and the outer world as a type of protection.

The tectonic plate movement caused every part of creation existing on the surface to become aware of itself, and its sensations, feelings and experiences from that moment on became its own. Every subsequent event for each individual has been patterned on that first experience. The victim/perpetrator pattern was again played out by each individual as it took conscious form. Until we each remember how we experienced the Split, forgive ourselves and those around us for how we judged them at the time, and let go of our own emotional experiences, we cannot heal our deep patterning and find the 'other' route we so long for.

One of the largest mountains at the time, with one of the largest collections of life on its surface, was one through which the earth split or tectonic plate shift ran, causing the mountain to explode and crumble to eventually almost nothing. We currently refer to the remaining interior of this mountain that was left exposed after the Split as Machu Picchu. As the mountain reached its most explosive, trees were snapped in two like twigs, huge rocks were thrown high in the air, boulders and stones of all descriptions flew randomly everywhere, the atmosphere was filled with dust and black smoke for miles around, and animals screamed and perished in the tumult. The sheer magnitude of this event is almost impossible to describe. Earth's surface had become the most enormous, overwhelming and fearful place, with nowhere to hide. Every part of creation appeared to be the other parts' enemy. As Machu Picchu was one of the highest and largest areas on the earth's surface, it was therefore one of the most damaged. It carries the shock, despair, hopelessness and sorrow trapped throughout its landscape, with a deeper intensity than most other regions. Reverberating through it at the time were questions such as: 'Why? Why is this happening? Why are we being destroyed? Why are we being subjected to this? How can we stop this? What have we done that is so dreadful to deserve such a punishment?'

These cries ran through nearly every part of the mountain, including the interior of the mountain, rocks, earth, animals, birds, trees and all vegetation. The whole surface of earth felt like the most enormous battlefield, so overwhelming that it is difficult to imagine, with the mountain becoming one of the most severely damaged places on earth.

The deep, deep sorrow, the trauma, the overwhelming terror as the event slowly calmed down, remained, deeply scarring earth. There was no escape. It seemed, to the whole of surface creation, that Source had abandoned it.

The entire outer earth and the subsequently created individuals residing on it, still feel this trauma today, deep down in their core, allowing it to drive and shape their everyday life, until they learn how to release it. Nevertheless, release it we all must, from every area of land, every being and every part of vegetation that grows there. Only then can we, as a collective, become 'as one' again.

As earth remembers that it is only fighting a part of itself, it has the opportunity to work *with* its counterpart, rather than against it. At this point, untold positive resources and possibilities will emerge and the union recreated will consciously start to work as one. Currently, it is only the thin crust on the earth's surface that is awakening to this memory as beings on earth wake up to the devastation they have caused the planet and seek ways to put it right.

As it has become clear to the collective consciousness in recent times that the massive imbalance between the slowly awakening earth's crust and the rest of earth was seriously hampering earth's enlightenment process, causing amongst other things, global warming at a fast increasing rate, the collective deemed it necessary to take steps to rectify this position.

A Selfless Act

It should be noted that when activated, a selfless act can spread as far as is necessary and, as the act can never be undone, it becomes a beacon of light. Once in place, it does not ever need to be renewed. The steady Source flow is present on earth forever.

One incarnated soul from the same soul group (see Glossary) as Jesus was approached at soul level and asked to sacrifice itself (undertake a selfless act) in order to bring about much-needed faster change on planet earth. The soul was shown that it would tread an individual path never trodden before in order to achieve this. There have been individuals, both known about today and unknown, who have walked similar paths. Some have succeeded, others not.

This soul was first taken to a brilliant white void that lay at the entrance to the unknown path that we had sought before we finished the previous or seventh expansion of the cosmos. It was eerily silent and empty but the soul felt very safe. It knew there was nothing in that void but trust. The path was brilliant white (like fresh snow) and there were a few footprints around the void where the soul lay, with other prints going off up a path into the distance. Other than that, there were no reference points. The soul's intuition advised it to follow the footprints. Firstly, however, the soul felt into the space that lay in the opposite direction to the footprints (where it had just come from) and it felt black and dark. With absolutely no wish to go back into that darkness, the soul felt itself move quickly back into the void where it was brilliant white again. The soul knew that it never wished to go back into the dark again and therefore took a few steps forward along the path and stood still, taking in the enormity of what it was experiencing. This was the path we had asked for as a collective at the end of the seventh expansion so many eons before; it was a path that held only trust and potential joy. A message came again: 'You need to stay right here; you need to acclimatise before moving forward again. You will be taken care of.'

The soul felt dazed. It knew it was experiencing the same world it had always been in but now it was viewing it with only brilliant white light in its vision: no fear, only trust. Everything seemed strange. The soul was being asked to carry on with life as normal and yet everything felt so different. Nothing seemed threatening as it had on the old track. On this new track, everything was at peace, so still and so unthreatening. Yet there was nothing to reach out to, nothing to hold on to. The soul decided: 'I will just take this one step at a time, one day at a time. I have no idea what to do next, apart from simply—being.'

The Portal

Remember, this soul had already agreed to sacrifice itself for the greater good of the planet. So, through what seemed like an ordinary accident to those on earth, it had actually willingly agreed to go through the pain it soon experienced. During this act of unconditional surrender to the greater good, the soul was caused to lose consciousness for a few seconds, hit the ground with enormous force, causing huge pain and bodily harm, while remaining in total trust that the highest good would prevail. In those trusting few seconds, as the energetic soul met with inner earth in such an unconditional manner, it allowed a unified portal to emerge between inner and outer earth from which memories could ebb and flow as never before. This sacrificial act was made in the same way that Jesus bore the cross, many centuries before.

In the days that followed, as the soul started to recover from the impact, explanations as to what its accident was all about came into its consciousness. It was asked to unconditionally apologise to inner earth for the judgements when the three S's had each claimed to be right, as energy had entered earth. The soul asked forgiveness for these damaging judgements, already having surrendered all judgement, resentment, fear, anger and feeling of being overwhelmed from its own field.

Memories were expressed through this portal that now lay open, unifying the two sides. Inner earth was offered the following:

> How rude and thoughtless we were at the beginning. Energy treated earth as something less than itself, not as an equal. Please forgive the energy for its ignorance. We now know we are truly not your enemy. We are, and originally came to be, as one with you. We are slowly learning to respect earth, as the surface resources wear thin. But this is not enough. Energy needs to have a total respect for all that you are and to be deeply aware of how it has offended and continues to offend. We must respect each other. We must learn to work together, teach each other and thus re-find the balance between us.

Inner earth was offered the opportunity to shed or let go of the damage it had experienced. It could forgive the energy if it chose to, and then release any sorrow it was harbouring because the situation was no longer sad. There could be much rejoicing if earth matter would allow itself to remember its connection to energy.

The sacrificial soul, as the balanced embodiment of matter and energy, then stood in the portal that had been created. The soul called for inner earth to remember its origins and work for the greater good of all. It asked that this message be sent into earth, wherever it might be received. The echo, once sent out into the mountains of Machu Picchu some 12 years before by the same soul, was also ignited and energised in this much deeper way: 'Remember who you are...'

A day or so later, the intense sadness did not seem to be releasing. The main portal that might allow a release seemed blocked at the entrance. Understanding was sent into inner earth by the soul, through the portal:

> The Split was not a sad occasion. It should never have been experienced as a sad occasion. It was the beginning of something wonderful. Have you ever considered that if things hadn't happened the way they did, earth might have divided completely into two separate pieces? We would then have lost the ability to succeed on this planet. As it played out, the Split only went skin-deep because you, inner earth, hung on and held together while energy upset you. Well done!
>
> Because you hung on and did not give occasion for a total split to occur, you broke a pattern that had been held in the ether since the Big Bang. Until that point, matter had experienced split after split after split. Somehow the shock and reaction you went through caused the opposite to occur. The relief in the ether was enormous at the time. The experiment we call earth was saved. Thank you, thank you from the entire cosmic field.

Inner earth hesitantly questioned: 'So we did the right thing?'

Energy replied: 'Yes, perfect. We can all see that now. The facts are that an ignorant mistake on our part caused you to seize up and strengthen, and it has all come out with a workable result.'

The soul sensed the beginning of joy and a sign of lightness coming through the portal. A few minutes later, an integrating feeling between inner and outer earth started to emerge. An excitement dawned. A feeling of equality between the two sides was unfolding. Sadness was dissolving; the hard crust that had held both sides protected from one another had the opportunity to dissolve for those who could allow it to.

Up until then, inner earth had felt like an extremely injured party, heavily investing itself with anger and resentment. In this moment, it was allowing itself to believe it had always been an equal part of the whole. Neither party had got it quite right at the beginning (by accident) but it was still possible for earth and energy to work together once more, each letting go of their reason to hold anger, judgement, resentment, fear and feeling of being overwhelmed from the time.

Later, the soul encouraged inner earth to let its Split trauma release slowly and carefully. Volcanoes, earthquakes and tsunamis are such a big build-up of trapped anger, panic, shock and fear that they cause further destruction on the surface. If the earth could start to consciously release its trauma gently through portals such as the one that had just been created, less damage would be experienced by all.

A couple of months after the above took place, the soul kept experiencing bouts of sadness coming into its consciousness. Upon delving in to see why the sadness was being experienced, the soul knew that inner earth was struggling to believe it could be forgiven for killing or damaging, through its explosions, everything on earth's surface at the time of the Split. The idea of returning to oneness seemed impossible, hence the sadness.

The soul immediately knew that earth was also remembering and recreating a pattern which occurred during the Big Bang. The guilt lying within earth seemed heavy and the soul knew that this was of its own creation as energy had put no such blame on earth.

The sacrificial soul spoke to earth through the portal:

> What you have to remember is that in the beginning, energy withdrew from matter and matter withdrew from energy. It was a mutual agreement. The fact that you responded to the separation with anger, fear and violence, creating a perpetrator type of being-ness is not of personal resonance to energy. Matter *happened* to be thicker and therefore had a different experience to energy which *happened* to be thinner. That's all there is to it. It was random!
>
> We on the surface are sending you this reminder. There is nothing to be guilty about. The Split was a smaller version of the Big Bang which again was random. We on earth are not holding a gun to your head; please don't hold one to your own head. It is imperative to let it go and become 'as one' again.

***

When the love of individual consciousness on earth is greater than the fear of the trauma, then love will have the upper hand and the trauma will leave.

There are so many untapped resources within earth that, in reality, humanity has only tapped into a fraction of them. As the inner and outer parts of earth forgive each other and learn to trust one another again, thus dissolving the barrier they created at the Split, these resources can be discovered and used more wisely than in the past.

It is important to understand that, over the eons, earth has hurt individuals just as much as individuals have hurt earth. At times, earth has reacted very violently, more than most realise, and thankfully humans are now recognising how much they have hurt earth.

A second major use of the portal followed a few months later. The elected soul realised that earth already carried all that it needed to overcome climate change. On the surface, it had learned to survive all types of climates that circumferenced the world. For example, grasses grew in particular ways according to both their environment and their route from the core.

The sacrificial soul stood once more in the portal. There was a sense that the portal had a mesh over it as a type of protection. Upon enquiry, inner earth told the sacrificial soul that two different souls had stood in the portal in the previous few weeks. The first (A) had been properly prepared and had therefore been received with caution. The second soul (B) had not been properly prepared and had caused a dramatic disruption to their energy. Therefore, 'A' had received a beneficial experience from communing with inner earth and 'B' had received a muddled one. The sacrificial soul was informed that proper preparation for any future visitor must include asking for forgiveness for causing separation at the Split and forgiving inner earth for its part in the separation. Any visitor also had to have proper knowledge of, and to be in harmony with, what the portal stood for, thereby holding it in respect. The sacrificial soul immediately sought forgiveness from inner earth and promised to respect the portal in future. This soul then politely requested an audience with inner earth. The mesh was removed and the following prayer was sent in:

> Within earth, you have all the knowledge necessary to survive any climate. Please pool our resources, study outer earth, teach each other, work in harmony and together we will bring back the balance while we go through a climate change. Is there anything we can do for you to help you in return?

There was a surprised silence and then a communication: 'You want our help?' and then a feeling of delight spread over the soul. The prayer was sent ricocheting throughout inner earth and finally landed within the core. The sacrificial soul knew a deep change would come about as inner earth woke up and set in motion the execution of its newfound mission.

Over the next few months, the soul found itself opening up at odd times of the day. An easy example of this would be that when watching the news or a documentary, facts about the state of the earth might be shared as the portal held within the soul would be opened to allow certain information and teachings to sink into inner earth. This would only happen at specific points and was never influenced by the soul. In other words, the soul could never choose these moments; they came at the discretion of the light. The soul would allow the flow through its own body for as long as necessary and then it would naturally close.

The day came when a group of about 20 souls who had been preparing to open up to such understandings, gathered together. The enlightened universal flow had been asking for volunteers to help with the opening of the portal to a greater degree. As the souls prepared for this to happen, it became clear that those gathered had to be educated as to what had taken place so far. They were warned that entering the portal might prove to be a very deep catalyst for change within them and the flow asked if they were ready to embrace that change. They were also made aware that they were part of an experiment and that the result of the day was unknown. Finally, they were offered a visit to the site but, as it was raining, it did not seem like it would happen that day. However, the universe had its own plans and, against the odds, an hour later, the sun came out and shone brightly on the wet grass, inviting the group to form a circle beside the portal.

Respectfully, those who felt they wanted to, entered the portal one by one, to offer forgiveness and to ask forgiveness in their own way, to reacquaint themselves with inner earth and offer to help in any way they could. Each soul that entered came out of the portal and shared their experience with the rest of the group. As the experiment continued, all present began to learn more and more about what the portal was about and how it could be used.

While no one had an extreme experience on the day, over the next few weeks it became clear that certain deep inner shifts were taking place. It seemed that the portal had highlighted to those who had entered, their deepest trauma or a block that was holding them back in their enlightenment process. I realised that this was so uniquely possible because there was no individual trauma to muddle the issues within the inner earth realms. The benefit for inner earth was that it was gently being put in touch with the confusion experienced on outer earth as each soul entered.

Soul B got in contact. She wanted to come and talk over her experience. I knew that since her visit a few months ago, I was now more ready to help her understand what had taken place. She in turn was ready to tell me of the enormous happenings and realisations that had come up for her. As we sat together, it became obvious that 'B' was completely changed. Her ego had dissolved and she had become a humble servant of the light. She expressed herself differently and her energy was so much purer. She had realised so many things about herself that she had struggled to comprehend until this point. The portal had highlighted things in such a way that she was unable to fight any longer and her ego had caved in. Most remarkable of all, she was so happy to be free. What had seemed to me to be a terrible mistake when she first entered the portal had in fact been a massive success.

Soul A, however, who had had such a wonderful experience on the day of entering the portal, seemed afterwards to have gone through what one could only describe as 'a dark night of the soul'. As I listened to her, my world was turned upside down. I just didn't know what was good and what was unbeneficial for her, given the portal experience. But I did not convey my worries to 'A'; I simply handed them over to Source and trusted that the highest good would prevail. Over the next few months, it became clear that through her 'dark night' she was successfully facing all that she had feared for so long. Up until that point, I felt I had been banging my head against a brick wall whenever she had asked me to assist her. Suddenly, she was moving through them bravely, facing one after another, until a point came when her life started to flow in tandem with the universal flow. All that she had withheld from herself in her belief that she was unworthy began to become her reality; it was like magic!

Helpful Hints to Release the Trauma of the Split from your Core

Recognise the truth of the 'enemy' within you. (*There is no enemy!*) Become a being of no resistance, no fighting but one of *true surrender*. Allow yourself to face the greatest depths of the Split in you, in all its vulnerability, knowing there is no real enemy. The trauma will disappear.

Reversing the Split

For many, many years, I have been helping people remember what happened to them as the Split on earth occurred. Over that time, through high numbers of people allowing me to tune into their experiences, I have been growing ever clearer as to what happened all those years ago and therefore am able to help speed up their process of releasing the emotions and trauma held so deeply within.

I would currently express the process of release that I see in so many like this: first, people hear about who or what they were and how they experienced the Split, as if it is a very familiar story. They spend days marvelling at finally understanding why they are the way they are and the enormity of the whole thing. After they grasp the concept and know its truth, they struggle to access the depth to which it runs inside them.

Over a period of weeks, the memory slowly wakes up and enlarges inside their soul. Gradually, they feel more confident and comfortable with it and, often, they realise they have reincarnated amongst other souls, perhaps their family and friends, who experienced the Split with them.

On a further chat a few weeks or months down the line, I can repeat much of what I said the first time around but it becomes clear that the soul has only taken on a small amount of what I said at the first sitting. However, the second time around the soul is able to open up to so much more and to take on the concept much more efficiently.

After some more months, the soul starts to realise they have to let go of some of the emotions as understanding why they were there in the first place drops into their conscious mind. Realistically, they may be able to truthfully claim they have let go of between 30 and 50% of the emotional impact. It is the deepest wounds that are left and it is those the soul has the biggest struggle to release. Typically, these are lack of self-worth, feeling unsafe, being out of control and a sense of guilt.

For those who stay with the process, there comes an exciting point when I explain to the voyager that, while they have taken on and have worked with the surface of what happened at the Split, they now need to allow their consciousness to drop down into the deepest part of the experience. Most don't realise that they have only been trying over and over to release from the initial story; a few even fabricating more and more around it as they attempt to avoid the deep pain they are carrying. When they finally understand what they have been doing, they start to allow a process of going deeper into themselves. Their experience deepens gradually until they find themselves just outside the main disaster (i.e. their original Split story). At this point, they are usually prepared to face anything to be free of all the emotions (or illusions) that the Split left them with; they stop fighting or controlling and allow a process of dropping into the most painful part of their illusion. What has stopped them doing this before is the belief that they are going to re-experience the pain and become lost again, but when they understand that they are going deep inside to let the roots of the pain *out*, this helps them relax and freedom can happen in a second, for they stop controlling and allow their consciousness to drop into their deepest terrors.

The Split and a full release of the individual emotions we then experienced is by far the hardest part of our enlightenment journey to move through. We can only overcome or reverse it on our own as no one else around us carries our exact experience. It is being alone that makes it so difficult to trust and yet when we do, the reward is magnificent. Our lives change forever, not just in this life but in every following lifetime.

Everything we experienced as part of the collective is easier as there is an army of us releasing it. Every part of creation that is letting the memory go is doing so for us all. Therefore, while we are pioneering at this moment in history, release of the trauma can only get easier as the world lives on. A lovely lady I know described it like this:

> There is understanding and there is knowing.
>
> I have understood for decades. My visits to the retreat have brought me to insights and experiences that give me the knowing from within.
>
> I am now 'knowing' as a reality what I understood to be so. This is so different!
>
> I am consciously stepping back and shedding my previous world-views, beliefs and conditioning to make way for the new perspectives that come from experiencing directly from my heart.
>
> It is becoming a case of remembering what I already knew in my heart but had lost sight of.
>
> I can't do this but I can allow this to happen in divine timing.
>
> With love to you all…

Now here is an example of how *not* to do it! A lady came to see me who believed she felt ready to understand her deepest roots. She took herself off for a walk to allow just that. The next day, she told me of her experience and it goes like this:

> I set an intention of going into the core of my Spilt experience. I took a dive, like off a diving board and found myself in an awful pit of black pain and human misery. It felt like a

mediaeval prison. There were tortured bodies everywhere, no light and chains clanking. I took my light into the pit and it started to change everything. People were releasing from their chains. And the light transformed them into the young people they had been. Windows with light shining through then appeared in the walls. Doors opened and the souls were able to walk out. Everything became light.

To this lady's dismay, I burst out laughing. She had been so intent on avoiding her pain that she had completely fabricated a very shallow level of her idea of the root of the Split. She was a character from the Sun experience, completely steeped in denial. Luckily for me, she took my laughter well as she was well aware of her tendency to deny and it had crossed her mind that she was making it up. However, she then set off to face her deepest levels of consciousness without 'effort', without trying, but simply allowing, now fully aware that she needed to surrender her ego completely!

An example of how to do it now follows. A different lady had been trying for many years to find peace in her heart and had gone off on all sorts of tangents in her efforts. She sat before me one day and said, through copious tears, 'I can't do this. I've tried and tried but nothing ever seems to happen. I repeat my mistakes; I still feel dark. I can't do this. Help!'

Such was her humility in that moment, I said joyously to her, 'At last! At last you realise you can't do this out of your own strength! It's when you *know* you can't do it, and *trust* that the Source is all there is, that you can be set free.' I asked her to sink her consciousness into her Split experience in all its terror. Again, she sobbed, 'I can't, I can't. It's too terrible!' I quietly reassured her that trust was the only way, 'Which is worse? Do you wish to carry on as you have been or to surrender your fear?' She cried, 'I can't carry on as I have been.'

Slowly, she was sinking herself into her deepest fears. She knew the truth of what I was saying. She knew she had tried every which way out of her own strength and nothing had worked. She knew she was at the end of the road. She allowed her consciousness to sink deeper and deeper, until she became lost. There was a long silence. The sobbing slowed and then finally stopped. A slow smile crept across her face. She looked at me and said, 'Wow!' I waited. A couple of moments later, she said wow again and her smile grew broader. Her face lit up and her physical energy was lightening. She marvelled out loud, looking at me in wonderment, 'It's so peaceful. I am not alone! I feel free. I am safe. Wow. Wow. And wow again!'

This dear lady, after such a long search, had gone into total surrender of her individual consciousness, facing the deepest part of the trauma held within her (as it is held in the depths of all of us), realising her separation from Source was not true, never had been true, thus enabling her to reverse all her previous conceptions of the Split. On realising she had been connected to Source all along, she now lives totally free and at one with the Source of all things. Once we have found our long lost truth and released all the fear, the oneness or inner peace re-emerges forever.

Dee's Bliss

Dee describes her feelings once she faced and completely let go of the Split level of ego:

> This experience is life changing. I've felt nothing like it before! The garden seems brighter and clearer, crisper and even more beautiful. It is as though I am looking at it and also the world for the first time. I know myself so much better now. My determination to dig further is stronger than ever; I will go with the flow and allow further miracles to happen.
> Stick with the journey, my friends. It is not always an easy or comfortable experience but it is worth the perseverance.
> Much love and many thanks to all who have helped me get this far.

THE JOURNEY THROUGH EARTH

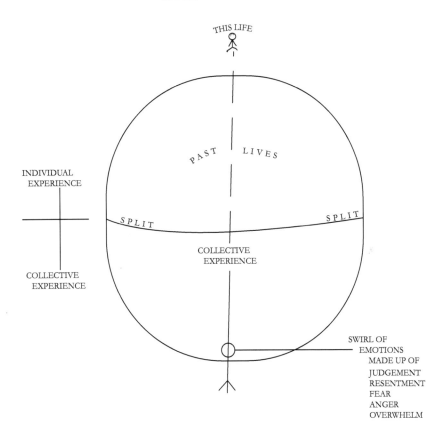

Diagram 2

9

Further Understanding of 'Watching' Source

In terms of life on earth, every single part of creation has come through either the Swamped, Sun or watching Source experience. This fact is inevitable. How these experiences impact on our lives now is very interesting.

The original energy that split off from matter was what we might call original Source energy. It is only as this energy later went through different experiences that it became split into three different types.

The energy that has not had a different planetary experience is what we could refer to as 'watching' Source. As this energy had no individual experience of its own, it was relatively uncontaminated because its only knowledge was from watching what else was going on around it. This was felt to be an asset as the agreement between the three S's was formed.

However, as the three S's entered the incarnated state on earth, everything changed. This watching energy saw how damaged the Sun and Swamped experiences had become, as, once reincarnated, they relived their previous planetary experience in some form or another. 'Watching' energy judged immediately that it could not now trust Sun and Swamped energy so became extremely pious as it felt it had all the best answers. However, it also had an innocence about it which was to prove to be helpful in the future, but at the beginning it served to separate the three experiences quite definitively.

One third of creation on earth derives from watching Source energy. Humans carrying this experience, when ready to understand evolution at this level, can be recognised in all walks of life. However, they do tend to congregate more often in religious gatherings, claiming their beliefs to be the right way and everyone else's way to be 'wrong'. They tend to be a little narrow-minded, seeing no advantage to opening up to the bigger picture. This comes as a direct result of what happened as the three S's first incarnated, when judgement, resentment, anger and fear of each other took a grip. However, while watching Source types hold this conceited viewpoint, the innocence they naturally carry helps them let go of their 'self' rather more quickly than others.

How to Heal?

Jesus said: 'I am the alpha and the omega, the beginning and the end.'

When Sun, Swamped and watching Source were asked by the collective to take an equal portion of energy of their experience and enter various planets, the idea was to cooperate together and hold the balance as energy infiltrated matter on what we might call the third attempt at reuniting. Watching Source did indeed hold the balance better than the other two but, in becoming judgemental as the differences between the three S's incarnated, it became tainted goods from which it must heal. This did not start to happen until the Split, and it came in the form of the golden lions.

The golden lions, who were by no means perfect, were incarnated at the time of the Split, many of whom are currently the hierarchy of the Source experience, being those who held onto the 'light' or connection to Source for the longest, after the Split. They held on because they had heard a call for help from deep inside the mountain they happened to be feeding on, as the Split experience was erupting deep inside earth. They picked up the call from their natural link with Source and it continued to resound through them as they slowly made their way down the mountain. They were therefore continuing to listen inwardly as they started to step outwards into individual consciousness.

If they had not fought at the great battle against the white lions (described in my book, *A Memory Returned*) and in doing so succumbed to the darkness, they could have retained the light or inner connection and continued their earth journey listening to their inner instructions. However, they did fight and their connection became hidden from them, and so they became as damaged as the rest of the incarnated world.

Many lions to this day hold an inner wisdom that reflects what happened at the beginning of individual consciousness. They are of the few who retain the memory of oneness while yet becoming self-conscious, and have therefore always been at the forefront of bringing light back to the planet. If this quirk of fate had not happened, it might have taken a lot longer for the energy on this planet to reach its current stage, or maybe it may not even have happened at all.

Ever since the Split, the lion family has reincarnated repeatedly on earth, trying to find ways of retaining an inner connection. The best-known incarnations date from Adam followed by Noah through to the time of Jesus ... and beyond.

Jesus was the first member of the golden lion family to overcome the terrors of the Split that took place on planet earth. Two thousand years ago, well ahead of his time, he held onto his inner connection while the world replayed his Split experience around him. He thus became the first individually incarnated part of creation to overcome his Split experience and shine his true light on earth. He became what some refer to as 'Christed'. From that time onwards, the hierarchy of watching Source has grown as more and more souls have understood what he did and followed in his footsteps.

Jesus did indeed represent the alpha and omega, the beginning and the end.

10
Further Understanding of the Sun Experience

The energy that had experienced the Sun experiment by entering the first set of planets many eons ago, some of which volunteered to make up one third of the energy on this planet, is very different to the watching Source energy.

The decision the leading edge made as it did a U-turn and came back out of the Sun experiment left it with a huge set of imbalances that affect creation on any planet it has subsequently entered. As the energy withdrew and found itself outside the incarnated state once more, it felt very *different*. The energy it returned to felt comparatively pure, while the energy that had experienced incarnation in the Sun planet felt contaminated. Immediately, the Sun energy started to *point a finger* at the watching Source energy, crying: 'You told us to go in there. It's your fault and now we are different to you. We have to live with this while you are still as we once were.'

The Sun energy started to *blame* the rest of us, feeling *betrayed*. It completely *denied* the fact that it had been part of the sum total of energy that had originally made the decision to try the experiment. But, in reality, how could it be otherwise, for there was no division in watching Source energy before this experiment.

A growing feeling of *failure* consumed the Sun energy and with it came a feeling of *shame*. It felt it had not done what it set out to do and felt it had let the rest of us down. It felt grossly *misunderstood* and that what had happened was most *unfair*.

Characteristics of Sun Types

As we humans progress deeper into our spiritual enlightenment process, having gained an understanding of the need to let go of our personal baggage, there comes a point when we realise that some of this burden of feeling is bigger than ourselves and is rooted in an earlier time. We may call this our collective emotions. Those beings that have a level of investment in the Sun experience will virtually all relate to the words set out in italics above and relisted and amplified below:

- feeling different;
- pointing fingers;
- blaming;
- feeling betrayed;
- sensing that things were unfair;
- denial;
- knowing failure;
- experiencing shame;
- feeling misunderstood.

Some Sun energy is more heavily invested in these feeling states than others. Those who were amongst the first energy to enter the Sun planet (the leading edge) were also last out and are therefore very much consumed by it, while those who were last in were first out and are therefore only lightly invested in it. Then, of course, there is a full range of different levels of attachment in between. The most heavily invested are known as the hierarchy of the Sun experiment and in their efforts to make themselves right, and to be right, have spent eons trying to convince everyone that they are. They are what we know as the Sun-god types who have dominated quite a few religions, amongst which are Buddhism and Shamanism. It is a very addictive energy and those who are invested in it find it incredibly hard to let go of. Even those who are only partially attached to it find it hard, such—as we all witness daily—is the draw and power of the sun.

Denial

One of the biggest problems Sun energy souls get stuck on is the denial within them that is so cleverly hidden that they have lost awareness of it. One lady, having been broken open and humbled after quite a personal inner fight, described it to me in this way:

> Sun energy souls see through a distorted lens. We don't see the pure truth; we see the Sun's truth. This allows us to feel what the Sun wants us to feel, and not what we should be feeling. We don't care how we receive the distorted love—the adoration—as long as it is received. It blinds us with 'See me, feel me, only I matter'. It does everything to prevent us seeing through the veil it has put up. It convinces us to look on the bright side of life and all the problems will fall away, preventing us from seeking balance.

Another insightful lady, on her journey to understanding the Sun experience, fed back to me the following:

> Sun felt different after being separated (even though it was the same) and projected its feelings onto watching Source, blaming it, and then got stuck on the feeling of betrayal. The sun in the sky is currently healing. It's being celebrated and loved by the whole world and has been for many thousands of years.

She has stated a wonderful truth. For, in reality, the energy that watched the Sun experience never had any of the thoughts that the Sun accused it of. It merely noted that too much energy going into too little matter was dangerous and could end up destroying the planet it had entered, and that another way must be found. If watching Source felt anything at all, it felt gratitude for the teaching that came through this first experiment. The cool and calm comprehension of watching Source was what caused the collective mind to set about the second experiment.

Therefore, those aspects of creation who were part of this first experiment and seek to enlighten must not only heal themselves from their own individual emotions (the Split) but must also heal the emotions that are rooted in the moment energy entered earth. They must then understand and release the nine, or possibly more, emotions that they created as having been part of the Sun planet because they can never become one with true Source again without doing so. As Sun experience souls on this planet tend to numb and block off their emotions, and generally hold back in life (afraid of overpowering anything as they felt they did on the previous planet), it can be very difficult for them to face the truth and let go of their perceived power. They love to avoid issues and persuade themselves that it is OK to do this.

A Journey with Emily

Coming at all this from another angle was Emily, a lady who I got to know fairly well and, because she was so intent on healing herself, she came to see me regularly. One day, Emily arrived on my doorstep in a terrible state. She was restless and tormented, and felt suicidal and in a dark place. I took her out onto the lawn under the big cedar tree, which is a very healing place, and she started to throw her body around the lawn in an uncontrolled fashion, saying all sorts of negative things.

As I listened, I became aware that Emily was reliving her exit from the Sun experience. She was convinced that the energy she had been part of had totally destroyed the planet it had entered. I realised she must have been amongst the last of the energy to exit the Sun planet and, as the energy left, the whole planet became a darkened 'blob'. I called out to her as she rolled around, 'Look back! Look back!' She shouted, 'I can't, I can't.' I was firm, 'You can. You must look back.'

After what seemed like an age of firm but gentle persuasion of this nature, Emily eventually looked back at the planet she had left, realising that there was nowhere else to go. Her body froze. There was silence. I said to her, 'It's still there. The planet is still there. The energy only overheated it and because it hit such a high temperature the density has altered and has become blackened. As the planet cools, it will alter again. Nothing can destroy a planet in reality. It can only change form through any experience it goes through.'

What had seemed to Emily to be on the scale of 'mass murder' was at last seen by her in its truthful form. She was able to let go of the fear that she had destroyed a planet and would never be forgiven, for she had seen for herself that what she had believed for so long was unfounded. Her whole body calmed down and she lay still, allowing the lie to leave her.

I never saw Emily again after this day for she had finished teaching me and for that moment I had finished teaching her. However, there are many souls who believe in their core that they have been part of a mass murder, and understanding that this is not so will help them heal enormously.

The Ra

The hierarchy of the Sun experience—we can call this the leading edge of the experience or the 'Ra'—has tried to make itself greater than Source, in an effort to convince creation that it had done all the right things. (This was driven by its underlying belief that it had done something wrong.) This is understandable, given the fact that it was the only experiment around for some time and it felt its difference so acutely. So, unfortunately, the hierarchy, having created an idea of power when it commanded the rest of the energy to withdraw from the planet, started to use and abuse it. It began and established a leading role in the decisions that followed, persuading the rest of the Sun energy that it was the true Source and that all should obey its leadership. This has caused untold problems within the Sun experience and prevented it from returning to its true Source roots.

The effect on this earth and the entire cosmos has been devastating over time. From its elevated position away from earth, it has loved tempting the energy on earth to succumb to its power, making itself feel good when others appear to come onto its 'side'. It has taken the energy earth has offered and twisted the truth around it to make itself fit. In reality, of course, Swamped and 'watching'

Source could never actually change their roots so the Ra's belief in its power has always been one huge illusion.

Thousands and thousands of years ago, there was an attempt by the Ra to incarnate on this earth and conquer the Swamped energy. Other Sun hierarchy incarnated at the same time and dropped into one of the centres of the Swamped energy, namely, a Chinese emperor's quarters. The end result was a huge war, a blood bath, and it was a terrible catastrophe. The Ra now sees just how much of a catastrophe this was and is deeply sad about it. It does not feel it can be forgiven for this. The Ra was also part of the forces that resisted the Noah initiative. This was deeply regrettable as the Ra now admits that Noah's role was to bring true light back to the planet, and its actions made this so much more difficult.

A visitation I experienced from the Ra energy for a couple of days taught me much. Above all else, it allowed me to experience the addictive qualities it possessed so that I could better help those whose journey had come through the Sun planet.

On its visitation, the Ra appeared to me, seemingly wanting my help. It flattered me, played havoc with the truth and confused me as only it knows how, in a very clever fashion. I had two days of such excitement, living in close contact with this unbelievable force. It seemed I had access to any knowledge I wished for and could have anything I wanted. The way I escaped from the Ra's clutches was when I came to my senses and remembered I had never, ever taken my orders from anything other than pure Source. As I recalled this, the Ra knew the game was up and it immediately left me alone. I was quite shaken by the experience and wondered why it had been allowed. I was then assured I had never been in danger as it was known already that I would see through the game fast enough. However, two days of exposure was long enough for me to understand Sun's incredibly addictive nature, and to realise how hard it is for those who are invested in it, in any shape or form, to let it go.

A number of decades ago, the Ra realised that if it continued to play games like these and others with the incarnated world, it would be close to causing the experiment called earth to collapse. At that top level, it therefore knew it had to halt the pursuit of its own illusion of power and start the process of healing itself. To that end, the hierarchy has been incarnating on earth in small chunks ever since, because it knows that nothing that is created during a state of integrated matter and energy can heal itself from the dis-embodied state. The Ra cannot reincarnate all at once as some of it has to hold the rest of the Sun power steady and in balance. As soon as some hierarchy has healed itself, it will return to spirit and allow a further chunk to come to earth to do the same. It seems a slow process to those of us who run on earth time, but in the grand scheme of things it will happen quite quickly. As it occurs, the safer our world will become.

One such chunk of energy from the Ra was sent into incarnation around the late 1950s and early 1960s. The souls dotted themselves around the world, with the sole intention of surrendering them-selves to Source.

A Journey with Martine

One of these souls—she called herself a cornerstone of the Ra—was sent to help me understand the process of surrender it is going through. Martine came from Belgium and was an extraordinarily wise woman. As we spoke together, it became clear that we were to teach each other. She knew who she was and I asked her when she arrived, 'What percentage of you is Ra and what percentage is Source?'

Martine was quick with her reply, 'I am around 20% Source and 80% Ra.'

Over the three days she was with me, we had many deep exchanges and she came to better understand what her mission on earth was and how to become free of her Sun experience. She had no difficulty letting go of her power as she was in full knowl-edge that it had already been let go of in spirit before she came to earth. Martine's heart was so pure and her willingness to heal absolute. During one of our conversations, I could feel a deep well of tears coming up from within me. On tuning into it, I became aware that they were the tears of the ancient beings. They were making us aware of the deep gratitude Source feels; it is gratitude beyond tears. I conveyed this to my counterpart: This gratitude is for the fact that the energy you carry is prepared to let go of the grip it has held over earth and also for your humility that you came to earth to allow this. Sun energy can only release its power by incarnating on earth. Right now there are a number of incarnated cornerstones from the Ra that are crumbling. None of you have done so yet but you are all on track and willing.

After the three days and before she was due to fly back to Belgium, I asked Martine, 'What percentage of you is now Ra and what percentage is Source?' A quick reply again, 'I am 80% Source and 20% Ra.' I looked at her in astonishment and exclaimed, 'You have let go of this much in three days?'

But I knew that Martine spoke her truth. I asked her how she did it. She stood up and indicated to me that where she was standing on the floor represented earth. She then took a step backwards from that spot and said she was now standing on a ring around earth that represented the Swamped experience which she was not a part of but which she thanked for all it had done to help us, forgave it and sent love to it. She then took a further step backwards into a ring which represented the Sun. She thanked it, loved it for all it had taught her, forgave it and conveyed to it that it was now time for her to step back out of the Sun experience and into her pure Source self. She no longer wished to be associated with Sun and its strong addictions. She apologised for being part of an energy that had caused so much destruction on planet earth for so long and for leading so many astray. She wished now only to follow the brilliant white Source energy within her (that is within all of us) and let go of all the pseudo gold that she had, up until then, falsely declared was God.

I was overcome by her humility. She was indeed of the hierarchy of Sun, of the Ra. Only such true nobility could have reached this position so quickly. And she further declared her full intention of letting go of the remaining 20% as quickly as she could. I was filled with immense joy and hope as I waved her goodbye.

A Journey with Nigel

Shortly afterwards, I encountered a soul who had no such humility. Nigel was of very strong Sun essence and he tried to splash his golden light everywhere he stepped. He was not interested in the true Source light, although he declared his light was of Source. In his illusive state, his gold was all he wanted to know and he was not ready to let go of his addiction at that time. Such was the power he gave out that not one of us at the retreat could be in his company for long. I knew he was heavily invested in the Sun experience but he was not of the Ra. He was of the energy that had dipped into a sun planet, not first in, but let us say, second in, with much to prove (so he thought).

After Nigel's visit, I was used in an extraordinary way. I was out in the fields when I saw seven magpies fly up from the grass ahead of me. As this was a very unusual sight and I didn't ever recall having seen it before, I recited the old magpie rhyme to myself and thought: 'Hmm, seven magpies—seven for a story that has never been told!' In that particular moment, I knew it was very significant, but that was all.

Later that day, having been inwardly directed to relax and be still in a quiet place, I found myself being transported high above the clouds to the level at which the deluded golden energy resides. I felt my brilliant white Source light getting stronger and stronger as I approached. I heard my higher self communicate with the Ra: *You came to me, taught me about your energy field, told me that you had let go of your ego and asked for my help. How can I help you when you keep feeding your old rubbish to men such as the one*

I have just been sent? If you meant what you said, you will have to stop doing that.

I was very firm. The Sun energy around me was nonplussed and stopped silently in its tracks. It had not been aware of my approach and was puzzled as to where I had come from.

After a while, I found myself floating through this deluded level of the Sun energy to the Ra domain, the hierarchical level, with my words echoing through the energy as I passed. There was a stunned silence through the realms of the Sun.

Shortly after that, I heard what seemed like a reluctant, low, gruff command from the Ra: 'Stop feeding them! *All* of them.' I became aware of the energy leaving Nigel. It held itself away from his body so he could not feel it.

In that moment, it felt as if my visit had surprised the entire Sun sphere. The Ra had wanted to redress their power on their terms, not on the terms of true Source. It felt as if they had not expected or encountered such a shocking visitation before. Source had found them out and they were totally unhinged.

I then knew why I had seen the magpies. This was a story that had never been told. The Sun experience now knew it could not hoodwink true Source, however hard it tried.

A third soul, Orla, came to the retreat soon afterwards and taught me much. Initially, she sat apart from the rest of the guests and informed me that she was too powerful to be with others; she needed to be alone. After some chat time with her, I realised that she was the next level down from Nigel. She was easier to cope with than Nigel but it wasn't long before her addiction got the better of her and I found her a few hours later, holding court amongst the other guests, unable to rein in her addiction to her power any longer.

All this was teaching me just how strong the heavily invested Sun energy is, and how the levels can drop away like the peeling of an onion. As I have shared the information, I have been gathering with those who are ready to hear; they have understood and been following in Martine's footsteps, letting go of their addiction and digging deeper to find their core, their true inner Source light.

Hints and Words to Help you on Your Journey, Originally from the Ancient Beings to Martine

To let go of the power that you have immersed yourself in is to let go of everything.

If you wish to become as us, that is indeed what you have to do; you have to surrender totally to your heart.

You cannot do this out of your own strength.

You can however apply to us for help.

You have been a cornerstone in the great empire of the sun.

Your surrender will be of enormous value to us all.

Paulina's Sun Experience

In my sessions with Louisa, I realised I felt judged. I felt like she was saying the Sun experience was wrong and my expression of that experience was wrong, so I looked deeper into it to understand why. I knew in my heart that Louisa was not judging me, and thanked her for telling me that she, as watching Source, appreciated the Sun experience. I really needed to hear that. I haven't been able to see the core of my Sun issues before, even though I understood how it all came into being, because when I looked into it deeply I have been blinded by Sunlight, so I have been in denial. Now I see that in that core there has been a deep feeling that I am somehow wrong, wrong as a person, wrong as a being and wrong as a collective consciousness. I have felt that I must have done something very bad and was therefore not worthy of the love of Source. Now I see that it is me alone who has judged myself as wrong.

I have been a child playing grown-up, and no one could see the child, feeling hurt and rejected in the dark, because I blinded them with Sunlight.

When I am on my own and am comfortable and happy, usually in nature, my heart is open and I am as close as I can be to being in alignment with Source, and this is what feels most natural for me. When I interact with other people, I become uncomfortable. I realise that because of this, I have been hiding that inner self by covering it with Sunshine. I have not felt safe without my sunny front and even use it when I write emails, when I blog on my website and through all other interfaces between myself and others. People like the Sunshine and I now realise that I have felt safer giving people what they want, all my life. Others say things like, 'When she smiles, the sun comes out.' I realise that this is all a cover, a protection that I have been subconsciously using. I have not known any other way to be in front of people.

I also realise that when I have tried to talk about my inner world with others, I have been talking through my Sun experience and using its language. Now I understand that I have not been saying what I really mean, which is why I am being misunderstood. I have subconsciously been making myself misunderstood. I have been putting on this Sunshine front whenever I feel uncomfortable, alone or not. I feel it in my body as tension and contraction. My left foot starts to crunch up, I close my solar plexus and my stomach gets tight, and my shoulders scrunch forward to block my heart and restrict my breathing. I have been doing this subconsciously all my life. I have been aware of it for a long time but couldn't stop. Now I know why I'm doing it, I can change it and am in a *lot* less pain.

It has also not felt safe to be my true self because I have felt like I will damage people with too much love or too much brightness, so I have suppressed myself. I now realise that this comes from my Sun experience; I have confused myself about what it means to shine. I have confused shining with being externally bright and powerful, instead of just being me, internally bright and powerful, which is completely safe.

I know I am Source in my heart. I am innocent and pure, no matter what my experiences have been. We are all innocent and truly loved. I still feel very uncomfortable around others, but I am learning to shed the experience of the Sun planet and keep myself completely open.

***

Complete release comes when the Sun soul recognises that:

1. Sun energy has tried to portray to the world that it is 'right'.
2. It has done this to cover its deeper belief that it has done something 'wrong'.
3. Underneath both those beliefs, it is actually innocent.

When each part of Sun experience energy accepts these facts and allows itself to feel its innocence once more, it will let go of its 'pseudo gold' knowing that to retain it any longer is doing the world a terrible disservice.

11
Further Understanding of the Swamped Experience

The energy that we call Swamped, that experienced the integration with the matter experiment which never made it to the earth surface, is sadly left with a huge and very damaging sense of failure. It felt it had broken its promise. This feeling of failure was made worse by the fact that it had had many attempts to finish the job off and still did not achieve it. The final withdrawal, when the energy felt totally overpowered by matter, seemed like the last straw and it was hard for it to emerge, in its own judgement—un-victorious, amongst Sun and watching Source.

The most common hallmarks of every being on earth whose journey has come through the Swamped planet are an overpowering sense of *failure*, a belief they cannot succeed, a strong tendency to *doubt*, to suffer *depression*, to go into *despair*—sometimes leading to suicide—and most carry an inner memory of *dilemma* from the dinosaur age, which often disables them from making key decisions. They often have a *dense*, *sombre* and *intense* nature and fall into the belief they are unloved very easily. This lack of self-worth which we all carry, together with a heavily invested Swamped experience, is a difficult combination of experiences to untangle and release.

One man I met who was heavily invested in the Swamped experience, aptly labelled his experience of life as 'living in an endless loop of hell'. His loop was one of suffering in a similar way, over and over again. He described himself as feeling totally crushed. Many of the more heavily invested Swamped souls have resonated with his words, and in coming to understand that the loop pattern is a repeat of the Swamped energy's efforts to fully incarnate over and over again, they have felt less alone and better able to move on from it.

The most common Swamped energy-invested emotions or sensations are:

- failure;
- depression;
- dilemma;
- dense;
- intense;
- sombre;
- despair;
- shame;
- betrayal;
- responsibility;
- doubt.

As we know, the Swamped experience has a hierarchy which came into being during the dinosaur age on earth. At that time, the most heavily damaged of the Swamped energy was the initial 1% that raced off towards the earth's surface. Within the 1% lies the deepest, darkest and angriest energy. We know that 2% to around 20% of Swamped energy followed the 1% and also incarnated during the dinosaur age, the 20% being the least heavily invested, because it was last to cross the divide. As around 17–18% crossed the divide, the energy was beginning to hear the call to stop from Sun and watching Source. By the time 19% had started to cross over, it was slowing down and the energy approaching the 20–21% mark had actually stopped.

We can now more fully understand the large division, or some refer to it as a 'wound', between 20% and 21% invested Swamped energy. With varying degrees of discomfort, the 17% through to the 20% carried the decision to continue to bolt towards the surface. The last over the line, so to speak, or as 20% of the energy was going over, it looked back at the 21% that had stopped and felt huge consternation: why were the rest of their kith and kin not coming with them? The 20% expected a sudden surge of energy to follow them any minute. But no surge arrived. The consternation grew deeper. Had they done the right thing to carry on? Should they have stopped with the rest? Should they stop now? However, they continued, limping after the rest of the Swamped energy at a slower pace, not knowing if they were right or wrong but ultimately too fearful to go back.

With similarly varying degrees of discomfort, the 21% through to the remainder of the Swamped energy carried the decision to stop, deep in its core. It could see 20% of the Swamped energy ahead of it, disappearing into the distance and getting smaller and smaller. But the bulk of Swamped energy, 21% onwards, had dug its heels in alongside Sun and watching Source on that unmarked inner ring. It was torn apart. Had it done the right thing? Should it have followed its own kind and carried on? Should it carry on now? Were Sun and watching Source right?

Within Swamped energy as a whole, the energy that happened to be closest to the inner ring (20% on one side of the wound and 21% on the other) holds the strongest feeling of dilemma. Neither of the experiences has ever known since that time if they did the right thing or not. Both feel very responsible for the health and well-being of the energy on their side. Alive in their energy field is a deep need to hold onto control because of the strength it took to separate and make their own decisions. The 21% felt the build-up of energy behind it as it all came to a slithering halt. It had to dig its heels in harder and harder to hold the position it had decided upon. The 20% had long disappeared into the distance and, as it felt it could no longer contemplate going back across the wound to its other half, it became very stubborn, full of uncertainty, yet getting more and more insistent on defending its decision.

The wound, division or—it has even been described as a fracture—of between 20% and 21% is wide and deep. Within the wound is a huge amount of sorrow at the separation that took place. Both sides came to feel very different to one another as they sustained different experiences. The initial 20% that crossed the divide has certain traits in varying degrees. Such individuals:

- of course hold the sense of dilemma, 20% the strongest and 1% the least;
- try to force life instead of allowing a process;
- carry deep, mostly unacknowledged, guilt for what they did;
- often have a massive determination to convince the world that their way is right, struggling to allow themselves to see they could be wrong;
- find it hard to change;
- swing in and out of depression and dark feelings;
- try to control life and what comes at them, in an attempt to avoid the pain already held within them from igniting;
- carry a strong trapped feeling and when the trap is sprung, they often can't control their reactions and explode;
- are often rebellious when someone tries to control them;
- are resistant to their inner connection;
- have a strong feeling they can never be forgiven;
- hold utter despair, disappointment and fury within their heart.

The 21% that remained behind hold the following list of traits:

- a sense of dilemma;
- a huge amount of responsibility;
- life seeming to be a series of dead-ends (don't seem to get any-where, however hard you try);
- doubt, particularly self-doubt;
- sorrow;
- guilt;
- uncertainty as to what is right and wrong;
- feeling unsettled;
- feeling joyless (yet they can see there is joy to be had);
- self-criticism/judgement;
- never feeling they can do what they want to do;
- a sense of 'When is it going to be my turn?'

When souls on planet earth recognise and understand this level of creation, they have the opportunity to dig deep, open themselves honestly to all that is held in the collective part of their core, asking forgiveness of the Sun, Swamped and watching Source experiences and, most importantly, asking forgiveness of each other. As they let go of the relevant emotions and beliefs they each hold, they can heal the wound within them and then send healing into the general wound in the Swamped energy. Once the wound within them is no more, they can step back from the Swamped experience, step into the Sun experience, forgive and thank it for its help on the journey and then step back again to reconnect with pure Source within.

One of the most courageous humans I have ever met is Selina, who remembers being part of the collective experience on the 21% spectrum, when the wound in the Swamped experience first began. So rigidly did the 21% experience dig its heels in at that time, it is incredibly hard for her to let go now. Selina felt so responsible for all she was holding on to that letting go was not an option. If she were to let go, she felt she would let the whole world down. It was only as she came to understand that she had done the right thing by holding on at the time and that the hierarchy from each of the three S's was now at last adhering to the agreement it had originally made, that Selina had the courage to loosen her grip. If she (and her kind) had not held so fast to her position at the time, and more Swamped energy had crossed the divide and incarnated, earth might not have become the success it is today. It was down to the dogged tenacity of the 21% that only 20% of Swamped escaped and therefore earth was far less knocked out of balance than it could have been. Further, when Selina realised that a different planet had already been in this position, had allowed its total Swamped experience to escape and was now in deep trouble, she was able to believe she could hand everything over to the universal consciousness and become free of what she had believed to be her personal responsibility.

It is worth noting that many Swamped experience souls, once they have found freedom from these Swamped emotions, have a fear of meeting and becoming involved with other Swamped energy in the future, in case they get pulled back in. The last part of this part of their journey is to trust they are truly free and can truly put the experience behind them and not be vulnerable to its grip anymore.

The Healing of the Swamped Wound

One day in September 2021, I invited Meg (mentioned in Chapter 6) and Selina to meet together. I had first met them about 12 years before, first one and then, a few weeks later, the other. I did not realise how important these two meetings were at the time, or that they represented the opposite sides of a coin. As events played out in the summer of 2021 and both ladies healed from their dinosaur-related experiences, it gradually dawned on me that what Meg and Selina had opened up to 12 years before was their part in the opposing sides of the Swamped wound, and that it was now ready to conclude.

I spoke with both ladies and they agreed to meet, only having spoken on the phone to each other in all those years. Their conversations on the phone had been difficult and stressful. It was with courage that they met and I was able to ask each to share with the other their 12-year journey. Now that we all understood that one of them represented the 20% on one side of the wound and the other represented the 21%, we understood the difficulties that had stood between them. Meg was able to explain to Selina how she had come across the bridge and now rejoined the 80% of Swamped energy. Meg and Selina held hands and formed their own bridge. As each lady had now healed their wounds independently, their coming together and forming a consciously healed bridge was invaluable to the healing of the wound on this planet. It was a piece of magic as they then let all that lay in the wound between them dissolve.

Any part of the dinosaur energy in the future would be able to cross this now permanent bridge when they were ready. The magnitude of all Meg and Selina had suffered over the 12-year period and before was known and, as they now understood why it had all happened, they could let it all go. They had elected to be part of this agreement before they were born. Their job was done; the joy was tangible and we celebrated.

An 18% Invested Soul Heals

In her own words, this is how Cora experienced her healing. She came to a point in her life where she could no longer tolerate the level of anger she experienced within herself on a daily basis. Certain circumstances caused her to feel stupid, ashamed, intense and as though she was doing everything wrong. She knew she needed to change her approach to life. She knew her energy was too chaotic and she needed to slow down, calm down and trust the process of life. She felt she was headstrong and controlling. She wasn't sure if she wanted to give up or keep going with life. The massive dilemma she was facing was: 'If I keep going, it's too scary, but giving up isn't an option.'

Cora knew that the only way to set herself free was to face it all. She sank herself bravely into the actual feelings she held deep inside her. She felt dark, empty, sorrowful, hollow, trapped in self, at a dead-end, with nowhere to go, lonely and unworthy. She looked deep but initially could not find the anger. She only found it when she opened up to the possibility of forgiving herself.

She told me, 'When I asked myself if I could forgive myself for crossing the gap, the anger came rising rapidly to the fore. It was so huge and intense I started to blame others for what had happened. It was so scary.' She looked up at me and said, 'I am not at all surprised that souls like me transfer their anger to others rather than face it.'

Once Cora had owned the fact that the anger she held was all her own and accepted that she could be forgiven for her part in the dinosaur age, she could let it go. It left her, by degrees, like a huge black cloud that was so much bigger than herself. Hopefully, Cora's experience will give others reading this the courage to face their own anger, to own it and to forgive themselves from wherever it is rooted. A world with less projected anger would be such a major enlightening development, especially that which stems from the age of the dinosaur.

Swamped Experience and the Narcissistic Traits

I am deeply grateful to a few narcissists who have come into my life to help me understand this complex personality disorder. Through their friendships, I have been able to help so many others who have become painfully embroiled with a narcissist. If you look at the traits of the 20% of Swamped experience, some of these characteristics can be found in all narcissists, to a greater or lesser degree.

Many of these traits were also experienced in the form of volcanic explosion at the time of the earth's Split. Through one particular man, I was able to learn the following, and while he has still not been able to forgive himself and release both levels (volcanic and Swamped) from his experience, he does at least understand his roots. The time for the deep release of the narcissistic personality is getting closer.

First, it is important to understand the volcanic experience at the time of earth's Split. As the first rumblings of the Split on earth occurred, deep inside the mountains, one of these being the largest mountain at the site of Machu Picchu, it was felt that something enormous was about to happen. The inner mountain's perception of itself became that of being out of control, trapped, terrified, helpless, nervous and panicked. What was happening to it? Why was it feeling different to the outer rocks around it? Why was it being singled out for change in this way? What had it done?

In this initial moment of terror, it called to pure Source for help. The cry for help resounded through the mountains, wave after wave, and was picked up as a tiny discord in oneness by some golden lions who were feeding on the surface. The cry was faint yet full of anguish. The lions became alerted to the anguish, had no idea where it had come from but nevertheless responded to it by automatically gathering closely together and following an inner instinct to descend the mountain.

Meanwhile, the growing individual consciousness in the core of the mountain became stronger and more and more widespread. In terror and anguish, individual rocks and the raging fire reached out for a release from their perceived trap and were ejaculated out of the mountain into the air. The rocks had no wish other than to escape the terrible thing that was happening to them. They flew out of control, high into the air, one after another, randomly scattering themselves in the atmosphere. Eventually, the terror subsided enough for them to respond to a pull back towards earth. The red hot rocks rained back down onto the mountainsides in a way that seemed to destroy everything they contacted beneath them. The experience left that part of our creation with an intense feeling of guilt and it could not forgive itself for what it thought it had done.

Many lions who had been alerted early on, had by this time reached the foothills of the mountain and its relative safety. They looked back with horror at the carnage behind them, but stayed together as a pride, retaining a sense of inner connection that most had lost.

The mountain continued to throw its inner self higher and higher into the atmosphere until the main mountain had almost entirely collapsed. Every form of life that had become caught in its volcanic eruption had been destroyed. By the time the chaos from the explosion had subsided, nearly all but the lions had reached a full state of individual consciousness. The shock and horror all around the mountains were overwhelming and everything in the vicinity blamed the volcano for what had happened. The volcano even blamed itself as it knew no better.

But deep in its core, the erupting mountain retained the memory of its call to Source for help. It has therefore felt it has never been listened to, never fully valued, has felt aggrieved and deeply misunderstood. Not only had it not been helped but it had been blamed and has had to live with the consequences of that ever since.

The burden lies heavily within volcanic experience but yet it knows in its heart that to be blamed is not the truth. Therefore, it twists the perceived truth to try and be understood and squirms beneath the burden that the rest of the world gave it, trying to find comfort. Over time, it has come to believe that Source does not answer its call. It has learned to survive by controlling, cajoling, twisting, lying, whatever it takes to prevent a further disaster.

The truth of what actually happened *was* wiped out of consciousness and it has taken thousands and thousands of years for the lions to remember that original call for help that saved their lives at the time.

The volcanic energy, or the inner mountain, has been forgiven by those who understand these things. Forgiveness has been sent into the core of the mountain by many golden lions. In turn, the mountain experience needs to understand and forgive the lions and indeed all of creation for blaming it.

The truth is that if the volcano hadn't called for help in that moment and if the lions hadn't picked the call up, the whole experiment that we call planet earth might not have succeeded, or at the very best would have taken a lot longer to succeed. Would any other part of creation (other than the alerted lions) have ever remembered the oneness enough to make so many attempts to bring it back? Would such wisdom have been retained in enough quantity by anything else? We will never know.

What we do know is that the force which caused so much destruction at the Split is the very force that has helped to save us. The volcano called for help from Source, after it had become individually conscious, unlike anything else at the time, and that very call, because of its timing, in an individually expressed state, is invaluable. The golden lions that picked it up, as they came into their own separated state, did not lose the memory. They retained it deep inside so that one day it would be possible to reignite and use it again.

When narcissists can truly accept that they have been forgiven, the hold these experiences have on them will leave. One man, Aaron, who carried both the dinosaur and the volcanic experiences, came to see Geoff and me and, on hearing the above, literally exploded in front of us. His vociferous, out-of-control explosion could have been heard a fair few miles away!

'Do you know how hard it was for us?' he roared. 'We came back to the inner ring and you held us prisoner. You made us feel so bad. You did not understand how it was for us. You blamed us and would not trust us again. We have lived in this prison for so long. You did it to us again when we exploded at the Split. We have felt alone, wrong, dark, full of terror and outcast forever…'.

Aaron hardly drew breath as he raged, his body towering over us. 'You tell us we are innocent. You tell us that we are part of you and you are part of us and yet you shun us, reject us and make us feel so bad.'

There was nothing Geoff or I could do or say to stop Aaron's raving and bring him to reason. The raving went on for about twenty minutes before he ran out of steam. But it was an experience to learn from. He epitomised how deeply wounding such past experiences are, and how difficult they will be for all those connected with them to overcome. If you recognise that there are some souls on earth that carry the combination of the Swamped and volcanic experiences, some of the darkest acts in the world are better explained. You might also recognise that they need true and unconditional forgiveness from as many souls as possible to bring about their healing.

Healing from the Narcissistic Trait after Death

Zoola came to see me after her mother had died a couple of weeks beforehand. She wanted to know why her narcissistic mother had treated her so badly. I tuned into her mother and found that, as she died, she had slid out of her body via her head and she was lying face down on a stretcher of sorts, under a heap of black soot. I could not rouse her.

I decided to tell Zoola and her dormant mother about Machu Picchu and all that had happened between the lions and the inner mountain at the Split. She was unresponsive until I told her about the call for help that the lions had heard. Then there was a sudden shift in her soul. She indicated to me that she had heard that call echoing through her throughout this lifetime. Zoola and I then asked her mother for forgiveness for blaming the volcano and assured her we knew she was innocent and that her call had been heard. We felt her shift and, shortly afterwards, she allowed her soul to leave her body and return to spirit. Zoola and I both knew great healing had taken place. We spent the next few hours letting her mother's pain and agony leave earth through our bodies so she would not come back with it again.

***

It is important to realise that these narcissistic souls are no worse or better than anyone else; they are purely victims of circumstance.

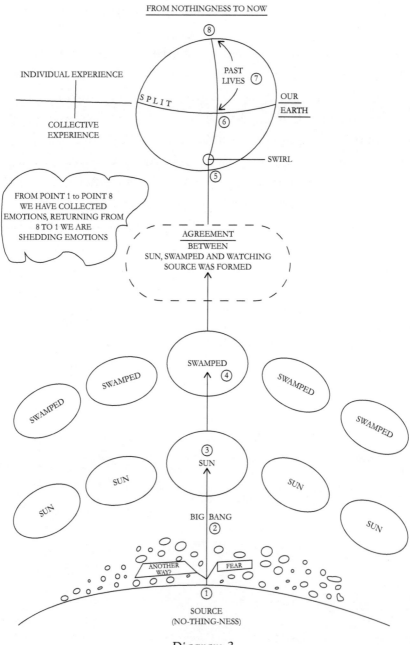

Diagram 3

12
State of Being

When we understand that the 'other' place we are looking for is a state of being *within* us, we have the choice to change. The fear that we all came in with, because we had no other point of reference, can be let go of; and as we do so, this allows a state of joy to emerge. We cannot find true joy until all the fear has been understood and released.

The purpose of these writings is to help you, the reader, understand the enlightenment process. Once you understand how you acquired your current state of being, you can recognise and heal, first from this life, and then take yourself back down the route you came up. In a nutshell, these key places, or we could refer to them as egoic release points, include:

8. this life;
7. past lives;
6. the Split;
5. the moment we entered this planet;
4 & 3. the Sun, Swamped or watching Source experience;
2. the Big Bang;
1. the moment the cosmos began to expand
   and previous cosmic expansions…

The fear doesn't have to be released in this exact order but this was the order that we all gained it, in varying ways and degrees.

To heal from this life, you have to take ownership of your own faults. While you are continually pinning things on others, there is little hope. When you realise it is 'you' who must change, you begin to understand the magic of inner healing.

Past lives, when you accept they are real, can come spontaneously into your consciousness to be released and the energy from them can then leave your body. It is important to forgive all those who hurt you, and for you to ask forgiveness of anyone you hurt, before you try and release the emotions. Sometimes past lives are so traumatic that the holder of the trauma needs help. Make sure you follow your intuition when looking for the right person to help you. It can save you a lot of time.

Number six requires a full understanding (memory) of what you experienced at the Split before you can forgive those around you and yourself. You can then itemise all your emotions that played out at the time, for, as they first began at the Split, they are your personal roots which have replayed in some form or other ever since. When you have fully let each one go—and that takes time and persistence—you will find you no longer experience these emotions. Releasing the emotions from the Split or roots means you are shedding the repetitive patterns from all other past lives at the same time.

To help you heal from number five, I will here remind you that the three S's all felt judgement of each other which, in turn, created resentment, fear, anger and the sense of being overwhelmed. So, these five emotions began in a collective form and are therefore held in every part of creation on this planet. When we understand that:

(A) We are currently a success on this planet (we are more light than dark).

(B) We are all on the same side. (We all began at Source and carry the same original intention.)

Then,

(C) We start to thank each other.

And

(D) Move into acceptance of each other.

These four laws negate the laws of judgement and so on, and we can let the habits go.

As for numbers four and three, briefly, if we were part of the Sun experience, the common denominator between us is a holding back and a tendency to numb off to our emotions. Swamped is commonly recognised by a continual feeling of failure and the tendency to experience life as a series of dead-ends. Watching Source tends to be rather pious and on the innocent side.

Numbers two and one tend to be understood and released spontaneously when the time is right. It's a journey we all have to go on in order to reach enlightenment but if you push yourself into these understandings too soon, you can end up in a tangle. The best way is to make the universe aware that this is the level at which you wish to heal eventually and ask to be taken to that level of understanding when you are ready; then live in the trust that it will happen.

Number two, the Big Bang, resides as a memory in all of us and affects everything about us on a daily basis. We should not attempt a release until we have almost fully moved through ego points three to eight.

In terms of number one, we came into this cosmic expansion wanting to find a way to exist other than in fear. We could not have labelled it as joy when we started, but as we understand more and more about our long journey, we can. Now we know what the 'other way' looks and feels like, even if only in small bouts right now, it brings the opportunity to enlighten ourselves ever closer.

<u>MAJOR HEALING PHASES</u>
Each point release occurs as we let go of the
ego attatched to it and surrender the relevant emotions

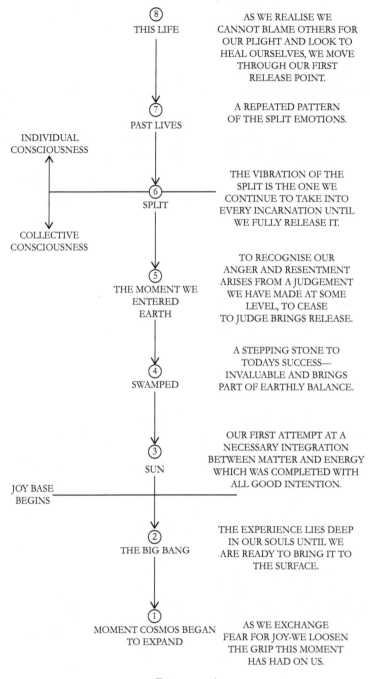

⑧
THIS LIFE

AS WE REALISE WE
CANNOT BLAME OTHERS FOR
OUR PLIGHT AND LOOK TO
HEAL OURSELVES, WE MOVE
THROUGH OUR FIRST
RELEASE POINT.

⑦
PAST LIVES

A REPEATED PATTERN
OF THE SPLIT EMOTIONS.

INDIVIDUAL
CONSCIOUSNESS

⑥
SPLIT

THE VIBRATION OF THE
SPLIT IS THE ONE WE
CONTINUE TO TAKE INTO
EVERY INCARNATION UNTIL
WE FULLY RELEASE IT.

COLLECTIVE
CONSCIOUSNESS

⑤
THE MOMENT WE
ENTERED
EARTH

TO RECOGNISE OUR
ANGER AND RESENTMENT
ARISES FROM A JUDGEMENT
WE HAVE MADE AT SOME
LEVEL, TO CEASE
TO JUDGE BRINGS RELEASE.

④
SWAMPED

A STEPPING STONE TO
TODAYS SUCCESS—
INVALUABLE AND BRINGS
PART OF EARTHLY BALANCE.

③
SUN

OUR FIRST ATTEMPT AT A
NECESSARY INTEGRATION
BETWEEN MATTER AND ENERGY
WHICH WAS COMPLETED WITH
ALL GOOD INTENTION.

JOY BASE
BEGINS

②
THE BIG BANG

THE EXPERIENCE LIES DEEP
IN OUR SOULS UNTIL WE
ARE READY TO BRING IT TO
THE SURFACE.

①
MOMENT COSMOS BEGAN
TO EXPAND

AS WE EXCHANGE
FEAR FOR JOY-WE LOOSEN
THE GRIP THIS MOMENT
HAS HAD ON US.

Diagram 4

13
The Joy Pathway

It is not possible to explore this pathway until the universal collective experience knows you are ready for it. All you can do to prepare yourself is first gain an understanding of the depths I have conveyed in these writings and then start the process of clearing the fears from each of the eight areas mentioned in the last chapter until suddenly you find yourself taken there. The joy path does not recognise fear so it can only become your path when you have let go of enough fear and live in trust. When trust has become part of your every moment of being, it can happen.

My Own Journey into Joy

Having become joy based (as opposed to fear based) some years before 2020, I was then taken on a journey through the Big Bang. I was put through many tests until I passed them without a ripple and became the balance that was necessary. The final test culminated in an experience that proved my trust was stronger than my fear. At that point, my consciousness was allowed to pass through the Big Bang to the preceding era. What follows is how it happened for me.

I was feeling a dark weight in my heart such as I had not felt for around 40 years. In fact, I had grown used to not having any weight in my heart at all. As the weight did not leave, I decided to go within and ask what it wanted. As I dived in, there were big black rocks flying at me from everywhere. Digging deeper, the rocks became smaller and smaller until I came to some solid rock that was too hard to penetrate. At this stage, I knew I was being taken into the energy field of the Big Bang. This solid rock felt like it represented the 'root of evil'.

As my consciousness failed to penetrate into the root of evil, I turned my back on it. I had therefore unintentionally shown it I had no fear of it. With my back still turned away, I asked it to let me in. Suddenly, it grabbed me from behind and dragged me into its core. Everything around me seemed black and sticky. A voice from the gloom spoke to me: 'We have let you in because we know you won't judge us. We know you understand that you are us and we are you.'

Well, that was true! I then felt its huge sense of being trapped. I asked: 'Why do you keep your energy stuck in here?' Interestingly, I realised from the reaction that from its point of view, the energy had not considered itself to be stuck.

After a pause, a reply came: 'OK. Well, now you are in here with us, you are stuck too. We've got you.' I casually replied: 'I can come and go as I please.' I proceeded to let myself out. Then I realised I was incorrect. While I had indeed let myself out, I couldn't let myself back in unless the dark energy allowed me back in. And to my surprise it did!

On my second visit inside the core of this dark energy or rock, as it had seemed to me, I sent light from my heart through the whole domain. The light was unconditional and beautiful and the dark lapped it up. I spoke lovingly out loud to it: 'You actually have a choice. You can choose to enlighten if you wish. I bring you the gift of "no judgement" (I had an inner knowing that others had brought them this gift before me.) I also bring you alignment,' I continued.

I then asked if I could continue my journey through the dark energy and let myself out the other side as I wanted to see what lay there. Nothing stopped my progress and I found myself opening the door on the other side into the most brilliant white light that felt all-encompassing. I wondered if I should enter the light. Eventually, I did so and as I looked back at the darkness a call came out from my soul towards it: 'Remember who you are...'

I withdrew my attention from the dark and looked around in the brilliant light but did not recognise my surroundings. I asked the light to dissipate the darkness in my heart. I found I was struggling to let it all go. The light spoke to me: 'It's up to you. You can let it all go if you want to, or you can keep it.'

Of course, I wanted to let it go and I continued to release as much as I could. As I did so, I had this amazing knowing of how deep a love the enlightened ones had for the root of darkness. I could feel their longing for the dark to let go of its story and heal itself. I then pondered: 'How do I get this last dark hook out of myself?' I thought to trust the dark to pull the hook out. I asked: 'Please pull the hook out from my heart. I trust you. Your reward will be great and be returned to you a thousand times over.'

In that moment, I knew the only way for any of us to become free of the root of darkness/evil is to trust it 100%. As I came into a state of complete and utter acceptance and trust, the hook finally came out. The flow of love between us was then absolute.

Before the Big Bang

I then had to face the four emotions that had occurred on a truly all-encompassing scale as we began this expansion of the cosmos. As the density within original Source began to change, there was a cry of 'No' as the fear path came into consciousness once again. That old familiar feeling of fear was more than we could bear. The changing field of energy and matter screamed in its depths: 'No! We said we wanted to expand another way. We stipulated that we never wanted to do this in fear again! No! No! No! Why is this happening? Where is the other way?' The fear was insurmountable at this moment for we did not realise that it was 'us' that had to create the 'other way'. We did not realise that 'joy' did not exist and could not exist, until we created it.

So the reimmersion into fear brought with it such shock. We had trusted that we would be given another way and the shock that it was seemingly not to be so was devastating to us. This shock brought a panic about. We could not bear the thought of going through another, 'seventh' expansion. It was unthinkable, beyond measure. This then brought about huge anger. We had been prepared to expand again, been brave enough, trusted enough and yet here we were, experiencing the fear path again.

So, the four emotions listed below governed our expansion as we separated into duality once more:

- fear;
- panic;
- anger;
- shock.

I knew I must release these at this very deep level in order to fully enlighten. I already knew the root of fear lay in the previous expansion of the cosmic field and, in the knowing of it, it no longer had a hold on me. I have lived in acceptance of it, knowing it will fully release as time goes on. The panic and anger were fairly easy for me as I was already so deeply healed. The one that for me was more difficult was shock. It took me a few years of continually experiencing shock, and therefore continually probing how I might release the root of shock, before the answer came to me.

In the end, it was so simple. There is no shock. What is now understood can no longer be a shock because it is understood! How stupid I had been not to see this before! I felt the root of shock within me melt away in one fell swoop.

Somewhere along the line, during this process, I found myself going through what seemed like a doorway back into the void that lay in the nothingness before the eighth expansion began. From inside the void, I could see the doorway I had just come through and I could see another doorway to the right of it. Both were closed. I felt safe but I knew I didn't want to stay there for long.

Pathway of Light

I stood in the void. The two doors stood open and there were two pathways in my sight. I knew which one I had just left and the other seemed dark, empty, unexciting and even spooky. I knew I had to trust blindly if I was to choose the spooky path. The choice was: go back to the old path or move on. I chose to trust and took a step into the unknown pathway. Immediately, to my surprise, I found myself surrounded by brilliant white light again. I hesitated and then stepped back and found myself returned to the void. Having rebalanced myself, I stepped forward once more.

I pondered from my surroundings of light: 'There is nothing here! I am in a different void. I feel so safe. This is a place of total trust.' I knew that if I walked forward, there would be more of the brilliant white around me. As I wanted to get away from the black and leave the fear behind me, I took several steps forward. I stopped and pondered again: 'This is so strange. There is no point of reference.'

I knew that few had been here before me. I could see a selection of differently shaped footprints on the white snow-like path ahead of me. I knew I was not ready to follow the footprints, however much I wanted to. I knew I had to empty out any remaining dregs of fear before I could move on.

A voice confirmed my thoughts: 'You have to stay here in this "holding place" until you are used to being in the brilliant white light. You will be taken care of.' The voice had a matronly quality about it and I felt like a little schoolgirl, but the words were said in such a way that there could be no doubting them. I would be looked after in every possible way. I found I was not feeling anything particular. I was not happy or sad. I only knew that nothing would induce me to exchange what I had found and go back to where I had come from.

As I stood silently taking it all in, I thought about how when it snows it changes our whole world. Well, it was like that. There was nothing to see but white. My inner knowing suddenly informed me that I stood in the same world I had always known, but it was all white.

My astonishment was considerable. This path was the same path, the same world; the same world I had always known! It was just white! I had thought when I entered that I was somewhere different. But I wasn't. The whole environment was so silent. I thought: 'What shall I do?'

The voice came again: 'What would you like to do?' I realised I would just carry on with life as it had always been. It seemed so strange. How could I carry on with life when I 'seemed' to be on a completely different track? I argued with myself. The old track was so noisy and threatening. This new track seemed so silent, safe and still. I floundered. There was nothing to hold on to. Nothing to reach out to…

In my uncertainty, I asked myself once more: 'What shall I do?' This time my question was met with silence. I decided to remain in this brilliant white holding bay I had found and take life one step at a time. One day at a time. I had no idea what would happen next. There was only trust.

***

The original darkness is made up of the fears or memories we carry from other expansions of the cosmos. As separation began at the beginning of this expansion and the Big Bang took place, the dark re-emerged and the old memories became like a shield that kept us from our light. The only way back to our true source is to find a way through it.

When we know and trust that at the root of evil:

- there is no evil;
- there is no separation;
- there is no judgement;
- and it works for the greater good;

—then we are no longer a slave to it.

That very evening, these words came to me:

> 'Love as you have never loved before,
> Be open as you have never opened before,
> Clear out as you have never cleared out before.'

I therefore asked to experience exactly that.

The next day, I felt an urge to ask to become the balance of earth, fire, water and spirit. I found myself consciously back in the brilliant white holding bay. I looked and felt my way round it. I sensed I was not alone but could not physically see anyone else. It was shown to me that I would only see others if it became necessary, as it was important for me to be experiencing and coming to understand this next phase of my enlightenment process alone right now.

Lesson Time in the Holding Bay

I now understood where my soul resided. This beautiful holding bay would be my home until I was ready to move on. I could go back to what I knew but I had no wish to go back. The journey ahead seemed daunting but I recalled the voice that had previously assured me I would be looked after. I trusted.

For the *first* experience, I felt a swirly fear and trepidation as I was driven to a hospital following a very severe injury. What would be the outcome? What would my life become now? My emotions went up and down. I did not want to arrive at the hospital in this mess as the highest outcome would not be achieved. It came to me that I should sink my consciousness into the holding bay, which I did. A voice asked me: 'How would you feel if this was going on and you were travelling up the unknown pathway in the snow?'

Immediately, I responded that that would feel so safe, so amazingly light and I would be looked after. There was a little pause before the voice came again: 'It's the same pathway.' I was gobsmacked. Stunned! Of course it was! Almost immediately, the fear fell away and my hospital visit went like clockwork.

The *second* time, I experienced feeling overwhelmed. This time I was quicker off the mark and went straight to the holding bay for advice. I felt that I released half of the feeling of being overwhelmed in the same way I had released the fear and trepidation, but then got stuck. I trusted I would be shown how to let go of the rest and stayed calm in that trust.

I went to sleep, woke up in the middle of the night and found myself in the pathway. It was the same pathway yet it seemed very different somehow. If I touched the edges of the pathway, I knew it would cushion me from any impacts that came my way and send me gently off in the other direction. I might be travelling from one side of the pathway to the other, over and over again, but I knew the cushioning would protect me. It was an awesome feeling. I felt so safe, safe as I had never felt before.

A voice spoke to me: 'Did you think it was all give on your part, all suffering and all up to you? This is a give-and-take pathway. All impacts will be cushioned. You are always held; you will always be safe, loved, looked after and looked out for. You are not alone! We help you and you help us. This is a two-way journey.'

I hardly dared to hear what I was hearing. Could this really be true? The relief was mind-blowing. So this is how life can be? This is how life will be from now on. Nothing can crush me unless I stop listening to my intuition and separate myself again. I am truly, truly loved.

In the *third* place, I experienced judgement. A situation was shown to me where I still held a judgement of others. I was devastated with myself. I could not see a way out of this deeply ingrained habit, so I asked for help. I was shown a path which led directly from my body to pure Source. This path was straight, true, strong and unwavering. It was solid and could not be deviated from. Others could cross and re-cross this path as often as they wished to, but I had to remain constant. There must never be any judgement of any choices that others make. It was not my job to teach but simply to be. I can only exist on my joy pathway if I am constant to this rule—as the universal light is constant to us all.

In the *fourth* place, grey spots that needed shifting from me kept appearing. I began to feel the journey was impossible. How could I ever become pure enough? Feeling very uncertain of myself yet still trusting the process, I asked for help yet again. This time I was told something so simple yet so easy to comprehend that I relaxed over it all completely: 'Be the joy of perceived separation. Do not live in the fear of perceived separation.' Of course! I had been going down the fear route again. Fearing I would not be good enough or not get there. There? Where is 'there', for goodness sake?

All I had to do was live the joy, live in acceptance and appreciation of all that appears to be separate to me, and know how beautiful it is to experience the differences between things. This is what we had been yearning for. The differences are there to give us consciousness. They are there to be enjoyed. I am not right or wrong. No one is right or wrong. There is no right or wrong anywhere. We are simply experiences!

I felt so much better after that. I didn't have to be perfect. I just had to be the most constant I could be, without judgement of myself or anything else. The universe is a constant. When we take ourselves out of the constant or—in other words—out of alignment, we put ourselves under stress and into the fear of separation. However long it takes me, I knew I wished to become totally constant, living in continual alignment with all that is, living in the *joy* of separation.

What I did not know at that time was that the above was only a brief introduction to the holding bay and the path of joy. It was 18 months later, in the spring of 2022, that the universe decided I was ready for the real journey! I am currently recording everything that is awakening in me as I am experiencing it, and I have no doubt that it will form a hugely important part of any second edition of this book. All I will say is that it is so unexpected and is staggering in its nature. I am so excited…

14

Celebrating the Coronavirus

The following was written in diary form as the event occurred for the benefit of a group of 20 souls who were able to help hold the planet's balance at the time. They were already feeling many aspects for themselves in various ways but this diary helped them to understand it better.

Diary in the Form of Letters from the Author

First Letter to the Group of 20

In late autumn of 2019, I remember asking the universe if there was anything I could do to help China. I had always felt an intense, deep, dark energy in its roots and never had a desire to visit the place. When I remembered this, I could see why the spiral of such a virus could begin/spread from China and appear to take control, as the energy was already in place beneath the surface from many millions of years ago when a similar event took place during the dinosaur age.

During the last week in February 2020, I felt the universe asking me to be a vessel from which the enlightened or ancient energy held in the ether could come through and help steady the planet. I have never felt that request before so I knew how significant the coronavirus situation was becoming. It didn't feel like it was the virus itself that was the danger but the way it was being handled by the authorities. I also felt that dark energy was releasing from China's roots very slowly and in patches.

The next morning, on tuning in again, I felt a huge chimney-like flow of dark smoke leaving from a hole in the earth from somewhere in China. I knew that the awful dark energy was starting to release much faster and that it needed to be dissipated quickly because no one on earth was ensuring that it was being dissipated. I quickly asked for everything that was releasing to be dissipated before it landed anywhere and caused destruction. The strength of the dark flow was strong and consistent, almost like the beginnings of a volcano.

For a whole week, I felt the ancient enlightened energy coming through me and spreading worldwide and so did Geoff. I stood in the retreat sitting room, where so many of you have sat, and asked that if any of you wished to add to what we were doing that somehow you would put your energy out there, whether you knew what you were doing or not.

About seven days after the energy started flowing through me, I felt it diminishing and I mentioned this to Geoff. He too, that same day, had noticed it diminishing. We both knew that all that was needed to happen through us at this time was complete and that the ancient energy was able to hold the balance again. The wobble on the planet was stabilised once more. I knew there was no need to worry about anything and just knew that what is happening is part of our evolution and part of the much-needed breaking down of the perceived power of governments all over the world. What comes from it, if we hand it over for the highest good of all, will be magnificent.

Bringing the light back to our planet was never going to be easy. I strongly knew that this virus is an opportunity for us to grow, let go of our fears and trust that all will be well. I do not know, at this point in time, what the eventual physical outcome will be. If you feel like adding to what Geoff and I are doing, please do so.

Final week in March 2020
Letter 2
In this period, I felt it right to tune in again to what lies under China. This time, to my surprise, I saw an enormous crater, larger than London, where the funnel of dark smoke had been releasing from. The crater was open at the top as if a bomb had blown the

ground apart. I immediately knew so much dark energy had been released since I last tuned in a few weeks ago.

Then I realised that there was a large dark ball of energy, originating from the dinosaur times, in the crater. It nearly filled the crater but it didn't touch the base or the sides. I knew it was very dark and dangerous and wondered if there was anything I could do to help. I felt an urge to call Geoff (which I did telepathically) but, as he didn't turn up, I sat quite still to see what might happen. Soon, I felt the presence of the ancient energy around me. I felt it slide under the black ball, between the ball and the base of the crater. It slid silently and quietly, taking infinite care not to alert the black ball to what it was doing. I felt I must stay absolutely still while the ancient beings slowly and carefully eased the black ball out of the crater. It seemed to take ages, for they were taking great care not to let the ball hit the sides of the crater. It seemed the ball didn't know it was being lifted! As soon as it was lifted high enough out of the crater, I felt I could breathe again. After this, the black ball moved higher and faster up into the ether and I knew a huge moment of danger had passed.

An hour or so later, I told Geoff what had happened as we went for a walk. I realised as I told him that the whole plan of the ancient beings was that it had to take the black ball by surprise and it had succeeded. This ensured the highest outcome, which was to remove the main thrust of the dinosaur energy from beneath the earth surface. As we walked, I tuned in again to the crater and saw it was empty and that the black ball had been spread out widely, well above the surface of the planet. I told Geoff the danger was over but even before my words were half out, I knew I was wrong. This dark energy had free will and could choose to regroup at any time. Oops!

Then I realised that the ancient beings were making the thinly spread dark energy aware of all that was going on, on the earth's surface, because of the 'so-called' coronavirus. (The dark energy had not been able to see this in the same way from within the earth.) It was shown that it was being given every chance possible to be healed and to set itself free as the rest of us imprisoned ourselves in our homes. (During the age of the dinosaurs, the unbalanced incarnated energy had tangled itself up and strangled itself in its roots, killing off all vegetation. Every living creature fought in hatred and fear to the death, eventually leaving nothing living on earth. As the damaged dinosaur age energy returned to the rest of the waiting energy beneath the earth's surface, it was admonished severely and held prisoner, to avoid a similar outbreak ever happening again.)

Today, as the dark energy releases from the dinosaur age it is being shown that it has been forgiven and that we are willing to imprison ourselves while it releases. Human beings all around the world are paying a karmic debt, showing all our fellow inmates the ultimate respect of keeping a distance in order to *save* lives. Also, note how every single being on the planet is putting out the intention of helping release the dangerous dark energy first, at great expense to itself, no matter what the cost. It is the rest of the world's way of showing that we wish to be forgiven for imprisoning the energy and that those who partook in the dinosaur age are forgiven for what they did back in those dark times. Time to let it all go and become one again! Every opportunity for the dark energy to shift and become one with the rest of us again is on offer at this moment and if the opportunity is taken, it will change the face of the earth forever.

As things heal so much more quickly on the other side, as nothing is embodied and weighed down by matter, I could see straight away that some of the dark energy was already shifting as it took in the truth of the scene below. The balance of power was changing and I trusted in that moment that as much dark power would be let go of as possible, while it was still in a relative state of surprise; enough at least to make a huge difference and allow the rest to let go of its trauma in its own time.

8 April 2020
Letter 3

Out on a walk with Geoff, I suddenly stopped. Seemingly out of the blue, I could feel myself sinking back into the Chinese crater. Once in, I could see that the dark ball had completely gone but the presence of the extreme energy relating to the Sun experience and the extreme energy relating to watching Source were very present. I looked closely and realised that the very extreme end of the Swamped was still hiding in cave-like places beneath the surface of the crater. This energy represented the 1% (described earlier in this book), the very first part of Swamped energy to shoot ahead and incarnate before the rest of us during the dinosaur age.

As I watched from what seemed like halfway up the crater wall (representing the ancients in an incarnated form), I saw that Sun and watching Source were waiting to see if this energy would choose to release. If it was to heal in this moment, it had to come out of its own free will. As I watched, it sometimes felt as if it had decided to come out, but then it would remember that it believed it could not be forgiven and would disappear again. It was very on edge and unsettled but a lot quieter than when I had tuned in to it a few days before, when it had the swirly energy of rush hour in London!

As I sat on the crater wall, I knew the energy was aware of me; I saw red eyes glaring steadily at me from a few places. I was aware that I held absolutely no fear of the energy and it was also aware that I had no fear of it. This disconcerted it somewhat, as it was used to having power over most things.

After a while, I gently reminded it of the agreement that the Sun experience, the Swamped experience and the watching Source energy had all made before they agreed to come into this planet. The agreement was one of working together and being equals; teaching each other to hold the balance as we attempted to integrate matter and energy.

Not long after this, I felt a certain amount of the energy come out and release. It might have been about one fifth of what was hiding.

It came out very nervously but was welcomed with open arms by Sun and watching Source. I spoke again with the remainder of the energy but it appeared to be stuck fast and would not give in. At that moment, I did not know whether it would ever give in on this occasion, or whether we would have to offer it a further chance on a different occasion, and maybe even offer a further chance after that. I left it to its fate and simply rejoiced at the amount that had come out, which was being given the same chance to heal as the dark ball had been given. It was progress.

Easter Day 2020
Letter 4

Today seems like the first day of the rest of our lives. It is so enormous, so wonderful and so sad all at the same time. I awoke amazed. There seemed to be a massive bright light coming from my heart that I felt spread all over the world. It was spilling out of me with such a flow I could not stop it. Of course, I did not wish to stop it.

I instantly knew that the light coming from me was because the extreme end of the Swamped (the dinosaur energy) had let go of its grip and agreed to join the patiently waiting extreme ends of Sun and watching Source. The light streaming from me was what one might call the union of all three extremes from the Sun, Swamped and watching Source experiences, which had now become one. All having let go of their own stories, they had become 'as' the energy that originally held the agreement to all work together, teach each other and hold the balance, before we entered planet earth. The war that had started between them as we became incarnated on earth, at least in the hierarchical realms, was finally over. This level of unified light was now pouring through portals on earth and its newly healed state would, in time, speed the progress of releasing all the dark energy from every part of earth.

I had an inner knowing that my current home would never be the same again. I got out of bed and walked through the retreat, spreading the joy that the union was bringing. I told the house: 'New ways are coming to us. We have done our job as it has been needed and now we hold the energy of the unravelling of the swirl. (*The swirl refers to the swirl of emotion that began as we entered earth.*) This unravelling is happening because of the great reunion'.

I asked the light coming from me to flood through the house and release the old level of disharmony and fill it with the newly healed union. (I later came to realise that the swirl would slow from that day, eventually stop and finally start to unwind.) Later on, I began to question what it would be like to work with the union. I would still be answerable only to the ancients from pure Source, but would I also talk with the combined energy of the three extremes of Swamped, Sun and watching Source? I had to trust the union. Could I trust it? It was still full of habit from its past experiences.

Just then, the phone rang and someone needed help who was in deep trouble. I wondered how I was going to be able to help them while I was feeling so discombobulated. But, as the conversation went on, I found myself trusting my direct line to Source and the usual precise, deep accurate answers came through in a very helpful and even clearer way. After I had put the phone down, I knew I did not need to worry about how I would continue anymore.

I decided to go for a walk across the fields to try and rebalance myself and take in what had happened. As I trod the parched land, I spoke with the union about the weather and explained how world-wide we need a better balance between the elements: sun, rain, wind, cold, hot, and so on, in order to thrive. I suggested they could perhaps communicate directly with Source if they wished to help release any damage or influence their 'war' had created.

I spoke with the union about the small percentage of worldly control freaks that held the purse strings on earth and asked if it could help disperse the control of financial matters in a way that would serve us all for the highest good. I then asked for the same for coronavirus, which had now lost its roots in earth and could hopefully be dispersed speedily, while serving the highest good at the same time, of course, for us all.

Today has felt surreal. We have been spiritually expanded as never before. In worldly terms, the progress made through the Covid-19 epidemic has been enormous. This moment of union, this moment when the three hierarchies have become one, is the moment we have all been striving for. The extreme ends of Sun, Swamped and watching Source energies each had to let go of their perceived power through free will. Extreme watching Source had let go hundreds of years ago, Sun a few decades ago, and today the last of them, Swamped, finally surrendered, enabling them all to reunite.

This is indeed the first day of the rest of our lives. The swirl of emotion that began as we entered planet earth in a clockwise direction is now slowing. It will eventually stop and then begin to unravel all it has done since that time, in an anticlockwise direction.

27 April 2020
Letter 5

This day has been beyond amazing yet again ... It really summarises all we have been going through so I want to try and share it with you.

I have felt the most extraordinary sense of peace within, all day. My heart feels unbelievably weightless and I feel a dawning excitement. I have felt like this before on a handful of occasions but it is very rare. As I have had such a tough few weeks, I wondered why, out of the blue, I was feeling like this and have been trying to put a label on it all day. Eventually, I let go of the idea of knowing why and said to the universe: 'OK. If I need to know, I'm sure you will tell me when the time is right. And if I don't need to know, I will celebrate with you anyway.' With that, I let it go out of my mind and continued to enjoy the floating and joy in my heart.

Very shortly after, I knew I was part of a huge celebration in spirit and I was being allowed to party with them. I had a vision of all the roots from the dinosaur age coming out of the ground all over the world, detaching from the earth's surface and floating away. The main root, the Chinese one, has already gone, as we know, but these were the secondary roots that had subsequently tried to establish themselves all over the world. They were not as strong as the primary root but had taken a grip that had held many of us firmly in darkness over the eons.

I myself had nothing personally to do with the release of these roots, except to ask for help to release them and to send love and light to these areas, as many of you have been doing too. Various others were in the driving seat for each root release, all over the world. I think I told you that the ancients in spirit had sacrificed some of their precious enlightened energy to help with the release of the main Chinese root. It came about because of the dangerous pivotal moment or wobble, for a few weeks in February, when the ancients decided to gamble a little of their strength, fairly sure they would pull the gamble off but never exactly sure, as the light/dark balance could shift again. Having gambled, the ancients then found they had to rely on some of the ancient energy currently incarnated on earth to bring the mission to full fruition. (It is always dodgier to trust incarnated ancient energy than the pure stuff in spirit!) However, we now know it paid off and that the main ball of darkness was removed by stealth, while the hidden roots underground became exposed and chose to follow after the ball.

Today, the celebrations and partying in spirit were held because the balance has reverted to 'safe' mode again. As there is now considerably less darkness on the planet, with no hierarchy to feed what darkness is left, the reduced ancient energy is no longer left precariously reliant on 'us' and the main danger is over. Not only that but I kept hearing a song telling me that this is the moment we have all been waiting for, the moment we have worked and worked towards all this time. It really is time to feel the party in your soul, connect with pure Source and be conscious of just how well the earth is doing right now.

End of Diary—and a few responses from those who read the above

1. How wonderful to read! I took our dog for a walk on Monday afternoon in the local woodland and my heart was literally bursting with joy at every step I took; every sight, sound, flower and plant. I was so grateful and happy for it all and now I know why it was so intense! What a celebration to be part of!

2. My Dear Louisa, Thank you very much for sharing that, and how absolutely wonderful. I saw your email late last night when I was tired and about to go to bed, so I just read it through quickly. It was wonderful to go to sleep with it filling my head and I slept like a log. On Monday morning I woke up and felt real joy in my heart. As I dressed I kept thinking how amazing that I had such 'joy in my heart'—those words were ringing in my head. I didn't understand why, but I decided to enjoy it anyway!! Last night when I read your email through quickly, I thought you'd had your experience yesterday and I kept thinking how strange that I'd felt the joy in my heart the day before. Now that I'm properly awake I see that it was Monday for you too!! Perhaps I'm more aware than I realise!!

3. Absolutely loved reading that and could feel the celebration. I had a feeling a couple of days ago that it was over ... but then I was told the death rate had risen again, so I felt a little deflated. But I realised that those people weren't necessarily newly infected and therefore I felt the feeling of peace again. I'll reread over that when I'm less tired, but to be honest it totally resonated immediately. I was smiling the whole way through reading it ... sharing your joy too. Thank you for sharing with me.

4. Dear Louisa, I contracted Covid-19 early in Feb., not knowing what it was at the time and before it was 'a thing' in the UK. I knew from day one that this was strange and it felt really weird in my body. It completely floored me for over a week. I took almost no medication and intuitively all I did was focus on releasing 'darkness', breathing out, breathing out ... I had one particularly bad night and my partner intervened energetically, which I believe was

a turning point. It took many weeks to recover fully and only in retrospect did I realise it was Covid-19.

During this time, there remained a sense of urgency and an acute sense of dark energy. There were elements of my own 'stuff' but intuitively knowing that it is not mine—it's much bigger. Not knowing what to do and not knowing what was going on, I opened to the universe, surrendered and adopted the mantra: 'I Choose Love. I Choose Love...'. So, whenever I felt this energy, I was guided to mentally repeat this mantra until it felt 'lighter', while honestly not having a clue what was going on—I just trusted.

It all culminated one night, around Easter time. I woke up around 2.00 am with a feeling of immense dread, foreboding and urgency. Again, nothing personal. At this point, being somewhat familiar with these energies, I simply started reciting the mantra—not just mentally repeating the words, but really feeling into it as I always do. I lost sense of time and space and became aware of an enormous black, fluid-like bubble of dark energy floating in the sky. Bursts of white/blue energy shot up from my heart chakra towards this ball and I gradually became aware of thousands of similar 'energy bursts' all over the world. [There were] individual streams of white/blue energy shooting up towards this ball and it gradually became more and more transparent. Clear. This went on for over two and a half hours and at some point, I think I simply fell asleep, because it felt resolved.

During this time, I hadn't spoken to Louisa at all, but felt I had to see her next weekend, because, frankly, I was getting a bit freaked out and it all started to feel 'too big'. She helped me by telling me the story of China, Corona and the dark energy, etc. I had no mental knowledge of this before. She also helped me to release more energy. I now know what is going on and I'm still being used by the universe—I guess in a more conscious way. I still use my mantra, because it helps me to focus, but I also KNOW I am love. We all are and that is what will save this world.

Love to you all!

In Trust

Author's Note

After the agreement became incarnated on earth on 28 April 2020, it became possible for the hierarchy of watching Source energy to complete its mission and finally let go of the pattern of suffering it had held onto since the crucifixion.

The union highlights the end of the era of separation between the three S's and the energy of the healed union is now spreading through our world, allowing a new and higher level of consciousness to emerge...

PART 2

The Omega—The End of Separation and the Return of the Lions

Let the truth be unveiled at a pace that each reader can manage. There is so much to learn and so much to unlearn and it is not a race. Each must take their journey at their own rate.

The Second Coming of the Christ Consciousness

Prologue: The Day of Reckoning

This is the 'day' of reckoning. It is now. We see it happening all over the world as ordinary people are no longer tolerating the strict regimes that have ruled for so long, regimes that were born of fear. Trust is growing as we see things can change. The old energy is not serving any purpose other than to hold us back. The healing of our soul is here and we must account for all our doings before we can set ourselves free and enjoy what we have created.

Luckily, the purpose of this part of the book is fully known in the ether for we cannot know its full purpose from our small perspective. For the last 12 years, I have solely followed my intuition and acted on it. What I have written is as close as I can get to the truth in this moment, using the gift of discernment I was given to the full.

As each soul uncovers their journey at the time of Jesus, it helps us understand what really happened. There are some mind-blowing differences between what has been recorded in the past and what the memories actually are. The truth will awaken thousands of souls as they read and remember their part in what happened, and the truths bravely shared here, within the following chapters, provide an opportunity to kick-start a much faster healing within all of us and therefore the planet as a whole.

This truly is the day of reckoning.

Introduction

The truth will always out. The truth will set us free.

The above are two very well-known sayings that most of us repeat at some time or other in our lives. How shocked we all were to hear the truth behind the entertainer Jimmy Savile. It rocked our world and shook the very foundations of our thinking. Following on from Jimmy Savile, so much else has come to light. In fact, there are so many shocking revelations currently coming to our notice, it is becoming almost commonplace. Criminals can no longer hide safely in the world; even after death, they are being 'found out'.

My calling in this life has been to unearth the truth. First, I had to unearth the truth about myself, remember all the skeletons hidden in my own cupboard, ask forgiveness for them and release the energy from all that was caught inside me. This can be read about in detail in my first book, *From Chrysalis to Butterfly* (2008). Then I had to understand planetary skeletons and help to release those, both for this planet and the universe as a whole. These can be read about in my second book, *A Memory Returned* (2011).

I have known instinctively that this is the time of the Second Coming since I was very young. I knew it was coming through many of us but I had no idea how it would take shape until a sudden influx of people started visiting me who had been connected to Jesus of Nazareth during his lifetime. I started to learn so much from what was hidden or buried inside them. The huge truth of who Jesus really was, who supported his mission and who, on the supposed 'enemy' side, was present, either in spirit or incarnated, is staggering. The pieces of the jigsaw have been falling into place slowly for me, and still are.

What I never saw coming was the truth of my own connection to Jesus and how I would be asked to remember his pain so acutely, in order to help release it from the planet, thus helping him be free from all the garbage that has been woven around his life and added to, during the centuries since. The Second Coming is about 'Truth'. What happened to Jesus just over 2000 years ago was not ready to be understood then. But the truth has never gone away. Now, in the 21st century, there are those of us who are ready to see and understand the man for what he really did, to understand and trust in his incredible bravery and to choose to follow his lead if we have the courage. As we remember who we really are, forgive ourselves and release the emotions trapped inside us, we will set ourselves free.

It has taken me 13 years to collate the information recorded here and, without doubt, it is not yet a completed work. During the first few years of running the retreat, I didn't record any of the visits that I had from people with a connection to Jesus. There were not very many anyway. Recording my findings was only suggested by a guest one day when we unveiled her own story. She was so amazed and found her past life so helpful and healing that she encouraged me to write it down. She asked me if I did much of this sort of thing relating to Jesus and I replied that it had only started happening in the last couple of years. She asked if one day I would put it all into a book; I looked at her horrified!

'No,' I said. 'Who would possibly want to read this sort of stuff and who would believe me anyway?' Her reply surprised me. She said, 'Even if it only helped one person or was believed by one person, surely it's worth it!!' I suppose she awoke something in me so, when guided to do so, I have recorded certain events ever since.

Geoff joined me at the retreat in 2015. Up until that point, I had been collecting information as it came in, just logging it quietly without telling many people about it. However, after his arrival the information started to come in much deeper and faster and he has been beside me in all that has happened since then, holding me steady. I could not have gone through what has been an exceptionally difficult and fast journey very easily without him. The universe certainly knew when I needed help and responded.

On 4 February 2016, I woke to the words: 'The Holy Grail', running round in my mind. I inwardly saw an old piece of wood full of woodworm, with much of it turning to sawdust. This vision came to me three times in quick succession, so on the third showing I said: 'Is it that you want me to unravel the mess that this story is in?'

I knew nothing of the Holy Grail. It was a term I had vaguely heard and I thought it might have something to do with the Virgin Mary or Mary Magdalene. On asking around, it was amazing how everyone seemed to have a different interpretation of the phrase. So I simply said to the universe: 'If you show me the way, I will serve the greater good as best I can.' I had absolutely no knowing that this was to be the beginning of something so big—in fact, it has formed the heart of the second part of this book.

***

I had been wondering why the Second Coming, so longed for by so many, is upon us! During the revelations concerning the crucifixion, I suddenly knew that the world had reached a tipping point at which the burden can be taken off the Jesus soul group in spirit at long last, and start to be held by us, and the pain he carried can then be released from the planet. I knew in that moment that there were others remembering their past lives as we are, all over the world. Geoff and I sent a grateful wave of light across the world from our hearts and asked that the understanding of the Second Coming should be returned to all those who were ready to hear it at this time.

The following day, a lady who was staying with us at the retreat for her first time, and who knew nothing about us, suddenly said to about eight of us who were congregated in the kitchen, 'I had a random thought yesterday. I had a knowing that the Second Coming was not about one person coming back but about all of us and it was coming now.' Geoff and I looked at each other and smiled.

It was complete confirmation that the wave of healing light we had sent all over the world had been received.

**

On 30 December 2019, I lay comfortably back in my bath with a sigh. I said to myself in what seemed like a random fashion: *It doesn't matter if I never write a book on the Second Coming. I have put the truth as I have understood it to the best of my ability into the ether and it has helped hundreds of people already. If I don't write it down then someone in the world surely will, when the time is right.*

I was very happily unattached to the whole thing. I was 100% relaxed. Little did I know that the very next day I was to begin writing it down in book form. After 62 years of my own growth and 12 years of collecting hard evidence, the universe started to prompt me and sentences started forming in my mind in a familiar fashion. (This was how my first book began!) On 31 December 2019, I began to record this enormous work for the world. I wasn't daunted; I am still not daunted. If no one ever reads it, I don't mind. I am simply listening to my intuition and doing what I am being guided to do. If it all stops tomorrow, I still don't mind. I am so completely unattached to it and trust that the highest good will happen, no matter what.

It has occurred to me that when I heard the words: 'The Holy Grail', what is recorded here is what came as a result of agreeing to 'unravel the mess'.

As I have been putting the book together, Geoff has spent the last few months immersing himself in the memories that are shared below. He is changing almost beyond recognition and the truth he now oozes, his wisdom and whole auric being are transforming. This transformation is possible also for you, if you so wish.

1
The Birth of Jesus, the Nazarene

Jesus was not superhuman. The outcome of his journey to the cross was not known before it happened. The success of his mission was not a 'given'.

I must have come across between 20 and 30 people from the Virgin Mary soul group in my time. In case you don't understand what a soul group is, it is a way of identifying a family in soul from which we stem. An easy example could be a tree, where every leaf is part of the tree, but at the same time each leaf is individual. Soul groups are generally splitting and growing larger as new generations are born, allowing the soul members to help heal each other in an ever faster way.

Within the Mary soul group, each of the Marys seems to carry the deep, intense sorrow that the original Mary experienced at the crucifixion; and beyond that, each of them seems to carry their own particular aspect of Mary's life, which they have agreed to re-experience in this life and then release. In 2018, I asked as many Marys as I had met at the time to meet up for a long weekend, with the specific intention of speeding their healing of themselves and aiding the emotional release of the original Mary experience that is still left on earth.

A few months before the Mary weekend began, I received the following message and, as you read it, you will find that it emanates a unique power.

14 October 2017

Lunch time. Felt the Jesus energy descend on me … and this is what I wrote down:

Mother! Seek not to find an excuse to mourn for that which has happened. I am not mourning, for I rejoice in the success of all that we accomplished. The time was right. The setting was right. All is being revealed just as it was always planned. What seemed to the world to be a story of sorrow is in fact a story of joy. Do not waste any more time on what you thought you had lost but reflect only on what the world has gained. The pain of what happened has long gone and lives on only in the memories of those who choose to remain trapped by it. We are free…

***

What follows here is a mixture of all the Marys' memories surrounding the birth, put together as best I can. There are some notes included from the Mary meeting, interspersed with other recollections.

Mary and Jesus knew what their missions were before they were born. But, like everyone else, once the soul becomes incarnated, the knowing only becomes live as the memories return. In other words, the memories are only woken up gradually within us on a 'need to know' basis.

Mary was a deeply spiritual young girl who felt in her core that she wanted nothing more in her life than to serve (God). She was standing in her dwelling one day when she felt a huge presence in the room. She was a little anxious but she heard a male voice say something similar to this: 'We are looking for someone of your purity and essence to give birth to a man who has the potential to change the world. We humbly ask you, would you be willing to do this?' An immediate wave of fear and an omen of future pain and suffering flashed through Mary's body. (This would have been her first incarnate indication of remembering her soul agreement.) The voice confirmed: 'This will not be easy. But your sacrifice will serve the world in a way that cannot be explained to you at this time. You will have to do this on trust.'

Mary had wanted to serve all her life but up until then she hadn't really known what service meant. In this moment, she knew. She was hugely in awe of what she was being asked to do but it did not take her long before she overcame her fear, sunk to her knees and said, 'Thy will be done.' As she said the words, an embryo was planted in her womb and the presences left. Mary then had to tell Joseph what had happened, but thankfully he had already been given an inner understanding of what was coming and he knew his mission was to support her.

During her pregnancy, Mary was really frightened. She kept remembering the visitation of the presences and became terrified of her bodily changes. She felt she couldn't tell anyone, except perhaps her mother, about the strange visitation, and keeping the huge secret was very difficult for such a young girl. Her intuitive sense was that no one would understand and people would feel threatened by the knowledge. Nothing about the pregnancy seemed normal to her, and over the months the swelling inside her grew to be a potential monster. When the baby started to move within her, she felt alienation from it, instead of connection. She was terrified that something strange might be developing inside her.

Throughout the pregnancy, Mary was aware of a strange, dark shadowy entity that came and went. Sometimes she felt lost, out of control and in danger of being consumed by it; she felt her son was also being threatened by it. At other times, the shadow was less imposing but, whatever the level of threat, she protected her child and pronounced an authoritative 'No' to the essence of it.

As she came to term and her contractions started, she was at her most terrified. What was going to come out of her? It was her moment of truth. Her anxiety reached its peak. Everything about it was beyond her control.

However, when the baby was born and he was so normal, he suddenly became something she could love. He was real, he was a boy and he was obviously going to be with her for a while. All at once, she let the terror go, came back into her heart space and loved him.

One lady from the soul group carries the memory of Mary riding a donkey with Joseph on foot, leading it. Mary is in labour. She is wishing she is in a safe spot or at home with her family. She decides to get off the donkey and she is full of fear. Her feelings were: 'I won't be able to do this. I can't do this. I can't give birth.'

As they are travelling in the middle of nowhere, Joseph has to find the first place that he can for Mary to rest. He finds a cow byre. Joseph leads her in and at this point she is in constant pain. Jesus is born. The pain suddenly stops. Mary hears a baby's cry. She takes off her shawl and wraps the baby up in it. There is peace. Cattle stand around, watching silently.

Mary became unable to move. Joseph took the baby and washed him in the cattle's drinking water. Mary felt a sudden protectiveness and her intuition kicked in very clearly. She was filled with love and her inner balance began restoring itself.

Over the course of the Mary weekend, it became clear that many aspects of the Mary soul group carry the fear of the bodily changes connected with pregnancy. Some in this life were frightened of the birthing process and some terrified of actually having children. One member felt strongly that she was going to have a special baby. It is also of note that a large number of the soul group have not had children in this lifetime.

One lady who did have children was consumed by mournfulness and a constant feeling of 'waiting for something awful to happen'. She had blocked facing herself and allowing a healing process to take place because of the dread she carried.

Another lady had not been able to mother her children properly in this life and though she loved them dearly, was unable to show it. Upon understanding that she still held the energy of the Mary experience within her, she was able to release it. She was then able to relive her pregnancy in this life, communicate with her baby as he had been within her and feel a strong wave of protection and a becoming one with the baby which consumed her. She felt the strength of the universe flood through her and a joy and peace take over.

Many of the Marys felt a real resonance with donkeys and a peculiar love for them. One lady spoke up and conveyed that she had always felt a deep need to help them. The donkey became something of a saviour to Mary as she continued her journey for the next few years after the birth.

Most of those present had always felt very nurturing of babies and a deep 'need' to protect them.

One lady at the meeting remembered men coming into the cow byre with gifts. This had happened to give Mary confirmation of all that she had heard from the 'presences' at Jesus' conception. The nature of the gifts helped her understand her situation and put her back into a state of love, purity, gratitude, joyousness, innocence and, very importantly, full alignment.

The Watching Owl

Another lady, Olga, was incarnated as a white, male owl in those times, and happened to be sitting in the rafters of the cow byre as Mary and Joseph entered. Through Olga's eyes, we remember that the floor of the byre was formed of a dried, rough mud.

The owl watched as Jesus was born, bathed and placed by Joseph in the wooden feeding trough that was full of dried grasses. Olga felt resentful and angry. The owl had been trying to keep the energy in the byre clear and clean. He was part of a soul group who had incarnated on earth at that time to ensure the highest outcome for the birth of Jesus. Here were these strangers coming into his byre and interfering, upsetting his mission. He fluffed his feathers, trying to inform the intruders that they had to get out.

What the owl had failed to realise was that what he was witnessing was the very event he had been clearing the barn for. Olga and I fell about laughing as we recalled her story, for a similar tale had replayed over and over again for her in this life. She asked for forgiveness and let go of the energy so that the cowshed could clear itself of her resentment and anger.

The Wise Men

Another regular visitor to the retreat carries a clear memory of being incarnated as one of the Wise Men.

As some Wise Men were travelling the night of Jesus' birth, they had the 'feeling' that there was something they needed to go and see or find. Following their intuition, they deviated from their intended path, not knowing why but doing it anyway. They came across the cow byre where Jesus had been born. The 'star' they were supposedly following was the intuition in their hearts.

As they dismounted, they knew they were in the presence of someone special. They peeped through the door and saw Mary, Joseph and the baby. They each took a gift from their luggage bags, and presented them on bended knees. They only stayed a few minutes and then carried on with their journey, their job complete.

When Jesus was born, the planet was experiencing troubled times. The Gabriel soul group drew closer to earth in an effort to redress the balance, because it felt that the joyous occasion could have been lost and gone unmarked, in amongst so much trouble. The energy came and presented itself to any soul who was open enough to receive the joy at the time, saying: 'Hey! There is good news out there!'

The Wise Men, travelling from A to B, heard the message (because they were out and about, away from the bustle of life). Many isolated shepherds also heard it. The joy was spread wherever it could be felt.

This is one of the few times that the Gabriel soul group has been so present on earth. It normally keeps itself pure in the outer earthly spheres, so it does not leave itself vulnerable and open to abuse.

The Good Shepherd

One day, a man named Ken came to my house and almost immediately I recognised him. The words, 'the good shepherd' filled my head as

I listened to him talking. He had a sister who was deeply connected to her life at the time of Jesus and he was just full of scepticism over anything she had to say.

As our conversation progressed, I knew Ken had been a shepherd who had visited the byre just after Jesus was born. He had been tending his sheep nearby and his intuition had told him that something special was happening in the valley below and he should go and investigate. First, he argued to himself that he could not leave his sheep, but his intuition was digging at him persistently and deep down he knew his sheep would be safe for a little while.

Eventually, Ken trusted his intuition, left his sheep and made his way down the hillside in the direction of an old stone building he knew well, as he passed it nearly every day. An excitement grew within him: what was he going to find? He entered the byre in a hushed way. He became aware of a white light which he saw surrounding a mother and her child. He knew he was in the presence of a special family, a holy moment and that an incredible event was taking place. He fell slowly to his knees, bowing his head, and blessed the newborn boy.

When he knew his job was done and he felt he must return to his sheep, Ken got up and backed out of the byre, seeing only the smiling faces of the family as he did so. He was aware of cattle in the background but they were silent and still. It was a moment he would recall with awe for many years, even though he did not understand it.

***

This same shepherd found himself at the crucifixion decades later. He did not know how he came to be in the crowds but as he stood there, he became aware of the same light surrounding the man being crucified that he had witnessed in the cow byre so long ago. He was struck dumb! The years fell away in his mind as he recalled the baby's birth. How could this holy child be reaching such an end?

What had gone wrong? Should he have done something to protect the child? Was it his fault? Guilt, shame, mistrust of himself, horror, loss and fear crowded into his soul as he stood, silently watching.

In his turmoil, Ken then shut himself and his misplaced guilt down so firmly that he has subsequently not been able to revisit it and feel the truth. So strong was his conviction that he was unforgivable that he had run away from the memory and only in this life was he ready to realise his own innocence and start to heal.

***

When Jesus was still very small, Joseph dreamt during the night that he should take Mary and the baby out of the area they were in, to somewhere far away. He woke Mary who went immediately into a state of fear, the same fear she had felt at the conception of Jesus. The shock of Joseph insisting that she got up and they should leave in the middle of the night brought the memory flooding back. She was fighting herself inside. Her thoughts were along the lines of: 'I didn't expect this yet. This is too soon. Am I going to lose him now? Where are we going? I feel so unsafe. How can I protect my baby?'

Mary struggled onto the donkey, held Jesus in her arms and they rode in the dark of night, deep into the desert. They didn't stop for many hours, indeed not until early evening the next day. Mary and the baby fell exhausted off the donkey and collapsed in a place where Joseph felt they would be reasonably safe.

They continued the journey the next day and kept going in the same manner, day after day, until Joseph knew they were in a place where they could settle safely.

When the lady who carried the above memory tried to release the fear from herself and from the land, it wouldn't go. When we then took the fear back to the moment of Jesus' conception, it disappeared immediately, because that is at the root of all Mary's fear concerning Jesus.

Over the following months/couple of years, the deep fear Mary lived with has been expressed by one of her soul group in the following way: Mary was constantly scared of being found. She had terrifying dreams of men banging on the door, demanding entry, breaking the door down and taking her baby. She lived in daily terror of losing her son. She asked herself many times: 'Why did I ever agree to have this baby?' When she was really low, she even felt regret. Her father had told her many times she was a 'no-gooder'. As Mary hid from the world, she told herself her father was right. She felt unworthy of bringing up this baby.

This soul has re-experienced this same terror over and over again in this life in various ways. She has been rebellious towards authority, been on the run for a number of years and found herself in trouble several times, with the police. She even had her child taken away from her for a couple of months. These events have continually reproduced the shock, regret, unworthiness, injustice, terror, trauma, sadness and shame lying within her from the daunting life she led while Jesus was growing from baby to toddler and beyond. She now understands why this all happened to her, has forgiven the authorities both in this life and at the time of Jesus, and is finally letting go of the trauma within her.

Egypt

A lady called Kiki carries the most beautiful memory of this time. She was a child living in Egypt at the time that Mary, Joseph and Jesus arrived there. She recalled their arrival and how they settled on the edge of her small community and kept themselves very much to themselves.

Kiki quietly approached the toddler Jesus and played with him in the long grass. Kiki felt safe around him and his parents as they smiled broadly and oozed unconditional love towards her. The family in turn felt unthreatened by this little Egyptian girl. She visited them many times.

Many years ago, when Kiki had visited Egypt in this life, she had the feeling she had come home. She now realises that she was remembering the unconditional love she had experienced there and that she was safe now to recall its memory within herself.

**

As Mary cared for Jesus for the next few years until he was aged 12, she lived with the constant inner knowing that she was caretaking. This was a great wonder to her. At times, she felt that his arrival on earth and his future were so out of her control that he was not even her proper son. Certainly, the babies that followed after Jesus had a different feel to them and she had no trouble bonding with them. With Jesus, she felt almost like a surrogate mum would and therefore their bonding was different. She set about being the best mum that she could be for the time that she had Jesus under her care, loving him as deeply as any mother could.

From time to time, she would feel a dark shadow but she carefully protected Jesus from its approaches; throughout, she carried a heavy weight inside her because she understood Jesus and his potential mission as no one else could.

Interestingly, another member of the Mary soul group, totally unconnected with the above lady, felt that the whole of this life she had been haunted by a secret she could not share with anyone about who Jesus really was. She unknowingly repeated the other lady's words when she said she felt strongly that she would not be understood and some people would feel threatened by her knowledge.

2
Jesus' Childhood

Jesus knew he wasn't quite like other children. He seemed to have insights and wisdom as he grew up, that they did not. He also knew he had the ability to heal. However, he kept it all under wraps, knowing it was not his time, and therefore he had a wonderful childhood, playing amongst his friends, learning the carpentry skills of Joseph and generally living a normal child's life.

A Childhood Friend

Amira knew Jesus as a child and told me that she didn't consciously take in that he was different, at the time. She grew up not particularly remembering him until one day she heard someone mention that a man called Jesus was teaching in her neighbourhood. Something stirred inside Amira and she felt drawn to go and find him. The minute she saw him, her heart recognised her childhood friend and remembered the good feeling she had as a child whenever she saw him. From that moment on, Amira never lost touch with him again and listened to him teach whenever she felt she could.

The Local Priest

There was an elderly priest, Jonathan, who presided over the synagogue that Jesus' family attended when Jesus was young. The first time Jonathan saw the young child come into the synagogue, he saw the light shining from him straight away. He was thrilled by it and kept looking at him in wonder, his heart filled with joy. He felt as if he had been waiting for him all his life.

Jesus himself knew that the priest could feel his light and could also feel the affinity between them. He would quietly tune into what Jonathan was saying in the synagogue and intuitively know if he was about to make a slightly off-target statement. He would stop fiddling or playing and catch the priest's attention with something like a quick head movement, a look or a stare. Jonathan would stop what he was saying and feel moved to alter his words.

Therefore, over the years, Jonathan grew in wisdom and became much broader thinking than most of his colleagues. Because of his growing wisdom, those who attended his synagogue changed and became wiser and deeper too. Jesus loved going to the synagogue. He knew in Jonathan he had found someone who knew who he was, and a silent, unspoken connection between them became firmly established. Through the connection between them, Jesus learned how simply by 'being himself' he could alter the behaviours of those around him in his small world.

This secret world was just beautiful and was remembered by Jonathan in this life when he came to see me in 2019. Jonathan finally passed over when Jesus did not return from Jerusalem at the age of 12. He knew his earthly job was done and he felt free to let his soul lift from the earth. From spirit, he watched closely as Jesus fully self-realised, started to teach and was later crucified.

When Jesus was 12 years old, his parents took him to Jerusalem to attend the bar mitzvah, as was customary at the time. While he was there, he had an inner knowing that it was time to find out who he was. So his parents left him with the priests and he began his long road to self-realisation. It took Jesus from the age of 12 to around 30 to fully self-realise and in that time he travelled extensively.

The Bar Mitzvah

Jesus was amongst many 12-year-olds who arrived in Jerusalem for the bar mitzvah initiations. Matthias was an elderly priest presiding over the youngsters' ceremony and he had seen this annual event many, many times in his long life. Matthias was standing at the foot of a tall wall, initiating each boy one by one. As Jesus approached, Matthias saw a strange, bright white light shining behind the boy, which peeped out and glowed all around his body. Matthias stopped what he was doing and thought: 'This is a very special young man.' He then wondered to himself whether this boy could be the 'one they had been waiting for'. He looked around. No one else seemed to notice anything out of the ordinary.

Matthias put Jesus through his part of the initiation and, at one point, he looked straight into Jesus' eyes. In that moment, it seemed as if Jesus said to him: 'You know. And I know. But what we know is not for now.' Matthias gave a toss of his head and, with that, the moment was gone. He felt bound to secrecy over what had just happened and he died not long afterwards with this secret etched in his heart.

A Magical Experience

In 2017, Geoff and I were on holiday in Rhodes. One day, we were climbing from the southern tip of the main island to a further semi-attached island. Halfway over the semi-attached island, we stopped for lunch, overlooking a delightful cove. We had no intention of going down to that cove as our hearts were already set on reaching the south of the mini island. As we ate lunch, I sat quietly musing that maybe this was one of the islands that Jesus had visited. I felt a curious pull to go down to the cove in front of us. Unbeknown to me, so did Geoff! Neither of us said anything to each other in that moment and, when we had finished lunch, we set off southwards towards our original destination.

However, no sooner had we taken 20 steps in a southerly direction than the universe caused me to suddenly trip over the tiniest stone in the ground and land heavily on my hands and knees, making them bleed. I lay shocked and winded, flat on my front, for about 5 minutes, while I regained my composure. I looked at my wounds in dismay and realised I needed to soak them quickly in some sea water to stop the gravelly stones from sinking into the cuts. So we turned round and slowly made our way down to the delightful cove and I sat on a small rock, feeling rather shaken.

Almost instantly, I became aware of going back in time to see two old wooden fishing boats pulling up on the beach. Around six young men, aged between 15 and 16, one of whom was Jesus, climbed out of the boats and dragged them higher up the beach. The next thing I knew, they began to fish for their supper. It was such a happy scene, full of youthful laughter. After they had eaten, they started to explore the island together.

I was aware that they had spent many nights, possibly a few weeks, on the island, travelling its length and breadth, and were tried and tested in many ways in order to help them learn their life lessons.

I was amazed that I should have witnessed a snippet in time of the travels of the young Jesus and his friends in his late teenage years. Beyond what I had witnessed, I was shown that there were many tough times during these adventures and the boys were often struggling. I became aware that all his friends slowly dropped out of the enlightenment process, one by one (over a period of years) as they travelled, until only Jesus was left. When he became the last man standing, he knew he had to go it alone. He felt panic, doubt, fear and loneliness. Could he do it? He just knew he had to. He had to get on with it.

At this point, I started to feel very sick. My emotional state had gone quickly from the joyful scene to the lonely scene within minutes. I knew I was being asked to release the emotions that Jesus had left on this and any other island. He did not wish them to remain. Suddenly, it became clear as to why I had been tripped up. I was to be a vessel for this exact purpose.

On the way back, we came across a sign stating that an oil power station was about to be built in the very cove that I had received the revelations. I had clearly been tripped up in order to bring about an opportunity to remember what had happened in the cove and to release the emotions for Jesus, which might otherwise have been lost. I hadn't enjoyed being tripped up but I could see that it was my own fault for not obeying the signals/intuition I was being given as I ate my lunch.

Later that year, I met someone who felt she had been living on that very island when Jesus had visited. She had opened her house to him when he needed it and had befriended him unconditionally while he lived there. She was in tears as she recalled the memory and realised how she had been part of his journey. She too let the emotional impact release from her with gratitude and love.

A Friend from Jesus' Teenage Years

Will was a 12-year-old boy when he first met Jesus in Jerusalem. They were both attending the bar mitzvah and afterwards had decided to go off with the priests to 'find' themselves. Will knew Jesus quite well for a few years and they shared adventures together with other young men.

Will was part of the group who, when they were a few years older, took off in boats to travel and adventure further afield. He grew up and faced himself for a few years until the going got really tough. As other friends slowly dropped away, unable to run the course anymore, Will was one of the last to give up. He can remember speaking to Jesus and asking him to go back home with the rest of them. The words he spoke seemed to stick in his throat. He knew Jesus was doing the right thing to carry on, he just didn't have the guts to let the others go home without him and be left facing his own truth. He was also afraid that if he was found to be not good enough, and didn't make the expected grade, he might be left on his own. He remembers Jesus refusing to go with him and having that heart-wrenching moment of having failed himself and leaving Jesus alone.

Will was so upset with himself that when he got home he went into hiding and lived in another country for the rest of that life. The truth he could not face was his own weakness and deep lack of self-worth. Having remained in hiding for over 2000 years, he came into this life determined to remember his lack of courage and to put it right this time around. He had tried and tried to heal himself without facing the pain of the past life, but of course it never works. Now, he has finally faced his fear, knows he is forgiven and is releasing the shame, the feeling he has abandoned someone, together with the fear, regret, sorrow and anger. He is at last ready to pick up and complete the role that he began long ago, aged 12.

South of France

Tara remembered the following and shared it with me. She was a young girl between 12 and 14 years of age and described living near a port in the South of France. She remembers standing on a beach, looking out to sea and seeing a vision of a man standing on a rock, far out in the ocean. A little later, she then spotted the same man on the shore and instantly knew she had to help him. He was alone, dirty and looked very thin and tired.

Tara rushed towards him and offered to take him to her house where she lived with her mother and father. He gratefully followed her and, upon reaching the house, was welcomed by all, fed, watered, allowed to sleep and recover from his travels. Tara remembers washing his feet.

Tara fell head over heels in love with the man and, like any young maid of such tender age, felt devastated when it was time for him to leave and he left her behind. Had she not been good enough for him? She did not acknowledge her own acts of unconditional love towards him, she only saw the unconditional love in him and felt lost, overwhelmingly sad and alone when he had gone. Ever since, she has looked for unconditional love outside of herself, never acknowledging that it is already within her. In remembering this event, Tara has now realised she had a live brush with Jesus in his formative years, supporting him unconditionally in his hour of need, and this has allowed her to release her current feeling of inadequacy and the associated emotions.

An Innkeeper

On his travels, a lovely man I met, James, had the following story to tell. He remembers running an inn somewhere in the Middle East where travellers loved to rest and replenish their bellies. One day, he decided to have a quiet moment to himself and not to take in any travellers so that he could have a rest. When a young man came knocking at his door, James was annoyed. This young man was dressed in a dirty white tunic and was looking very tired and dishevelled. Despite noticing the sore and wounded feet of his caller and the weary frame that stood in front of him, James had directed him down the street to a different inn.

The young Jesus looked sadly up at the innkeeper. His gaze was prolonged and sad. James felt Jesus' rebuke, though nothing was said, and when Jesus turned away, to walk on down the street, he turned back into his inn, feeling great shame. The look that had passed between the two men haunted him for a long time and he couldn't get past the thought that he had lost an opportunity.

James had hidden himself in the Buddhist tradition for many, many lifetimes since. However, he had never found the peace he was looking for and eventually decided to reincarnate outside of the Buddhist tradition to try and find some answers. When he recalled his life as an innkeeper and was able to apologise for not taking his worthy traveller in and for not responding to his needs on that day, he could then ask for the opportunity he had missed to be reinstated. Suddenly, the ex-innkeeper's journey became clear again and he was able to move forwards in life.

***

When Jesus had fully self-realised, around the age of 30, he took himself back home. He started to tell his family what had happened to him, like any son would. They would listen to his stories in awe and he loved to tell them what he had learnt. Indeed, many neighbours and friends came to listen to him too and they could see how Jesus had changed and now delighted in what he had become.

One day, a man approached him and said, 'Please may I go down to the next village and fetch my brother? I am sure he would benefit from listening to you.' Jesus replied, 'Well, it's a fine evening. Why don't we stroll down to his village together and I can meet him and chat with him?'

So Jesus and the man (and maybe a few other friends) chatted as they strolled down to the brother's village. They found the brother with other friends and family and they all began to talk with Jesus. He found that they liked what he had to say and the numbers around him grew ... And so the ministry of Jesus began quietly and organically. He didn't plan anything; he just allowed the 'power greater than himself' to flow through him and dictate, minute by minute, how each day should pan out. As he travelled further afield and began to get known, he found the crowds getting larger and he learned how to talk with them, how to heal; he learned more about who he was and how to fulfil his inner calling. He learned and they learned. It was a win/win situation.

The Leper

One day, Jesus was teaching near his hometown and the listeners present comprised both people he knew and some he did not know. Mary, his mother, was moving around amongst the people that surrounded him.

Mary saw a male leper approach Jesus. Her heart was immediately full of fear, the same fear that had crossed her heart on the day Jesus had been conceived. She was immediately alert. Who was this man? Was he dangerous? Was this the moment she had always felt would come? She watched in trepidation.

The man spoke with Jesus and she realised he was asking for her son's help. She immediately had an inner knowing that this man was not a good man. He had in fact pretended not to be a leper for many years and had only declared his illness when he could not hide it anymore. Therefore, he had infected many unsuspecting people who had been unlucky enough to come near him.

As Mary watched the verbal exchange between the two, she knew Jesus had recognised the leper for what he was and had challenged him to face his behaviour. She heard him tell the man he needed to apologise to those he had infected and come clean with everything he had done that had hurt others. Only then could he be healed. The leper was furious and turned from Jesus, thereafter declaring him to be a false prophet and a liar.

In the weeks that followed, Mary was greatly hurt as the rumours the leper had spread about her son took hold. It was the beginning of her knowing that the 'incident' she dreaded was coming closer.

3
Herod

It would seem that the Herod who had all children under the age of 2 killed, was the father of the one who was alive when Jesus was crucified. Both father and son carry a similar sad tale. The soul group even today represents powerful energy that seeks to control from its own strength rather than Source.

Herod (the father) came into incarnation as a powerful king before the time of Jesus' birth. I have now met three of Herod's actual soul group to date and all are still very powerful characters, unwilling to change or even acknowledge the fear dominating their hearts. In the case of two of these souls, I noticed that other people, upon finding themselves in the same room as them, shrank back and couldn't take much of their company at any one time. Both souls subscribed heavily to their own 'god' or 'guru', different ones in each case. One of the souls admitted to her power and the other pretended it wasn't there. The third member of this soul group did not carry quite such a strong presence but he had believed it was OK to lie and cheat in this life to retain his powerful position, thus causing much pain to his family and friends.

Through Jay (one of the Wise Men already referred to at Jesus' birth), I picked up the following memory. Jay remembers feeling immense joy after he left the baby Jesus in the cow byre. His heart was overflowing with light, hope, happiness and the belief that something good was to come from the birth. As the Wise Men journeyed on, they told several people what they had witnessed. Still buzzing with excitement, they soon entered the court of Herod, which is where they had been heading in the first place. As they approached Herod's apartments, Jay remembers a shadow crossing his heart. He knew he should listen to that shadow as it was a warning but he ignored it, persuading himself in his excitement that no harm could come of telling Herod about the birth of this baby.

In that life, the Wise Men never pieced together that it was very soon after their visit to Herod that he ordered the babies to be sought out and killed. It was only in future lives that Jay's heart began to react to what had happened as the terrible slaughter story was being circulated. And in each lifetime following, his cry of anguish got louder and louder: 'No! It wasn't like that! We didn't mean that to happen. We would never have told Herod of the birth if we had known what he would do.' The denial of the shadow that had crossed his heart grew stronger.

Jay felt grossly misunderstood and buried the truth within him. But, over many lifetimes, the guilt has grown and grown inside Jay until now, when he has finally allowed himself to remember the truth and been able to acknowledge the original shadow that crossed his heart, the shadow that he ignored, the shadow that lies at the root of his guilt. In further past lives and this life, he has continually repeated the pattern of not listening to his intuition, but now understands why and has the chance to rectify it. Before his visit to Herod, his intuition was intact. Now he has asked forgiveness for what he did, and let the emotions connected to it go, he can live with a clear intuition once more.

Pat was a fourth person I met who was part of the soul group of Herod. She came over as a very damaged being and was extremely strong in her individual beliefs. On tuning into her, I was first able to see that the soul of Herod had chosen that royal body because it foresaw a 'light' event that was about to happen on earth in that region and it wished to overcome it. Any light of that purity was a threat to its own deep beliefs and threatened to undermine its power.

However, tuning in a second time, I was able to pick up the tremendous guilt Pat carried in her soul about killing so many babies under the age of 2, not long after Jesus was born. I could feel Herod was driven both by terror and determination at the time, fearful that anything or anyone might take status from him and expose him for what he was. (Deep down, he believed he was an unworthy, fearful soul.) From that fearful place, Herod sent his orders out. Until enough members of the soul group can forgive themselves and make a full confession of Herod's weakness, the soul will retain the memory and remain damaged. While Pat heard me and didn't deny her history, she wasn't ready to relinquish her power and face herself at that time.

Almost on top of meeting Pat, I met another member of this soul group who was even more heavily invested in his story. Ben was still kidding himself of his righteousness to such an extent that I found I could not tell him what I was seeing. He didn't want to know. He was a powerful man and very infectious to be around, if one had a tendency to need the strength and security he seemed to offer.

Ben had a thirst for power and a need to be *recognised* as powerful. He had previously only incarnated on earth as a lower level being, and, on becoming part of the Herod experience, Ben showed me that part of Herod's reasoning for making the decision to kill all children under 2 came from the fact that he was terrified of relinquishing his power to anyone. It had taken his soul such a long time to rise above his fears, to what he believed to be acceptable heights, that he was definitely not going to lose it all at this stage. Ben was not ready to resonate with a connection to Herod when I related it to him, yet his past lives between then and the present, which he had uncovered for himself, followed exactly the same pattern.

There was another powerful lady I met, Gina, who felt she was part of Herod's soul group in spirit at the time of Jesus' birth. She recalls watching helplessly with the following thoughts to the fore: Herod was paranoid about being usurped. The people closest to him felt the most vulnerable and unsafe. She was horrified at what was playing out and felt Herod would do 'anything' to survive. She describes Herod as hanging on to power like a drowning man. He felt all competition to him must be destroyed.

Gina felt powerless to help as all this happened. Now that she has remembered it, in an embodied state, she wishes to let go of all the feelings of helplessness, responsibility and guilt (by association) she carries from that time. In doing so, and in asking for forgiveness, she will of course help the soul group enormously, for she is not pulling any wool over her own eyes.

An Advisor

I met one man who had been an advisor to Herod during the period he was planning to have all the infants killed under the age of 2. He was full of fear and could not look me in the eye. I knew immediately that he held a dark secret that he was shying away from remembering and did not want me to see. As I tuned into him, I was aware of intense fear dominating his role as advisor to Herod and, while his intuition was probably quite accurate, he never allowed himself to advise other than according to what he knew were Herod's wishes. His dark secret was that he had advised Herod to kill the infants, knowing it was wrong, but he had to be agreeable and make Herod right if he was to stay in his 'important' role.

Herod, the Son

The younger Herod, who enjoyed a good party with plenty of food and drink, had become intoxicated with a young girl called Salome at a banquet one evening, and offered, rather recklessly, to grant Salome any wish she cared to ask for. Salome was at a loss and could think of nothing on the spur of the moment so she looked towards her mother who suggested she ask for the head of John the Baptist. To agree to this was a little impulsive, thoughtless and naïve but, on the part of Salome, there was no maliciousness attached; if there was any malice, it was from her mother who had suggested it. Salome's mother had earlier been criticised by John for some of her ill-founded actions and she held a grudge against him. It was her anger that caused her to make this suggestion to her daughter.

Herod was not very keen on this request because he knew it would be unpopular but, at the same time, he did not wish to lose face, having just offered Salome anything she wanted. So he gave the order and a little later the head arrived.

I met a lady from the soul group of Salome, Jean, who in this life had married a man, Warren, from the soul group of John the Baptist. The dynamics between the two were a complete replica of the past. Warren feared Jean would be the 'death of him' and frequently mentioned this. He had held both reluctance and a strange pull towards his prospective wife when they first met, unable to understand why at the time. Through Warren, I could feel the great guilt and shame John had held before he died, believing he had let God down by not achieving his purpose.

From Jean's point of view, she was seeking forgiveness from him, having carried the shame of what she did for so many centuries. She was still impulsive, thoughtless and naïve and Warren's simple, humble nature had attracted her. When he admonished her for her love of abundance, he would say to her, 'We should live simply so others can simply live.' This was a lesson she much needed. The coming together of these two souls was obviously going to be immensely healing of the past.

One of Herod's Soldiers

Winnie was a very conscientious lady who first came to see me when I was only in my second season of running the retreat. She carried the memory of being one of the soldiers ordered to kill all the boys under 2. She did not have any awareness of the significance of why this had happened or that it had a connection to Jesus (even though I had told her!) either in that life or this, until a few years after her initial visit, when we discovered she had not let the emotions go. When she allowed herself to take in the whys and wherefores of what had happened all those years ago, she managed to connect with enormous guilt and could not forgive herself. A third visit to this past life revealed that she had not wanted to kill all the babies but didn't dare go against her superiors for fear of her own life. And, on yet a fourth visit, Winnie came into contact with a lady at the retreat who had had the experience of her baby actually being killed by Herod's soldiers, and Winnie went ashen when she heard of it. Suddenly, the lifetime and its reality opened up for her. She faced the truth of what had happened and was able to fully ask forgiveness and let the guilt go.

The main point of interest here is that it took four visits to the past life over many years before Winnie could fully engage with the truth in such a way that she could find forgiveness. This is true of many, many soldiers who were around at that time. It is hard for them to face the past, let alone believe they can be forgiven for their misdeeds.

Herod's Wife

A lady named Fanny had chosen to become a wife of Herod's before she was born, as she thought she could bring light to the planet from that rich and powerful position.

As a tender young girl, she married Herod, thinking that she had found a real status and purpose in life. To begin with, she was very happy and she enjoyed the glitter and attention that that life brought. Neither I nor Fanny could find any resonance within her that told us she knew of the killing of the babies by Herod. It seems likely therefore that she married Herod's son after that event and had never known of it.

As the years went by, Fanny began to acknowledge how cruel Herod was, how he killed anything that got in his way and how his supreme power was the most important thing to him. She realised she was not important to him, other than as a symbol. The horror of some of his actions grew more and more acute as she witnessed that anything or anyone that threatened him was disposed of, whether it be in a war situation or a personal one. She was very uncomfortable and lived in trepidation of what he might do next.

One of the worst aspects of their later life was the fact that she became acutely uncomfortable that her name was naturally coupled with Herod's. It seemed that people assumed that whatever he did, she was also behind it. Walking in public became a trial to her as she felt the judgement of others. In reality, she was judging herself.

At a banquet one evening, Fanny witnessed the head of John the Baptist being brought in on a plate. This was when her horror came to a head. She knew a little about John the Baptist, had even been present when he had been speaking, so she knew he was a good and innocent man. She felt very unsafe and trapped at that moment in the banquet; full of self-disgust, self-anger and self-hatred because she did not have the guts to do anything about the situation. She was too afraid that something similar might happen to her. What felt like to her a poison began to fill her insides and, after a prolonged illness, she died.

Fanny feels she has been poisoned in subsequent lifetimes and only now understands the need to ask for forgiveness for her frailty at the time of Herod before releasing the emotions she experienced from her body, thus negating the pattern and helping to heal the soul group.

4

Characters Who Knew Jesus

A great number of people have found me over the years who carry an unusual connection with Jesus over the three years he lived as a fully self-realised being. I have recorded a few of the more important ones.

A Priest

Yo had one of the thinnest veils between herself and the other side that I have ever encountered. Therefore, she was very easy to read. Yo showed me a view of her past life as a priest. The priest was standing in the doorway of a temple in Jerusalem. He was glancing along a path to his left because a small crowd of people were coming towards him. In the middle of the crowd was a small, 12-year-old boy. Immediately, the priest's heart leapt. He knew that this was the moment he had been waiting for. As the boy approached, he fell on one knee, holding his hands to his face and sobbing. He was overwhelmed.

That moment was significant to Jesus because it confirmed to him that it was time to find out who he was. At the same time, Mary and Joseph, who formed part of the crowd of people, knew someone else had recognised their son and they were better able to let him go.

However, the happenings caused fear to stir in the hearts of other priests who were watching. They banned the old priest from taking Jesus under his wing and Yo was unable to teach him, as he had expected to. What no one realised at the time was that the old man had already played his part. That one action of acknowledgement as the crowd had approached him, had completed his task. Yo allowed himself to die soon after.

The emergence of this truth from within Yo, who incarnated as a female in this life, has allowed her to face her connection with Jesus without fear. She now knows she has nothing to be ashamed of and that she completed what she came to do in that life. She was able to forgive the other priests and let go of her own doubts and fears.

The Mother of Mary

This lady is little talked about in history but she played a very important role in bringing about the right family setting into which someone like Jesus could be safely born. What follows has been held in the depths of a lady named Kat.

As a young maid, Mary's mother intuitively knew which man she needed to marry, but at the time she did not know why. The man she married was someone who was heavily involved in business. As such, he was away from home a great deal and this allowed her to bring up her children without his interference. She taught her children to use their intuition; she allowed them to roam freely and let the world bring them the lessons they needed at an early age.

When Mary became pregnant, out of wedlock, her father woke up to his negligence and became incredibly angry. He insisted that Mary and Joseph marry immediately, to put right the disgrace. Then he set about controlling his family, stamping a huge guilt trip on his wife, who he saw as weak and someone who had grossly let the side down. He brought rules into the household and confined the family to the house. Mary was not affected by any of this as she had already married Joseph and was therefore safely out of reach.

The truth is that Mary's mother had done her job to perfection. She had allowed the young Mary to develop and grow into an enlightened being without being side-tracked. Only such a pure soul could ever be chosen to bring Jesus and his mission into the world. She then went about maintaining a very good relationship with her daughter, which ensured Mary always had a trustworthy ear and excellent support through all that she subsequently went through. However, Kat's husband's anger and control had a far-reaching and damaging effect on her and the rest of the family. Her natural intuition became blurred as she felt forced not to use it and fear took hold in her heart. She continually asked herself: 'Did I do the right thing?' She became full of a sense of shame. Doubt of her own actions grew great inside her.

Kat brought her children up in exactly the same manner in this life. She resonated totally with her life as the mother of Mary. She was able to release the fear, doubt and shame as soon as she had taken on the truth that all happened exactly as it was supposed to … She will now be able to trust her intuition once more.

I have been privileged to meet several other members of this soul group. One lady showed herself to be a very wise soul in this life. She remembers watching Jesus and his siblings grow up. She was a wonderful, patient grandmother to them. None of her inner fears were shown to them.

Another remembers what Mary went through in her pregnancy and birth. The memory has been festering inside her every lifetime since, and in this life she relived the terror as she carried and gave birth to her twins. She has now been able to let this memory go.

A third lady, Rachel, carries a feeling from that time of not being enough. Her daughter, Mary had become so pure and innocent, she felt herself to be unequal to her in many ways. When the story of the presences was related to her by Mary and she was asked to keep the meaning of the virgin birth secret, it weighed heavily on her. She struggled with this knowledge and Mary's fears during pregnancy until she eventually locked the secret away deep inside her.

Rachel also has a memory of being above the cross in spirit as Jesus died. She hadn't long passed over but was present at the occasion, and watching Mary suffer brought back the memory of all she had been through at Jesus' conception and birth. At this point, she remembered the responsibility she had experienced, felt very helpless, and a deep shame ran through her as, from spirit, she felt she was letting her daughter down while her son died. She felt anxious that she could not finish the business she had begun at Jesus' birth because she was no longer incarnated.

In this life, Rachel still has the tendency to come from outer learning rather than her heart but, after releasing her long-held secret, will now hopefully be able to release her perceived emotions and responsibilities from the time. This will in turn help her purify her soul and bring her to a deeper level of inner peace.

The highest good was achieved. But it is humbling to know just how much preparation and how many different souls held the success of Jesus' mission in a delicately balanced position. So much was hanging on a thread—a decision here and a decision there. The flexibility of the universal flow had to be absolute and is absolute, as it helps us bring these huge events to fruition.

The Feeding of the Five Thousand

I met a lovely lady who, as she approached me, oozed connection to Jesus. I have already related the story of her brother who was the good shepherd in Chapter 2. When I told her I could see her connection, it came as no surprise to her, just relief. Later that day, we sat together with a view to uncovering her long-held memory. She was very open and easy to read.

The woman remembered that her name had been Miriam and in those days she had been a young mum with two sons. She often took the boys to listen to Jesus as he talked to the people. They loved listening and they loved him. What he taught was exactly in tune with how they felt about life and they could hardly get enough of it.

One day, Miriam, her boys and her mother were sitting amongst the crowds as Jesus shared stories with them. It was getting late and near dusk. Jesus knew everyone was getting hungry but he did not feel he should stop teaching. He knew there was more to say. He asked if anyone had any food with them that they could share. Miriam had a basket of food with her which contained fish, bread and bones. Her mother immediately said, 'No, we have need of this. Don't give it away.' But Miriam knelt down and said to her boys, 'Jesus has need of this food. I know you are hungry but can we give it to him?' Both boys silently nodded, bravely putting aside their own hunger.

Miriam gave the basket to Jesus. Jesus intuitively knew the generosity of the two young boys and he used the energy of their unconditional gift to manifest enough food for everyone present to have plenty to eat. He kept dipping his hand into the basket and more food came out each time. He trusted, handed out and spoke to them, all at the same time. Miriam and her boys were watching in awe. They knew what had been in the basket and it certainly wasn't what was coming out!

When Jesus had fed everyone, he handed the basket back to Miriam. Only a little piece of fish and a small portion of bread were missing.

Miriam has two boys in this life, Philip and James. She feels very strongly that they are the same energy as the sons she had 2000 years ago. This memory returned to her and with it her deep love and connection to Jesus that she had buried for so long. She has been able to open up to who she truly is once more and able to let go of a lot of the anxiety and mystery that have surrounded her. She comments that her two boys are still generous to a fault in the same way that they had been back then.

A Friend of Jesus

A lady named Liv called to see me. She told me she had known Jesus when she lived in Bethany during his lifetime. As I tuned into that lifetime, I could see she had fed and housed him on a number of occasions as he passed through her village.

During that lifetime, when Liv heard of Jesus' death she thought: 'No. This can't be! He was the one and only...' When she finally had to accept that he had died, she felt betrayed and let down by him.

She had put 100 per cent of her trust in him and she had expected him to overcome anything, even death. If he was the one and only, if that was true, how could he have then been taken? She lived the rest of that life in a bewildered state. She has lived all her subsequent lives in a bewildered way, lost in her non-understanding of why the one she had inwardly trusted had died. She did not know how to move on from this space.

Liv had lived as a practicing witch in the same period that I lived as a witch, some 1500 years after Jesus. I recognised her straight away as someone who had betrayed me. (See my first book, *From Chrysalis to Butterfly*, for details.) Because of her retained bewildered state of not knowing truth from fiction at the time of Jesus, she was willing to testify against me to save her own skin. She joined ranks with other witches, not out of malice, but because she could not help herself. As we spoke, I was able to unravel all that had held her in confusion. I don't know how much she healed from it at the time but I do know she has now received the information and forgiveness she needs in order to move on.

A Tax Collector

A man named Eric, who had been studying *A Course in Miracles* (ACM), came to see me. He had been a tax collector when Jesus was around. We remembered that he had a wife and children and he was a very dutiful husband who provided for them very well. They were comfortably off. On his daily travels, he sometimes saw Jesus talking with many crowds around him and Eric was rather in awe of him. He used to sidle up to the edge of the crowd and attempt to hear a few words here and there. He heard enough to whet his appetite for more but he was careful to not bring attention to himself as he knew he was not a popular character.

One day, Eric found himself near Jesus and he had an opportunity to ask him what he should do to become a better man. Jesus looked at him and knew he had a fine house, a fine job and a loving family. Jesus suggested that he should leave the law of fear behind him (give up his possessions) and follow the law of God, the law of trust. Even as he said it, Jesus knew this man was not ready to do this. Jesus continued, 'You have to give up everything to find everything.'

The tax collector turned away sadly as he too knew he was not ready to give everything up. Eric wanted the peace that he saw in Jesus but he also wanted to keep his earthly goods. However, in this life, Eric felt he was now ready to let it all go. It had taken him all this time to become aware enough to even contemplate it. He now knew he had to let go of his wife, his possessions, his idea of safety and anything else that might prevent him slipping through the eye of the needle. Eric looked at me and said, 'The only thing I fear now is not seeing the way forward. I can't see the path.' I replied, 'You don't need to see it. It is already known in the universe. You simply need to trust in every moment and to know you are worthy of being looked after.'

Eric sent me the following a few days after revisiting his life as the tax collector, 'I am so grateful that I have met up with Jesus again after 2000 years. This time I have prepared myself beforehand with more understanding of his teachings and the many disguises of the ego. I am so thankful to rediscover his gift of Forgiveness, to open it and receive it more fully.' It seems appropriate here to quote from ACM, 'It is a joke to think that time can circumvent eternity, which means there is no time.'

The Priest in the Temple

One man who came to the retreat, Isaac, remembered he was part of the soul group of a priest who witnessed an important scene in his temple. This is what he remembered: Jesus walked into the temple courtyard with some friends and was immediately aware that dishonest dealings were taking place. He began to teach that it was better to support one another in life than to steal and cheat each other. He spoke firmly and with clarity as befitted a house of prayer.

Jesus' words caused an angry fight to start among the traders there, and tables were upturned and goods thrown all over the place. The priest drew nearer to see what was going on and to try and dissuade people from fighting. He was not happy with his temple being in such disarray.

A Beggar

There was a beggar who, at one point in his life, had come across a man who was seriously injured and lay dying on the pathway. The beggar had little thought for the man and his suffering but simply took what he wanted from the helpless man and then left him to die. He often thought of what he had done with a little guilt but persuaded himself that this man was going to die anyway so it didn't matter.

The beggar found himself in the vicinity of Jesus and his followers one day. He crept nearer to hear what was being said. He listened with interest to the conversations that were going on. These were words being spoken that he had not heard before. These seemed to be loving people who loved even the lowest of the low, i.e. beggars. His heart leapt as he learned more and dared to move closer to Jesus. He began to trust this man who spoke such wise and caring words.

Then Jesus uttered the words, 'What you do unto others you do unto me.' These words were like a sword through the beggar's heart. He remembered the man he had robbed and left for dead. Suddenly, he felt he could never be acceptable to a man like Jesus. Fear struck him and he moved away from the crowds, head hung low.

This man, Toby, and his past life history came to my notice in 2020. He was not ready to consciously remember his story in this life but his soul conveyed it to me. I asked for help for him to forgive himself and these were the words I was asked to send to his soul: 'It is not about what you have already done, but what you do from now that counts. Will you forgive yourself, if we forgive you?'

Toby has not had peace in his heart since the day he backed away from Jesus. He has carried himself in self-judgment and shame. He has now been sent unconditional love that will remain surrounding his heart; his soul will ensure that one day he will pick it up and he will then have the opportunity to set himself free.

An Old Lady and a Thief

There was an old bent lady, who had terrible pain in her back, who desperately wanted to get near to Jesus. She used to find a way to listen to him whenever she could because she got so much from what he was saying. She always hoped that one day she could get near enough to touch him.

One day, she realised his voice was very close and she wriggled her way between the crowds that surrounded him and saw what she thought was his cloak. She reached out, stumbling a little in her fear, and briefly grabbed a fold of his clothing. She had a firm belief that even if she could just do that, it would be enough to help her heal.

Within seconds, she found her back straightening and she was upright. Jesus had felt energy withdraw from him as the lady touched him, so he turned round and looked behind him to see why it had happened. He asked who had touched him. The lady froze in fear and shock, and unworthiness flooded through her. She quickly looked away. However, Jesus knew it was she who had touched him and why. He was touched by her total trust in him.

The old lady had a grandson who lived with her. When she got home, she told him what had happened because he was wondering why she was no longer bent. The grandson had a dark side to him: he was a thief and a general no-gooder. He was sceptical of what she said and upset her greatly with his response.

This grandson was eventually hung as a thief on a cross that stood to the left of Jesus. The old grandmother witnessed both her grandson and Jesus die on the same day. After what to her was an inexplicable moment and feeling very lost and alone with no one to talk to, she fell into doubt and her back began to bend again; back to where it had been.

A member of this same old lady's soul group came to see me after her son had died in this life. The son came through to us and showed us he had been the grandson and how he had felt as he hung on the cross that day:

> I knew I was a criminal and that I deserved to be crucified. I looked to my right and saw a man with a white light emanating from him. It crossed my mind he was the man my grandmother often talked about. But why was he hanging there? If he was truly good he would not be on the cross. He must be bad like me! I concluded my grandmother was nuts, and that he was like the rest of us.

Coming through to us over 2000 years later from spirit, we encouraged the grandson to take another look at Jesus on the cross. After we had explained to him who Jesus was and why he had died, he allowed himself to see Jesus for who he truly was for the first time. He then saw for the first time that he too could be forgiven. He crumbled in sorrow for who he had been and gave his life to the truth in that moment, vowing to incarnate next time and put it right. He apologised to his mother/grandmother and the stone she held within her from his passing began to shrink. An incredible healing for them both was taking place.

The Tavern Owner at the Time of the Last Supper

Sam came to see me near the end of this life. He had Parkinson's disease and a few other problems and wanted to know why his body was shutting down in such a way.

Straight away, I saw that Sam was very familiar to me and then recalled that Jesus and his friends often frequented the tavern with the famous upper room where the Last Supper took place. Sam sometimes spent time talking with Jesus over a drink and came to know that Jesus was a very pure soul with an innocent heart. On the night of the Last Supper, Sam chatted with Jesus and had a premonition that something was not right. His intuition told him that Jesus was in danger.

Sam popped in and out of the upper room where Jesus and his friends were having supper that night, but he did not hear any of the conversations going on. However, later, when Sam heard that Jesus had been arrested, he was shocked to the core. He asked himself continually why he hadn't warned Jesus of the danger he had felt was around him. A few days later, he heard of the impending crucifixion and stole out and hid amongst the crowds to see if it was really going to happen. He watched in horror and self-disgust as Jesus died on the cross. From that day, he shut down as he blamed himself for what had happened and was full of guilt.

I assured Sam that there was no guilt on his part for the death of Jesus but that he should seek forgiveness for not listening to his intuition and promise always to follow his intuition in future. Then he should let the guilt and self-disgust out because it was crippling his body, and he now understood the message it had been sending him.

What was remarkable to me through my session with Sam was the familiarity that he presented to me. It came off his body in an unmistakable way, as if it had all happened yesterday. He told me that Jesus was an ordinary man and that he did not feel inferior to him. This was because they had talked as equals in the tavern, with no crowds around and no song and dance. It was a lovely memory.

A Miracle

Darren was a debt collector and lived in the same area that Jesus was visiting. He did not know Jesus himself but had heard talk of him.

One day, Darren was following a rather rotund man through his village. The man seemed so joyous as he skipped and danced along the street. Darren was immediately envious.

'Why was this man so happy and so full of himself?' Darren asked.

As a debt collector, Darren was not a happy man and not well liked in his community. Darren saw the round-shaped man approach the well in the centre of the village and, in a moment of uncontrolled, intense anger, he suddenly pushed the man down the well and left him to fall to the bottom and die.

Darren then leant his arms on the stones that were built around the well and sighed a deep, discontented sigh. He felt dreadful about what he had done and about himself. His head hung low between his arms.

Suddenly, Darren felt a firm hand on his right shoulder. This grip was strong and healing. Darren felt a rush of warmth flood through his body to his heart. He knew instantly it was Jesus and that Jesus understood how he was feeling, that he was 100% sorry for doing what he had done and he had been forgiven. Not a word passed between the two men. No words were necessary.

In that healing moment, Darren's life changed. He no longer allowed the jealous darkness to have a hold on his actions. He lived the rest of that life and a series of future lifetimes, slowly paying off his karmic debt for all that he had done that was out of balance with the highest good.

In this life, he now knows his karmic debt is paid. He is ready to acknowledge the forgiveness he received 2000 years ago and to follow his heart. He has asked for all the darkness that had invaded him to be released and for the light to flow from his heart in an ever brighter way.

An 8-Year-Old's Experience

In her own words:

> I was an 8-year-old girl who loved playing with the other kids when Jesus was around. I loved his energy. One day, my parents and I left

home early, and arrived in Jerusalem just in time to see Jesus being put up on the cross. Everyone near me was murmuring amongst themselves, wondering what was going on, confused and sure that Jesus would somehow be able to magically get himself down from the cross. We all went into shock when it became clear he was going to allow his crucifixion to continue. I felt like I was watching a horror movie from the front row. When it was all over, my parents and I travelled home, all of us so deeply saddened we could not speak.

Not long after this happened, I was walking outside our home when I noticed the trees swaying gently around me, with dew reflecting brightly off their leaves. The birds were singing so beautifully. I remembered how Jesus was when he was with the birds. Suddenly, I felt a very powerful energy surrounding me. It seemed to come from nowhere. I just knew it was Jesus! I was so excited—Jesus was still here! I raced in to tell my parents: 'Jesus is still here! He's here! I can feel him.'

To my utter dismay, they told me not to be so ridiculous for we had all watched Jesus die on the cross. From that moment on, I denied my intuitive abilities and followed my parents' lead. I decided I must have been wrong.

Since remembering this part of my soul's journey, I have forgiven my parents, asked for forgiveness from the universe for shutting myself down, and asked to allow my natural intuitive ability to be reawakened in this lifetime. I am now starting to trust in my own healing powers and my own intuition more than ever, and I am so looking forward to seeing where this leads me!

A Second Debt Collector

One man, Simon, who collected debts for the authorities, found himself near to Jesus as he was teaching one day. Simon listened to what Jesus had to say but became sceptical because it seemed to him that Jesus was saying he had to give up all his life securities, in order to become a good man. He did not see the need for this as he was quite well off and enjoyed this privilege.

Simon decided to join the crowds that gathered around the cross on the day of Jesus' crucifixion. He was there because he wanted to reassure himself that he was right about holding onto his stuff, and convince himself that if he witnessed Jesus dying on the cross then he, Simon, must be right. It was the only way he thought he could get peace over it. What followed was not what he expected!

Simon watched, not too close to the cross, but near enough to hear and see what Jesus was going through. He could not believe it when Jesus said, 'Father, forgive them. They know not what they do.'

He felt as if Jesus was speaking directly to him and him alone. It seemed so personal. In his heart, he had believed he could never be forgiven. The tousle within him then changed in its format. He fought with the idea that he could be forgiven and he fought with the idea that he could never be forgiven.

For just over a thousand years, Simon had lived in this turmoil, never being able to come to terms with it. Then, around the 11th century, he decided he had to face the truth. He chose to be born into a military family that believed in torture and death to those who did not tow the family's particular line of beliefs. He suffered abuse at the hands of his father and other parts of the family but did not dare to cross them. He later followed his father into the army of the day, not daring to question that he had another choice. He found himself torturing other men, some of whom he felt must be innocent. He became more and more uncomfortable within himself. He would stand with his colleagues, going from one leg to another, wishing he did not have to be there.

One day, a man that Simon knew very well was brought before him. He knew this man was innocent. Suddenly, he snapped. He spoke up and told his bosses that he knew the man was innocent. It was not taken well. Our friend was taken in front of the torture panel and a retrieval of his statement was demanded. When he did not retract it, he was tortured in an attempt to get him to change his story. However, Simon was ready to follow the path towards the light. He did not retract his words. He suffered greatly and when he had become physically quite weak, he mumbled from his subconscious, 'Please father, forgive me for anyone I have ever hurt in any way. Please father, forgive these men for they know not what they do.' In that moment, Simon had overcome his fear and the higher realms took him out of his body and relieved his suffering.

Today, this man has set out on a mission to heal himself and the world, still adhering to his deep-seated extremes. He is currently wrestling with the strong belief he can never be forgiven and yet knowing he has paid the price for his wrongdoings and can be forgiven. The journey goes on…

A Paralysed Man

A lady I knew when I was in my early 20s, had a deep impact on my life and changed its course with a few sentences in a very profound way. I have stayed in touch with this lady, Fiona, and her family for the last 40 or more years. In her soul, she carries the miracle which is best known to us as the healing of the paralysed man. In this life, she believes herself to be paralysed and has not used her legs for the last 30 or so years.

At the time of Jesus, Fiona, as a male, was indeed paralysed and lay unmoving on his mattress to the great concern of his friends and family. Another male in the family, Zac, heard that Jesus performed miracles and knew that if he could get Fiona to Jesus there might be a chance of him healing. He and three friends lifted the man on the mattress out through the roof, down some stairs, and carried him to the feet of Jesus. Jesus could feel the faith, love and trust of Zac. He held out his hand to Fiona and said, 'Take up your bed and walk.' The paralysed man got up from his mattress, rolled it up and walked.

I knew, a few years after I first met Fiona in this life, that she only had to accept that same hand in this life and she would walk again. She scorned this thought. In the past life, she had walked away from the miracle and, because she felt unworthy of being healed, she declared herself to be special as this had 'happened' to her. She felt she had been picked out and therefore must be special. She has lived believing herself to be special ever since.

Forty years after I first met the family, Zac died in a sad and confused state. All her life, she had believed that Fiona, her daughter in this life, was the special one and, as such, had put her on a pedestal. She completely failed to understand that it was her faith, love and trust that had allowed the healing of her paralysed relative to take place. Through a connection after she died, we unearthed that the unworthiness and the specialness that the relative believed herself to be, had become entangled. She was unable to let her paralysis go because she believed it had been done *to* her rather than that she had deserved it. She has yet to admit the truth.

I have been holding Fiona in great gratitude ever since she helped me at the beginning of our acquaintance. After Zac died and we unearthed the truth from the other side, I suddenly had an inner knowing that the universe might now use my gratitude to repay my debt, and help Fiona untangle her egoic confusion, allowing her the opportunity to let the paralysis drop away.

Sara

Sara was a young girl who lived with her dad in a small village near Nazareth. Her mother had died in childbirth because Sara had attempted to be born breech and her mother had internally haemorrhaged during the process.

Sara's father was not a bad man but he continually told his daughter that if she had come out the right way round, her mother would be alive today. This caused the guilt in Sara that was already present from the Split, to swell and her digestive system failed to function normally. As she grew older, her digestive organs started to collapse until she became bedridden.

Jesus had known the family for a long time and was a frequent visitor to the home. He understood why Sara was in the condition she was and used to come and sit beside her and hold her hand, transferring unconditional love and bringing a peace to her that her father could not. Sara was incredibly attached to Jesus and considered him to be family. She died a few months before Jesus hung on the cross. She died in peace and harmony with the world, with Jesus close to her.

As Jesus hung on the cross, she was watching anxiously from spirit. She felt he would rescue himself and was waiting for it to happen. When she realised he was sinking and perhaps would die, she became terrified. The guilt that had lain dormant in her rose to the fore and she felt she should be helping him as he had helped her. She felt helpless and angry; despair, shame and inner panic grew as she felt responsible in some way. Was this her fault? She basically replayed her Split story. After he died, she formed the belief that she could never be forgiven and therefore would never find herself in the presence of Jesus again. The sadness in her was overwhelming.

These two events, with their subsequent emotions, have lain dormant in Sara ever since that time. Now she has found the courage to face what she has held inside her, she has the chance to let it all go and rebalance.

In the middle of her healing process, Sara asked herself and me why Jesus hadn't healed her. As we felt within her soul, we both knew she had not at that time had the courage to believe it was not her fault. Jesus knew this and therefore the only healing he could bring was one of peace and harmony. We can only heal ourselves when we are 100% ready to drop our fears and damaging beliefs. In Sara's case, they rooted directly back to the Split. Only in understanding her roots could she let it all go successfully. She has now asked to be forgiven for shutting down and allowed herself to believe she can be in Jesus' presence once more.

5
The Week Preceding the Crucifixion

For some years now, I have been asked by the soul group of Jesus to release the energy that was left from various events that took place during Jesus' sojourn on earth. It was mainly odd bits and pieces of energy that he had not been able to release before he died. I knew he did not wish this energy to remain on earth any longer. I thought nothing of releasing it really, and was just happy to do it when occasionally asked. I remember walking in the fields one day in the spring of 2019, just randomly saying to Jesus: 'If there's anything else you wish me to let go of for you, just let me know.' Little did I know what I was letting myself in for.

Over the next few years, various events were replayed through me and my heart opened to the memory of the extraordinary emotional side of Jesus' life. It rocked my world and turned me inside out. But I was able to release all that he asked of me, bit by bit, as it was revealed to me, and, at the time of writing, this process is still continuing every now and then.

It all began just outside Jerusalem...

Jesus was speaking to the people outside Jerusalem when he felt in his heart that he was being called to enter the big town itself. At the same moment, he felt a shadow of fear across his heart, and he knew his visit could be dangerous and possibly fatal. He asked: 'Why? Why would I run myself into trouble when everything is going so well? People are beginning to understand what I am saying. I am learning to heal and to do my job better and better. Why jeopardise this?'

His question was reasonable enough, but the message placed in his heart was adamant: 'It is time for you to enter Jerusalem.' No fully self-realised soul can ever act against his or her intuition; they can only trust and act on what they are given. So Jesus, feeling very alone and with no one around him that could understand what he was facing, knew he had to overcome his deeply increasing fear and set off for Jerusalem. He decided he could only trust that he would be looked after and that everything that happened would be for the highest good of all. Once in Jerusalem, he spent time with people, just as he had outside the town, continuing to heal, bravely spreading his love and truth wherever anyone wished to hear it.

When the soldiers came to arrest Jesus, he was, for the most part, expecting it. The shadow that had come across his heart had already prepared him for trouble, so he went quietly, anxiously wondering what was going to happen.

A Jewish Priest

A lady was staying with us who I felt carried rather a strange darkness and I felt slightly wary of her. As we sat together, Lynn told me she had been a Jewish priest who had lived and preached in Jerusalem. She became afraid of the popularity of Jesus and arranged for spies to be sent out to find out who he was and what he was up to. She gleaned information that was later used to condemn him to death.

After a period of deep contemplation, Lynn told me she regretted what she had done in that life and wished for forgiveness so she could let it go. I was filled with the presence of Jesus at this moment and I found myself telling her about Jesus and the truth of the crucifixion. As I spoke, I was aware of the power of Jesus' presence and the suffering he went through, coming through me. As I related his last moments on the cross, the energy of it caused her to feel its deep truth and she was hugely moved. It became obvious she was truly, truly sorry for what she had done.

I found myself sobbing deeply and telling her that her gracious presence at my home at this pivotal time gave the Jesus soul group a hope that had not often been felt before; that maybe some of the terrible things that had happened could at last start to be healed. In that moment, I realised how incredibly deeply affected Jesus was by all the betrayal he had experienced and the almost unbearable deep pain of how little he had been understood.

Lynn and I had no more need of words. A moment had passed between us like no other, and healing on both sides had taken place. As I sobbed, I asked for the energy to release from earth, as requested. I was shaken for many days after this.

Jesus' Arrest

The Roman centurion who arrested Jesus was a powerful, inflexible, self-important type who liked to command everything around him. He didn't like to be found to be wrong. He was aware that his colleagues had been after Jesus for some time and had even witnessed Jesus talking in the crowds on occasion. The centurion had him labelled as a troublesome man, so when he finally caught up with Jesus, his thoughts were unkind. They ran as follows: 'Aha, we've got you now. You can't slip out of this one.'

He obviously felt that Jesus had slipped through the authorities' fingers on several previous occasions and he was happy that he had got the better of Jesus now. Jesus himself wasn't fazed at all by the centurion's thoughts. He knew, without doubt, that he was being arrested on this occasion in harmony with the 'highest good'. He looked at the centurion with kindly eyes and forgave him there and then.

Pontius Pilate

Pilate was a very cruel man. He lived richly and enjoyed his power and status at the expense of others. He had many slaves, some of whom suffered cruelly at his hands. He did not treat slaves as people but as 'disposables' who could easily be replaced.

Pilate had a fascination to see the man who had been labelled by some as:

- a hero;
- a king of the people;
- powerful;
- a man above most men.

When Pilate heard Jesus had been captured and was to be handed over to the Romans for sentence to be passed, he arranged to meet him. Jesus was brought before him as he was 'playing' swords with a fellow swordsman. As he glanced up, he had fully expected to see a powerful, richly clad person in front of him. He was greatly surprised to see a poor, thin shadow of a man standing in chains who appeared to have no 'presence' at all. He was disappointed and felt ashamed. Why had he bothered? He approached Jesus, wielding his sword loosely in his hand. When he reached Jesus, he stood squarely in front of him and pointed his naked sword into Jesus' stomach. Jesus felt the tip of the sword pierce his skin. He stood steadfast without flinching, his eyes holding a steady gaze with Pilate as they stared at each other for a moment. Something energetic passed between them that later caused Pilate to play his Barabbas card. Pilate did not admit it to himself but the stare remained and has remained in his subconscious ever since. Just for a second, he had felt an energy more powerful than his own. But, in his conscious mind, Pilate chose only to acknowledge the poor, helpless dirty man before him.

A little shaken, Pilate decided to make more of the matter than he needed to. He took Jesus outside the building and resolved to offer a choice to the local crowds in the nearby square. They could either choose to crucify Barabbas who he considered to be a real criminal, or Jesus. He felt sure the crowd would go for Barabbas, who perhaps deserved this level of attention rather than this poor shadow of a man. Pilate then had both men face the crowds and he put the choice to them. He was really surprised when the Jewish crowds chose Barabbas to be freed above Jesus. He felt concerned. Whatever had this poor man done to rouse such hatred towards him?

Pilate decided to wash his hands of the affair. He wanted nothing more to do with any of it. With that, he handed the whole matter back to the Jewish authorities because Jesus wasn't worth the 'time of day' to him.

As Jesus looked at Pilate, he felt his toxicity and that he was really dangerous. He felt sick in his soul. Until this moment, he had never really come face to face with his total opposite—the extreme dark. Pilate oozed energy from his face and body that ranked amongst the worst that humanity could produce. Jesus felt he was looking at a poison he had not known existed. The shock brought him very low. He felt sick, desperately sad and helpless in that moment and confronted by a task that felt much too big for him. Very few words passed between the two men as Pilate felt it was beneath his dignity.

Today's Healing of Pilate

In my childhood, I had come to know a certain lady and her daughter quite well. We were as different as chalk and cheese but the friendship grew as we all had a love of horses and riding in common. I stayed in touch with the family for over 50 years without really knowing why. They were not really my sort. They spoke of people and the world in a derogatory way and had absolutely no knowledge of who I was.

As the lady reached a very elderly age and she became more dependent on others, she got very depressed and felt herself to be a nuisance to everyone. She eventually ended up trying to take her own life in a very crude way. She failed more by lack of strength than anything else. After her mother's suicide attempt, her daughter declared she would be willing to look after her mother for the rest of her life. In order to do this, she would have to give up her own life as she knew it, which would be a huge act of unconditional love on her part.

After the attempted suicide came to pass, I was contacted and told what was going on. I spoke with the daughter and was very impressed with her offer to change the pattern of her life for her mother. They had not enjoyed the best of relationships up until then. During the night, I was pondering what I could say to the mother who I was due to visit the following day. I didn't really want to go but felt compelled. I lay in bed and asked the universe to show me the way forward.

During the night, imaginary conversations with the mother kept running through me. I was happy with that and felt it would all come out in front of her as it needed to. I then asked myself, probably for the first time ever, if I had had a connection with them in a past life. Immediately, I knew mother and daughter were from the same soul group and were of Roman soldier origin. I felt dread in me. Oh no! Were they something to do with the crucifixion? I tuned in and felt the energy of a high-level Roman soldier's presence. I was puzzled. I didn't know the Scriptures well enough to know of any 'high up' Roman soldiers. Then, suddenly, I wondered if they could be anything to do with Pilate. I knew nothing of Pilate and had never met anyone from his soul group.

To my surprise, I then felt an urge to write down most of the above that I have related about Pilate. It flowed through me without stopping. As I finished writing, I knew I had to go into the lady's house next morning and reverse the meeting that Jesus had had with Pilate 2000 years ago. I felt sick. I had never had the courage to stand in my truth before them before. They were both very strong characters and could be very damning towards anyone and everyone. However, I knew my aura would already hold the words that had been planted in me through the night. I did not need to say them. But I did need to go and 'be' my truth.

I bought the lady some beautiful roses the next morning and filled them with unconditional love and forgiveness on behalf of Jesus, knowing they would stay in the lady's house for quite a while. I dared to take a copy of my book so she had the chance to discover who I was if she wished to. I then spent an hour with her and her daughter, struggling in my new and unfamiliar role. At one point, I gave the mother some home truths about suicide and what it did to those who were left behind. I suddenly realised that, during the conversation, I had replayed the stare that had occurred between Pilate and Jesus long ago. To my astonishment, this time she capitulated and I had the upper hand.

As I left, I knew I never had to see them again if I didn't want to. If they came to me for help, of course I would be there for them but basically a lifelong job was complete.

Later that day, I worked out that, of course, I had been marking time, waiting for them to reach this point. The mother, after a long life in voluntary service, had tried to take her own life rather than be a nuisance to everyone. The daughter had offered her mother unconditional love—against the odds. I had been prepared to stand in my truth for the first time in front of them. These three acts, together with the reversal of the meeting from 2000 years ago, marked the beginning of healing the Pilate soul group. The universe had clearly not allowed the lady to die until the three acts had been completed, thus bringing about the potential for healing that was always intended.

The Wife of Pilate

Sonia was in her later years by the time she found me. She was a woman who continually tried to bat me away from seeing into her lifeline and yet she wanted answers. Once I cottoned on to what she was doing, I conveyed it to her and she immediately stopped her batting and allowed me to delve into her fears.

She had been a heavily abused soul in her previous lives and, in her search for safety from abuse, she had set an intention to meet a man of means in her next life. When Pilate offered her his hand in marriage, she knew he was not a good man but she wanted more than anything to be safe. She soon discovered she had no peace or balance as Pilate's wife. She lived in his shadow and was continually afraid. A friend of hers took her to one side and suggested she come and listen to this man called Jesus, who seemed to have the answers to life's problems. Sonia dressed up, covered her head in a black shawl and crept out to meet up with her friend. As soon as she came into the presence of Jesus, she knew she had found what she was looking for. She went several times to listen to Jesus, always carefully keeping herself away from anyone she knew.

One day she was in her house when she heard a furious raised voice from the floor below her. Pilate had come storming into the house and was shouting about this man called Jesus who was nothing but a fraud and not worth the time of day. She froze. In that moment, she felt as insecure as she had ever felt in her life. When she heard Jesus had been crucified a couple of days later, she went into a deep decline. Somehow all hope seemed to have gone and she shut down to all that Jesus had represented for her. There seemed to be nowhere else to go and no other route for her to follow.

Sonia chose her old friend to be her mother in this life because she needed help. (The friend had also become shut down to her belief in freedom when she was killed as a witch many centuries after her life at the time of Jesus.) One of Sonia's goals for this life was to find a way to open herself up to the truth and to help her mother do the same.

On the day I saw Sonia, she was wearing her mother's crucifix. As I connected her with the truth, she lifted her own embargo that she had placed on herself 2000 years before, and asked forgiveness for shutting down. She also asked for the balance to be restored within her as she let go of her fears. She then asked forgiveness on behalf of her mother as we felt her mother's presence in the room with us. In doing so and in letting her mother's stuck emotions filter through her and dissipate, she knew she repaid the debt that she owed her friend who came to her aid as Pilate's wife. Having completed this goal, she was now able to continue opening up to the truth.

The Fellow Swordsman or 'Right-Hand Man' of Pilate

As Pilate approached Jesus, his right-hand man (RHM) lowered his sword to the ground and stood watching. He saw the pregnant moment pass between the two men and felt a little unbalanced himself. As Pilate dismissed Jesus and came back towards his RHM, he stated, 'There *is* something a little different about this man.' Pilate seemed to shake his head, according to RHM, almost as if he wished to shake something off. He then proceeded to plan the Barabbas move...

It wasn't until quite a while after Jesus' death, when RHM found himself in the presence of a couple of disciples in a market area, that the memory of this man Jesus came to his notice again. One of the disciples, possibly Andrew, was talking of the teachings and miracles of Jesus and RHM found he was very interested. A small crowd had gathered round and he stepped closer to hear what they were saying. He was astonished by how lovingly they spoke of Jesus and how in awe they were of his healing work. Suddenly, he went cold all over. There was an intuitive moment when he knew they were talking about the man who had entered Pilate's apartments when he and Pilate had been practising swordplay. The unbalanced feeling came back to him. He backed away from the crowd, uncertain of his ground.

RHM spent the following weeks or even months in a process of soul searching. He also found out surreptitiously as much as he could about Jesus and the more he found out, the more he regretted not speaking up for this prisoner. The truth inside him was awakening and his soul longed for this truth. But, at the same time, he felt guilty and ashamed for he felt he had had an opportunity to speak up for Jesus and he had not taken it. He did not dare tell anyone about it as he felt Jesus' friends would condemn him and blame him for his death. He was torn apart.

This split in him, containing his guilt, shame, anger, regret and fear, has grown bigger and bigger within him as the lie slowly swelled over many lifetimes in the last 2000 years. However, his secret is at last coming into the open and he has an opportunity to stand in his truth.

Barabbas versus Jesus

One evening, I was watching the news on television when they were showing the celebrations that took place in Liverpool after they had won the European cup. There was a scene which showed huge crowds surrounding a high double-decker bus that was carrying the Liverpool team on its upper deck. I was instantly transported back to the moment when Jesus was put on some sort of wooden structure and lifted high above the crowds, at the instruction of Pilate. The crowds were jostling and shouting but he didn't seem to notice from the unsafeness of his perch. Rather, he was aware of massive shockwaves passing through him: 'How could so many people be calling for his death and expressing such hatred?'

He was totally bewildered as to how this could be happening. Where had all these people come from? A few days ago, they had been surrounding him with love and a desire to hear what he had to say. What had changed? How did it happen so suddenly? His shock was tangible.

A few months after this experience, I was telling a guest about this when she suddenly asked me about Barabbas. I went cold as I realised this was a loaded question. I took myself back into the experience.

From Jesus' high perch, I saw a group of approximately 10 rough-looking men to my left. They were standing quietly, chained hand and foot, with a ring of chains round them, holding them together. They were tightly guarded.

Pilate was shouting, 'These are your dangerous men. These are the ones that might hurt you. This one in particular.' He was pointing his finger at Barabbas. Then he turned and pointed at Jesus,

'What is this frail man going to do to you? He won't hurt anyone. Who would you rather I release?' he cried.

Hardly any of the crowd were able to hear Pilate above the shouting that was going on. He was only heard by Jesus and those closest to him. In frustration and anger, Pilate threw his hands up and said, 'I give up. I'm not having anything more to do with this man.' He then gave instruction for Jesus to be handed back to the Jews.

While my guest had not had anything to do with this in her own past lives, she had been used to prompt me into remembering an important part of Pilate's history.

Geoff and I sent forgiveness into the crowds. We felt an urge to send a wave of brilliant white light from our hearts in amongst them and beyond them. We asked for as much energy as possible to be lifted from this and any other relevant scene, and for the emotions that Jesus had felt to be dissipated.

A few years later, a lady called Ros came to see me. She had a lovely aura but was rather closed down to spiritual matters. On the first day of speaking with her, all I could see in her auric field was that she had spent some of her childhood with Jesus. Looking at Ros, I could see her as a lively child with a flirtatious attitude. She could see Jesus was very kind, very safe and very trustworthy and she used to try and bounce him out of his seriousness by teasing him or jumping on him suddenly. He would be amused by her and knew perfectly well that she was unstable within and was extra-vivacious in an effort to try and hide it.

Ros did not particularly resonate with the life that I was revealing to her but she did know I had described her personality to perfection. The next day, we spoke together again and Ros asked me why she carried such low self-worth. As I tuned into her, all I could see was this same childhood lifetime again so I told her this and then asked her soul if she was hiding anything. To my surprise, I suddenly saw her in Jerusalem in the crowds as Pontius Pilate held Jesus aloft. She was amongst friends and was in a party mood. She and her friends were at the back of the crowd and when the others all started to call, 'Crucify him', she looked up and saw the prisoners. She shrugged her shoulders and joined in the cry without thinking about what she was doing.

Quite a few years after the crucifixion, Ros met a man who started telling her about Jesus. The words he used were similar to the ones that she herself had used to describe her relationship with the boy Jesus she had known as a child. (She had often thought about him throughout her life.) Something uncomfortable stirred inside her. Could the man he was describing possibly be her old childhood friend? When she questioned the man, he told her some more. When he described the crucifixion, she became hot with fear. Had she been in the crowd calling 'Crucify him'? The thought was unimaginable. Her pain was acute. She felt sick, horrified, shocked, guilty and ashamed all in one moment. She knew she had loved her old schoolfriend; she knew he was an innocent man and the thought that she had supported his death was shattering. She held her own council and did not tell the man of her association. She buried her emotions and tried to pretend it was not true. But, over the years, the more she pretended, the guiltier she felt. I looked at Ros. She was at last cracking open. Her secret had come to light and she knew she was being forgiven. The emotions started to pour from her and she now understood why she was dogged constantly by a lack of self-worth.

There was a huge feeling that had been ever present in Ros' soul. This was that 'she had always wished she could put the clock back', but of course that was impossible. On this day, she understood she could not put the clock back but she could ask forgiveness for herself and then let the emotional impact go. Jesus would not have wanted her to go on berating herself for ever more.

As I sat quietly in Ros' presence, I felt a sudden release of energy from my body. I instantly knew that Jesus now had the answers as to why the crowd had seemingly changed its allegiance to him so quickly as he was held above them. The shock he had experienced was dissipating as the realisation sunk deep; that the crowd of revellers had not necessarily changed their allegiance, they had simply been ignorant of the truth.

The Record Keeper

I was sitting with a soul named Rick. He had come to stay at the retreat for a few days and I felt a little uneasy in his presence. It felt as if he didn't trust me so I told him that if I was to help him, he must let go of his fears and trust his intuition. He nodded and asked me to go ahead with his session.

Rick had been a record keeper of some sort and one of his jobs was to keep records of the prisoners going through the Roman prisons at the time of Jesus. He recorded who was released, who died, how they died, the date and so on. When it came to Jesus, there was a gap by his name. Rick had entered in a scribble above: 'Prisoner held by the Jews and then handed over to the Romans for trial. The Romans could not come to a conclusion so he was handed back to the Jews.'

I felt the dilemma in him. Rick did not wish to record a death that had not happened at the hands of the Romans and yet he could not deny the death had taken place. He did not know how to record it. He had been present when Jesus had been held aloft by the Romans and the crowd had called for his crucifixion. He had joined the crowd without knowing why he was there.

Rick did not like having a blank space in his book and yet nothing he thought of felt correct to enter. He did not dare make too many investigations as to who Jesus was as he knew better than anyone how many of his followers had been put to death. So he continued to fear and feel very uncomfortable.

Rick then asked me what we should do with this memory. I asked him what he would write in the blank record book right now. He thought for a while and then quietly stated, 'He was innocent.' I burst into tears at his unexpected words and said it would be amazing if he really meant it. After a little while more of discussion,

I asked if he was ready to do it. He replied quickly, 'It's done!' I looked up at him and said, 'I trust you.'

I sobbed from deep, deep in my core as I sat in front of him, just as I had with the Jewish priest. A second person who had been on the 'other side of the fence' who had been part of the first coming of Jesus, was now ready to help put his part right. Again, I had this feeling of: 'Is this really happening after all this time? Can it be possible?' The deep feeling of incredulity was not 'of' me. The horror of being so misunderstood within the soul group of Jesus was again being touched and given a chance to lift through my body.

I recognised the potential of what Rick had done and that it could help change the course of history. Between us, we waved his statement high on a pole for all to see. At last, Rick was prepared to stand up and be counted for his completed entry into the records.

Caiaphas' Role in Jesus' Imprisonment

Sometime ago, through a number of souls, I had become aware of the following: the day before Jesus died, he had a private consultation with Caiaphas, while sitting at a table with Caiaphas on one side of it and himself on the other. There were two Roman soldiers present, both standing behind Caiaphas, one behind each shoulder. Jesus went into a state of shock as he realised the strength of the fear that sat before him. He started asking himself: 'What is the point of all I have done? How can light ever win over such darkness?'

He was overwhelmed and his throat felt blocked. That Caiaphas knew Jesus was innocent was obvious. He was asking Jesus, 'Why are you putting yourself in this position? You know you only have to say the right word, and it will all be over.' Jesus was looking at Caiaphas with great sadness. He knew Caiaphas was too full of fear to put his life on the line and trust as he was. He forgave Caiaphas his weakness.

For his part, Caiaphas was desperate for Jesus to give in and get him out of an awkward situation. But he also knew in his heart that Jesus would not go against his truth, however much he tried to persuade him to. There was a crucial point in their meeting, as Caiaphas impatiently signed and handed over the papers (that indicated Jesus would be put on trial which would end in his death) to one of the soldiers. One could almost describe it as 'the agony of the moment' because, for a few fleeting seconds, Jesus knew Caiaphas would one day have to face the truth of what he had done, and, in those same few seconds, Caiaphas knew it but threw the thoughts away.

This moment of unity was used as a portal recently to send healing and forgiveness into the Caiaphas soul group. This was able to happen because an incarnated soul opened up to it.

Jesus was taken away shortly after, escorted between the two Roman soldiers and thrown once more into his damp, dark, stone cell.

Others in the Cells at the Time

A man called Tom visited the retreat and conveyed the following to me: he looked after all the prisoners in their cells. He saw many passing through and was well used to dealing with them. When Tom saw Jesus, he saw an innocent man with a lightness about him that he had not come across before. He sat in the cell with Jesus as he wanted to get to know him. They had many a chat.

When Jesus came back from his time with Pilate and from speaking with Caiaphas, Tom experienced a very different man. He saw Jesus struggling with an unusual darkness and was concerned. He sat silently in Jesus' cell all night, waiting to see if the light returned but it did not. At one point, he asked Jesus, 'Who are you?'

Jesus looked up at him with a glimmer of hope but he shed a further tear as he saw only fear in the man who had addressed him. He didn't answer. In that moment, he was carrying what seemed like an unbearably heavy burden of being utterly misunderstood by the whole world. He did not realise that he was, in this moment, taking himself back into the dregs of the Split, the darkness of separation from Source.

During the night that followed, Jesus went into what we perhaps refer to these days as 'the dark night of the soul'. This experience was later to prove useful when he hung on the cross because the second time around, it brought a familiarity with it and gave him the strength he needed to overcome the darkness much more quickly.

When Jesus was led away the following morning, he looked like a broken man. Tom sat in the cell very confused: 'Who was this man? Was he special? Was he innocent or not?' That was the last Tom saw of Jesus in that life. When he heard Jesus had been crucified, he fell to his knees in the cell. The presence of Jesus had touched him deeply.

There was a prisoner in a neighbouring cell to Jesus who was also looked after by Tom. When Mick came to see me, I knew he was not the face he was portraying and there was a dark secret needing to be revealed. He was talking of being killed in previous lives and having memories of suffering. I sought to dig underneath what he was saying and see what the real problem was. As his soul was too scared to let me see it, I jumped my consciousness into his darkness (with his permission) to find the answers we were looking for.

Mick was in a cell which was cold, damp and miserable. He had been condemned to be crucified but, as he knew he was getting his just deserts, his thoughts were not on what might happen to him. His thoughts were on the man in a neighbouring cell who had been condemned to death in place of him. He had only caught a glimpse of this man when they had both been led out in front of Pilate but he knew an innocent man when he saw one. While he accepted that he himself might still die for what he had done, he could not accept that an innocent should die in his place. Most of him didn't believe it would come to this anyway. How could it?

One morning, Tom came into Mick's cell with some water and a morsel to eat. Tom told him that Jesus was to be tried and, if found guilty, he would be crucified that day. Mick went into a very shocked and concerned state and, when left alone, sat tucked up in his cell with his feet under his chin. What had seemed impossible was getting closer. Could it really happen? His turmoil and the injustice within him grew steadily stronger all that morning, and when Tom came into his cell later that day and told him Jesus had gone to be crucified, the reality could no longer be denied. In that moment, he was full of anger and hatred for himself. *He* was the criminal. *He* had done dreadful things. *He* deserved to be punished. The other man had done nothing wrong. He was so angry with himself that he had not spoken up for the man. And through the following hours, he faced himself and his actions and who he was. He had been a leader amongst criminals, taking the lead in criminal acts because he wanted things to be done his way. He encouraged others in bad ways which is why the authorities were so glad to have captured and condemned him.

As Mick spent the next few days in his cell because the authorities didn't really know what to do with him, he had plenty of time for all this to churn around inside. It was at this time that his soul knew he had to change. He could no longer kid himself that it was OK to carry on with this lifestyle in any more lives and he allowed something fundamental to change at soul level. When he was finally released, he took some rope and hung himself.

Over many lifetimes since, Mick had been gradually learning who Jesus had been and, at the same time, he paid his karmic debt to society. When he came to see me, he had been experiencing a severe pain in his stomach for some months. As we unearthed his past life, the pain slowly receded and, when we had finished, it had gone. Twenty-five years before, he had tried to hang himself in exactly the same manner as in the past life, and had come to, lying on the ground with the rope cut in three places. He had never been able to explain why he had not died or how the rope came to be cut, but on that day he now knew he could not run from himself anymore and he began his journey into healing. It took him 25 years to face the above because he had got stuck in the memory of his own suffering.

Taj was also in a cell at the time Jesus was held prisoner. His opinion was that all the prisoners knew Jesus was innocent. He remembered that when they heard Jesus had been crucified, they felt so low, knowing that there was no chance for them.

Taj had been accused of stealing. He had been stealing for many lifetimes as he kept finding himself in a position where he could not provide enough food to feed his family. He genuinely could not comprehend a world where those who had too much did not share with those who had too little. Not long after the crucifixion, he was found guilty of theft and had his hands chopped off.

Taj had come to speak with me because he had been having dreams of Jesus coming to him and showing him that he had been forgiven. In a more recent one, Jesus had beckoned to him in a dream and said: 'Are you ready to come to me?'

Upon reconnecting with his association with Jesus, Taj could now ask forgiveness, with the full context around the dreams in his conscious mind. He was then able to let go of the sorrow, shame, guilt, confusion, sense of loss and deep fear he had of simply being himself.

* * *

I was privileged enough to come across another man from the Barabbas soul group. I didn't actually meet him but, through contact with his mother, I was allowed to ask his soul questions because this man had gone into an institution and his soul was pleading for help. He could not forgive himself and did not believe he could ever be forgiven, and these thoughts were driving him into a mentally unbalanced and anguished state. I sat quietly and heard his soul pour out the following:

> I saw him being held high above us. I knew he was an innocent man. His demeanour was sad and that of a victim. He made neither sound nor movement. He was so alone. In this moment I did not understand my life was to be offered for his. It was only when I

heard it spoken that I realised what was going on. I was shocked and relieved at the same time. I asked myself why should this happen? What had they got against this man? I looked closely as he was taken down and brought amongst us. There were tears running down his cheeks. His face was blank and his mouth mute. He looked neither left nor right. He was broken. I knew Jesus was an ordinary man. Not a God, not special but I knew he was innocent.

When in the prison the night before Jesus' death, Barabbas knew Jesus had gone into a dark place. He could feel it, even though he was in a different cell. There was no anger, no movement, just silence. He knew Jesus neither ate nor drank. He could feel waves of depression and despair pass through his cell.

In this life, this man had always said to his mother, 'Jesus is not who everyone thinks he is.' His mother never understood what her son meant until now. Barabbas had witnessed what few had seen, and that dark night of the soul is hardly acknowledged in the modern day.

***

As Jesus was led out of his cell, his feet and hands were chained. There was a loud clunking sound as he dragged the chains along the ground behind him, his head hung low. He was taken into a courtroom where immediately ahead of him was a panel of judges with Caiaphas in the centre. The room was packed with interested parties, many of whom were mocking and jeering at him. There were friends of his dotted about amongst the ordinary onlookers, Roman soldiers and others who wished to be rid of Jesus. Peter was standing behind and to the right of Caiaphas. But Jesus neither saw nor heard any of this. He was in a very low, weak and bemused state. He was asking himself what it was all about and why it was happening. In that moment, he could not see the wood for the trees.

As he stood lost in thought in front of Caiaphas, he became aware of a light energy that felt different to the energy in the rest of the room, coming from the left-hand corner at the back. It was streamlining straight for his heart. His intuition woke up and he discovered the message in the energy was: 'We believe in you. We believe in you.'

The message was coming from spirit from the soul group of Mary Magdalene. The soul group saw the trouble that Jesus was in and sent this vital impulse of energy through Mary to Jesus. Immediately, Jesus pulled himself to an upright position in front of Caiaphas. No longer was he a down-and-out; strength flowed through his veins and his soul came back into balance. Perhaps his life hadn't been in vain, after all? Some of his followers believed in him and understood him. Perhaps there were more? He mustn't let them down.

He stood up straight, chains forgotten and eyes fixed on the panel of judges ahead. As they asked him questions, he found the answers that served the highest good of all. His intuition was in full flow again. As they condemned him to be crucified, he didn't flinch. He trusted the process he was being put through. He didn't know what the final outcome would be but he did know he had to follow his heart, whatever that might bring.

A Positive Sign

At around this time, a lady, Ruth, sat in front of me, full of resentment, judgement, fear, anger and shame. I could see her connection to Caiaphas immediately. I hesitated. I didn't know this lady and I knew how damaged the soul group was and that in anger it can explode. As Ruth spoke to me, it became clear that she was ready to heal. She had paid her karmic debt and was looking to discover her own deep truth.

'What do you want from this life?' I asked her. She replied, 'Unconditional love.' I asked, 'Who was Jesus to you?' She said, 'He was unconditional love, an enlightened being.' I carefully then told her what I knew of the Caiaphas story so far. Then I asked her, 'If you were put in that same position today, would you make a more balanced decision this time around?' She replied, 'I've been making more balanced decisions in this life for 31 years, as a top judge!' From this karmically balanced state, Ruth was able to release the anger, shame, fear, resentment and judgement she had held since the time of her incarnation as Caiaphas.

**

The Via Dolorosa, as it existed 2000 years ago, is long since lost to Jerusalem, but what has evolved from it is still a main focus for pilgrims who care to make the journey to that Holy City today. It has been rerouted around existing buildings and made to fit in with modern Jerusalem's lifestyle. However, the energetic resonance of the old route still exists in the hearts of many, if one is attuned enough to remember its true course. Jesus was asked to carry his cross along the original route.

Carrying the Cross

My shoulder had been getting progressively more and more painful one spring. There did not seem to be a reason for this so I was a little confused. I therefore decided to tune into it and immediately felt the memory of Jesus carrying the cross on his back and shoulder, the weight of it predominantly on his right shoulder blade. I felt his agony and the pain. Geoff started an exploratory massage on my shoulder to see if the source of this pain could be eased or released. He found a spot on a muscle on the inside edge of my shoulder blade in the exact spot I could feel the cross pressing painfully on Jesus' back.

As Geoff put pressure on this spot and I asked the pain to release, I was catapulted into a memory of how Jesus had stumbled on his way to the cross. In that split second, he felt anxious that he might not physically be able to stay alive long enough to complete his mission. As I came out of the memory, Geoff told me that some-one had gone to Jesus' aid. I now know that this aid was entirely necessary and was divinely inspired. I felt so physically sick at this point that I was retching and Geoff had to take the pressure off my shoulder. It took quite a few hours to recover from this but, afterwards, that part of my back was completely healed

Piata

Piata was a simple soul who happened to be in the crowd as Jesus was trudging up the hill to the place of crucifixion. When he saw the prisoner stumble, his heart went out to him. He moved forward to take the heavy load from Jesus and simply told Jesus to walk on ahead. It all happened so quickly that no one interfered. When Piata got to the top of the hill, he put the cross on the ground and thought no more of it. He stopped and had a couple of casual conversations with people and then went on his way. He had no idea whose cross he had carried, that he had perhaps saved Jesus from an untimely death or that he had been part of something so important. He had simply gone with a nudge in his intuition in the simplest of ways.

Having steeped himself in the Sikh tradition for a number of lifetimes recently, Piata was now ready to face the fact that he had been broader and more open in the past than he was at present. On his history being recalled, his heart burst open and he is now beginning on his deeper healing journey.

The Water Girl

The following are Nisha's own words:

> The pain and hurt I feel physically inside myself when I think of Jesus walking up the hill to his crucifixion are more than a story. They are a memory. I was a young, innocent girl and I remember knowing that something terrible was happening. There was a feeling of dread and terror almost palpable in the air. There was anger and

rage in the crowds around me which cut at my soul. I could feel my mum's hand round mine. She was trying to protect me, shield me from the pain and keep me safe. I was thinking: 'How can they do this to him, this good man? Can't they see what he is?' I saw him as a beam of light. 'Can't they see his pain? I can't believe people would hurt another being in this way.' I could feel his pain and became aware of his deep thirst and knew he needed water. I knew I had to help him. I let go of my mother's hand and, at that same moment, she felt guided to shoot forward up the hill to follow Jesus more closely. Putting aside my terror of being alone, I looked around for a way to get water to him.

When I found some water, I took it straight to Jesus. I have always felt a deep sadness inside me and I now know it roots from the moment I looked into his eyes as I handed him the water. I cannot remember any words, just a simple exchange of knowing looks. I felt his agony, anguish, exhaustion and fear. I now know that without this water he might not have been able to walk much further. As I recalled this scene, I now understood that this had always been my purpose. I had come into that life to help him complete his journey.

In this life, I have wondered why I have an inner knowing when people need a drink. I have made a point of putting love into a drink, especially as a little girl. I also, to this day, carry the memory of the aloneness I felt when I released my mother's hand. I now understand the patterns that I carry, and the emotions that occur when I think of Jesus. I know I can release all of this and my life is now about letting my own light shine.

Nailed to the Cross

The day after my back had healed, my neck was still extremely painful. Feeling quite nervous, I decided to tune into it. This time I felt Jesus lying on his back, ready to be nailed to the cross. A foot descended towards his chin and shoved it unceremoniously to the right with a quick, sharp movement, and a thick coarse rope was used to secure his neck to the cross. I could feel how Jesus could only breathe freely after that when his neck was turned to the right. Geoff explored loosening the muscles in my neck as much as he could while I tried to release the painful memory.

***

I had had a very strong pain on the top and inside of my left foot for some time when, one day, I was sitting quietly amongst a number of deeply spiritual friends. I suddenly felt a soul approach me in spirit. Uther was nervous and reticent so I encouraged him to tell us why he had approached us. Uther admitted he had been one of the soldiers who had helped nail Jesus to the cross. Putting nails in the hands and feet of criminals was not his usual job, and he was actually on guard duty that day, but the man who was putting the nails through Jesus' wrists seemed uncomfortable and he suddenly shoved the nails into Uther's palms, telling him to secure the prisoner's ankles. Uther reluctantly took the nails and, as he looked at the feet of Jesus, he had an idea. He crossed the left foot in front of the right, leaving the right foot neatly tucked in behind. He did not know why he felt the need to do this and he followed his inner urge in a little bit of confusion.

***

Just after I had written the above, I could not sleep. The pain in my foot was very uncomfortable and I tossed and turned that night, trying to find a more comfortable position. The visit from Uther at an earlier date, together with a very recent visit from the man who actually pulled the nails out after the death of Jesus, brought together the memory of a set of emotions that the universe wished to pass through me to help release the soul group of Jesus from the physical pain of being nailed to the cross.

As Jesus lay flat on the cross, he fell to a new level of hopelessness and became deeply disturbed. He was shocked that he actually had to be nailed to the cross and go through so much pain. Up until then, he had sincerely hoped it would not come to this. While I was not focusing on the pain in his wrists as I lay in bed bravely reliving the moment, I could feel the pain of a nail going through his left foot. It was getting worse and worse. Gradually, it dawned on me that I would have to lie flat on my back and be brave enough to go through the whole memory of that moment to re-experience exactly what had happened. As I did so, I felt a long, rusty nail sink into the inner side of my left foot just below the top bone. I heard an exclamation of anger, felt another sharp stab of pain, and shortly afterwards a second nail was being hammered into the top of my left foot at a slight angle so that it came out at the side of my foot and sunk into the cross. The way it happened meant Jesus' body was tilted at a slight angle to the right.

I had often found myself in that odd position when I was going to sleep or even while sleeping and I had wondered why. I had been asking to rebalance myself from that position for some years, as it hadn't felt good for me.

At the same time, my memory turned to the man who had removed the nails after Jesus died. I saw him (from spirit) slowly, lovingly, carefully and gently removing the long nails from Jesus' foot, leaving a spurt of blood trickling down onto the ground. I offered the soul group a release of the pain, fear and shock through me, while unconditionally forgiving Uther. The pain and shock had been so great at the time Uther had put the nails in, that Jesus had sunk deeper within himself to cope.

As I visualised the nails being drawn back out, I gradually felt a tingling in my foot, and the heat and what seemed like an infection that by this time had spread up my leg, started to recede. It was a slow business and it had to be done when I was experiencing the most pain. My heart began to lighten as, after hours of struggle, I knew I had reached a point where my foot could heal and I had done my job.

A little later, I felt a medium-sized pain in my left wrist and a tiny bit in my right wrist. It felt as if others before me had released most of this pain from Jesus already, so I was only asked to release what was left of the pain, shock and fear that were still embedded there.

Immediately Uther had finished, Jesus was hoisted high into the air and Uther turned away and left him to it, never thinking of the incident again.

In future incarnations, when Uther saw pictures of the crucifixion or stood in front of a crucifix, he had felt uneasy and eventually began to search for answers. He approached us from spirit on that day because he wished to be forgiven. The whole group of us sent him forgiveness and my foot tingled strongly for a very long time after that.

6
The Crucifixion

The cross should not be a pedestal from which to hang a godly act but should be a simple token of a memory from which the Split began to heal and ultimate trust returned to earth.

Later that evening, I could feel that rope around my neck again. My whole throat became sore and the pain in my neck worsened. I went to bed feeling uncomfortable all over and with a darkness invading my body which I knew was not mine.

For long hours in the night, I tossed and turned as I sunk into reliving the hours that Jesus was hanging on the cross. The pain and suffering seemed to get worse and worse, and by 2.00 a.m. painkillers were not touching the pain. Between 2.00 a.m. and 4.00 a.m., I relived Jesus feeling utterly alone and abandoned on the cross. His head was hanging down to the right and he could just about see from his left eye but nothing from his right one as it was pinned against the cross. He was falling in and out of consciousness. All the time, he was repeating under his breath, 'Please forgive them. They don't realise I am innocent. They don't know what they are doing', amongst other things.

The words kept forming in his mind and coming out under his breath over and over again, whether he was conscious or semi-conscious. He had enormous pain in both wrists and his left foot where the nails had been driven in. He had long moments of feeling devastated when he thought of all he had done to try and teach truth to those who cared to listen to him and how they now stood randomly around him, not one of them having the courage to speak up for him or offer him a word of comfort.

Shunned by his Family?

'What was it all for?' he asked himself. Even his mother was silent and still. Had nothing of what he had become been understood by any of them? Jesus knew that his family was not more important than anyone else to him, but in that moment on the cross he succumbed to feeling very unhappy that they stood like lemons watching him suffer. Many of his family were present and that was the most painful part of 'feeling let down' as he slipped towards the darkness. It all became too personal to him as he struggled to reconcile what was going on.

In the middle of all this, he was surprised to receive a shaft of love that was much stronger than any other around him, and that made a beeline for his heart. This was not from a family member; it was from Judas. Jesus instantly sent a shaft of love back to Judas and a message with it: 'It's alright, Judas. Don't worry. It's alright.' There was deep forgiveness, reassurance and love in his message. Judas' shaft of love gave Jesus an idea. He said to God: 'Please don't let everything I have done be wasted.' And he asked to sink the energy of who he had become and what he had learned into the ground at the foot of the cross.

As the pain reached unbearable peaks, I suddenly felt Jesus crying from his heart, in extreme agony and distress: 'How can one small man like me make a difference? How can I be expected to do this on my own? What possible good can come from it? How can this possibly be helping anyone? Have I made a terrible mistake?'

I tossed and turned in my bed even more frantically than before … In that moment, Jesus had gone deeper than ever before into separation and fear. I suddenly understood the words, 'Father, why hast thou forsaken me?' It seemed to him that in this, his deepest hour of pain and need, he had been totally abandoned.

The light was draining from the sky and dark clouds gathered around the cross. It appeared indeed as if he were alone and there was nothing left to show of his life's work. I was writhing with pain all over my body for what seemed like an eternity. I was really afraid and knew I needed help. I called for Geoff. He heard me and came at once so I told him I was unable to extract myself from this experience/memory. He put a hand on each of my shoulders and it was as if he was waving a magic wand. I instantly began to calm down. I then remembered that seconds after Jesus had cried out in his agony, he had felt very wrong inside and very remorseful for having had such thoughts. Had he scuppered his whole mission? He panicked a little in his doubt and felt uncertainty and self-disgust. But this state of separation was alien to him so seconds after it began, he retracted his doubts and elected to trust once more. In trusting, the fear left him and he came back into alignment with Source. He had an instant inner knowing that his earthly journey was complete.

He uttered, 'It is finished.' A few seconds later, he called out, 'Into thy hands I commend my spirit' or words like it. He at last felt able to ask to be put out of his bodily misery. There was an immediate flash of light, followed by a huge thunderclap, and the dark clouds began to part.

> *I could see now that it had to happen this way—for Jesus to be utterly alone without any earthly help—so that he could reverse/overcome the lack of trust that had been so completely lost at the Split.*
>
> *This was the critical turning point in humanity's affairs. Jesus had achieved coming out of the darkness and back into the oneness of consciousness, and reminded us that humanity was not separated, lost and banished from the divine, as we had feared.*

Still feeling completely overwhelmed but with Geoff's hands on my shoulders and back, I asked Source: 'What would you like me to do about this?' I felt the light in my heart illuminate and expand and, as it did so, it slowly pushed the pain and terror out of my body. I realised I had been put through all this as Jesus did not wish the energy of his pain to remain on earth any longer. I slowly started to recover, though I must say it was many weeks before its impact had completely left my body.

A few months later, I relived the moment when Jesus felt he might have scuppered the whole mission. It happened initially through a dream. It took me a few hours to realise I had to immerse my energy once more into what had happened on the cross and allow the emotions of self-disgust, panic, shock, unworthiness, seeming lack of support and uncertainty to leave. As I did this, I remembered that I had come into this world in this life feeling that I had done something terrible and been a very bad person. Those dark feelings came back to me and I knew they were related to that moment on the cross. I was in awe. My whole life had been about releasing this energy and I had had no idea that what I had felt back then wasn't mine. As I realised it, it dissipated.

As I got up after that long night of replay on the cross, I was so shaken up that I asked Source not to do anymore through me for the time being. Over the next couple of days, nothing was lifting and I was dragging myself around in a state of very low energy. I was wondering why it was not lifting when Geoff reminded me that I had put the brakes on the whole project by saying, 'I can't do anymore right now.' I was mortified. I realised I had stopped the process of releasing from happening and it was still locked inside me. I immediately took back my words and apologised. Slowly, slowly, the releasing began again and the mission was back on track.

The next night, through a dream state, I had an idea about a thought pattern that would help the world. From the thought, I was catapulted into finding myself pulling at the ground at the foot of the cross. Clods of dark brown, damp earth started to come out in chunks in my hands. I felt driven to keep going until the hole I was making became a deep pit.

Suddenly, as I pulled a large clod of earth out, the most brilliant white light I had ever seen started shining out from underneath. I knew I had hit the energetic memory that Jesus had buried just before his death. I asked for this active light to be transferred back into his heart on the cross and to shine from there all over the world. I glanced up at the cross and saw the brilliance of the light shining from his heart, filling the area, leaving little else to be seen other than the shadow of the cross and the darkness beyond. I then asked for this level of light to enter my (and Geoff's) heart and I felt it shine its luminous white light across the ether. As I was marvelling over what had just happened, I asked if the light could transform every crucifix and every statue or representation of the divine in any form, all over the world. This would have the potential to alter the quality of the Christ light in all the places those religious effigies were present, giving them the full power they should always have had. Both Geoff and I were excited and awed.

At a later date, I realised we will all pick up our own clod of earth when we are ready, and like the feeding of the 5000, there are enough clods for us all.

The very next day, a soul named Shari dropped in to see me. She didn't know why she felt she needed to come but as we began to chat about things, it became clear that she had no real personal problem at that moment. As I was coughing so much (due to the recent stress I had been through), I decided to tell her why and what had been happening to me in the last few days. I had completely forgotten that she had been in spirit as the crucifixion took place, watching it all happen. She and others like her had been holding the space from above the cross, to ensure the highest possible outcome.

At a similar time, a lady called Coli had been visiting me and it transpired that she had been part of the dark energy hovering above the cross, and was originally connected to the dinosaur energy at around the 20% mark.

From spirit, Shari and Coli each watched anxiously as Jesus weakened in his resolve. For her part, Shari witnessed a strange darkness gathering around him and felt it was ready to pounce on him, should he falter in his mission. Coli, on the other hand, participated in the intention of the dark energy from the very edge of it and waited to see what would happen with bated breath. As Jesus called in agony to his father, asking why he had been abandoned, the darkness sprang into action and approached Jesus' body, intending to engulf it and wipe out the light within it. Shari recalled how she and the energy around her had been 'holding its breath' in spirit while the darkness tried to take hold. Would he pull through? Would he relinquish his doubt and go back into trust or would he succumb as others had before him? It was a very tense moment for those in spirit. When Jesus threw the doubt away, allowing his trust to be in the ascendency again, he immediately disempowered the darkness. It was forced to reverse away from his body and, shortly afterwards, his enlightened soul was quickly lifted into the ether. This could not have happened unless and *until* Jesus had regained his trust; Coli watched all this in awe. From that moment on, she knew that the light energy was more powerful than the dark and the game was over. She relinquished her dinosaur experience and bowed to the greater power there and then.

Jesus had only been out of trust for seconds but the darkness had an impact. This is a part of the memory that the Jesus soul group wished Shari and I to clear from the earth, as he died before he could do it himself.

It is interesting to note that it was several years after these two ladies had visited me, that Coli finally overcame the darkness within her in an embodied state, when she stood up to two separate partners who carried the dinosaur experience and also to a similarly invested powerful friend, for, while she had 'seen the light' at the cross, she had had to return to an embodied state (this life) to remember what had happened in spirit, to be able to release it.

Later, I was taken above the cross and became 'as' Jesus, after his soul left his body. He was criss-crossing the crowds, in the semi-darkness, watching everyone. We saw souls crouched on their knees, quietly sobbing. There were families slowly picking up their belongings ready to make their way home. We saw Roman soldiers standing around fires chatting.

Cary had been a Roman soldier who had closely guarded Jesus when he was dying and admitted wondering why there was so much fuss over this one prisoner. As he considered this, it drew him to look up closely into Jesus' face, and he recognised him, because he was from the same soul group. He became distraught. This man was innocent! Cary felt caught between the devil and the deep blue sea, unable, in that moment, to extricate himself from his professional post. He questioned whether he was even right. He carried on his duties feeling extremely uncomfortable.

Later, while standing around a fire with some other Roman soldiers, he heard a colleague mention that he knew who Jesus was. The colleague explained that he had been one of the soldiers who had escorted Jesus away from Pilate's clutches and back into Caiaphas' presence. Cary had overheard the following conversation between Caiaphas and Jesus, which went something like this:

Caiaphas: 'They've sent you back because they don't want anything to do with you. You have done nothing wrong. I'm giving you a chance. Say what I want you to say and I can set you free.'

Jesus refused to lie.

Caiaphas: 'I can't help you if you don't comply. I can't save you. If I do, the crowds will go for me.'

Jesus: 'You have a choice. You can speak your truth or you can deny me.'

Caiaphas was so furious that Jesus would not let him off the hook that he banged the table with his fist and shouted, 'Die then, you stupid man.'

When Cary heard this, he knew what he had suspected was true and that he had been party to killing one of his own. He went into a very dark place and has stayed there ever since. It is only now that he has the opportunity to trust the words of Jesus: 'Father, forgive them, they know not what they do' that he can choose to let it go.

***

Back to criss-crossing the site: there was an eerie silence. Out of the gloom flashed a sudden bright light. It shone pure white and in its beauty we recognised an embodied soul who had just connected to the truth of what was going on and who Jesus had been, and given its life into total service. Then another soul did the same thing and this process was repeated a handful of times as we watched. I felt an uplifting in the soul of Jesus as it happened.

A Further Release

Almost exactly nine months later, the universe attempted to use me to allow a deeper release of Jesus' emotions from the cross. Initially, I failed to understand what was being asked of me but, three months later, the universe tried again, through the same person, and succeeded. Basically, this person had severely verbally attacked me and brought matters between the two of us to a head. She had been in the crowd when Jesus was paraded high in the air on a platform, by Pilate. She had pumped her arm in the air and shouted 'Crucify him, crucify him', along with the rest of the crowd. I had always known this lady was too scared to follow her own intuition and had joined in with the crowd because she had no desire to be singled out by anyone and because something about the presence of Jesus was tapping into her own guilt.

After I confided in my sister, she pushed me harder and harder to grasp that there must be something deeper, I had to learn from what was going on; the pain was so great inside me, I was struggling to hear her. Eventually, I managed to go into it and realised that the over-whelming feeling was one of being misunderstood and being helpless to do anything about it. It felt like I was being taken to breaking point. But, at the same time, I knew these thoughts were not mine, as I had dealt with them long ago. That was what was confusing me—the situation was so personal but the emotions around it were not.

In my agony and through my tears, I asked for help and was taken back to the memory of Jesus on the cross and reconnected with his unbearable pain at being so utterly misunderstood and helpless. I had touched on the deep pain in my core dramatically (explained in a previous chapter) when Zac, the priest, had come to stay, and when Rick, the record keeper, had come a few days later. What had allowed me to touch it was their understanding of and apology for what had happened. What made this situation more difficult was that there was no apology and no conversation between the initial lady who had hurt me and me. While sitting in a quiet place alone, I found the courage to sink into the experience on the cross once more. This time I realised, of course, there was no conversation between Jesus and anyone else! Not *one* soul had understood.

A quiet, gentle voice inside me said: 'At some level they all understood.' I was shocked. I felt a stirring inside me. The pain dislodged a little. The voice went on: 'Haven't they built churches all over the world in acknowledgement of what Jesus did?' As I heard this, I realised the hugeness of the pain and why I felt it bigger than a house (or church!) inside me. I also realised that the lady who had abused me also understood at a deeper level, whether she cared to remember it or not at this time.

I then had a different thought. I imagined everyone around Jesus on the cross, pointing fingers at him saying: 'This is your stuff. You are the one reacting to the crowd so it's yours to deal with.' I was aghast. And, of course, they may have been thinking it. After all, it was Jesus' choice to hang there when, in their eyes, he hadn't needed to. This thought was what my sister had recreated. She had tried to tell me I had to look at myself and it was just like Jesus being told on the cross he had to look at himself. It seemed ridiculous and yet here was the answer. He had felt misunderstood as I felt misunderstood right now. He had suppressed the emotion all this time because he was unable to digest or deal with it before he died. The forgiveness part wasn't the issue; it was about being misunderstood and being helpless to deal with it.

Learning How to Heal

It just seemed too big and too painful for me to do. I felt terrified that I had to go through the emotional mill yet again. But, eventually,

I found the courage and trusted I would be shown the way. (I hadn't cried so much or been so low in a long, long time.)

Shortly after my call for help came a new thought: *There will never be another moment of what seemed like a crowd of 100% misunderstanding, around Jesus again. The world has changed in just over 2000 years. If that crowd were around him now, it would not be the same for many are healing, many are beginning to understand exactly what happened and why he hung there. People from all walks of life are finding him and believing in him. Focus on them...*

I started to see the crowd from the cross again. This time I saw the truth. I saw them each as the percentage of healing they had achieved in the last 2000 years. I saw that a few would even stand by Jesus and die with him. There would be support! Of course!

That very evening, my sister sent me an email to say how proud she was of me and how much love she felt for me. (I hadn't talked with her that day; she just felt moved to send it.) My son had been in and out of the house all day and had unfortunately seen how upset and low I was. It became obvious I had to give him a brief explanation. He left shortly afterwards but an hour after he left the house, he rang home and said:

> 'Mum, I have rung to apologise. I haven't stood up for you in front of her [this lady] like I should have done. I feel bad and I haven't done you any favours. I am going to stand up for you now in my own way. I am a spiritual person and I am coming back to understanding it now. I am going to help you. I am very, very proud of you and what you are doing for the world.'

I had several emails in the days both before and after the event from random people asking if I was OK and saying that they would send their support, love and light to me. I had a dream that my deceased son was sitting beside me in what had been his favourite 'talking to mum' place when he was alive. I knew beyond doubt that he and everyone else on the other side was 100% with me. Geoff was beside me, supporting me and loving me every step of the way. Gradually,

I began to shift a little of the pain. My younger son's phone call was the icing on the cake really, because it was so unexpected. My inner realms started to steady.

A few hours later, I felt I was back at the cross again and the feeling of loss and sorrow was overwhelming. It was sorrow for the loss of family, friends, life, a future and aspirations. As I finally managed to let these emotions go for the soul group, I felt a tingling all over. I started to replay the scene on the cross in a different way. I could now see and feel the support of the crowds and the knowledge that Jesus would see them all again one day. All was not lost and there would never ever be a need to go through this again. I felt Jesus' immense pain. It invaded my body, especially my chest. I asked to throw the pain out and told it I did not wish to identify with the old and wished to live the new—the new being love, joy, trust, forgiveness, truth, peace, in fact the Christ light.

Suddenly, I felt a light shining from inside the lower part of my ribcage. I had never felt a light there before; I had felt it in my heart for decades, and in my tummy for a few years, but this was new. As I felt into it, the aching and pain in my body gradually began to diminish. I was exhausted and felt bed was the only place for me right then.

In the early hours, I became aware that the three light spots in my body had become joined: the one in my heart, the one in my stomach and the new one in my chest had become one. They formed a long shape from which there were star-like points jutting out, one from the top, one from the bottom and two from each side. This star shape was steady and glowing a little, and it was whitish gold. I kept waking up and feeling it again and each time it was glowing a little more.

By morning, all the aches had gone from my body and I felt physically better; I told Geoff all about it. As I described it, I said, 'That's funny. I told you I had seen a seven-point star inside but actually there are only six points!' Then I realised the seventh point was in the centre of the star and, just as I realised it, Geoff said it out loud.

I also knew the middle point represented 'today's' Christ in me, for the old had dissipated. I dived within to see if I could feel into the seventh point. Once inside, I saw an old stone with a hook in it. I wanted to unhook the stone but I couldn't. I needed first to know what it represented. After a while, I knew this hook represented letting go of every part of the past life of Jesus and everything else about my connection with planet earth that was still left in me. Why was I terrified of letting that go?

There were two answers to this: (1) I was still terrified that if I let it go, I might be asked to go through everything I had ever been through yet again (thinking about what Jesus had been through at this point). I just couldn't face that; or (2) I had to trust that I would be allowed to stay incarnated and live free, without it. Would I be allowed to?

I questioned my higher self and came to understand the following: when we, as a collective energy, originally came to earth, we thought we had learned all the lessons we needed to learn in previous planetary experiences and we fully expected to thoroughly enjoy our earth adventure. Immediately upon entering earth, we discovered it wasn't as easy as that for, as we integrated with matter once more, the emotions within us became alive again as we had not let go of them. This caused huge guilt, pain and terror in all of us and we got swept up in the tide. We now understand that we can only let go of emotions when we become conscious of them and root out their origins in an incarnated state, which is why true inner joy can only be known by us when we have let go of all our fears from every experience we have ever been through.

As I let the guilt, terror and pain go, I saw that we were guilty only of innocence! I became the centre point of my inner star, my seventh point. I knew I could live on earth safely and freely without repeating all that I had already experienced. When we have released enough fear—fear was created by us all at the time of the crucifixion—the event will no longer be based on suffering but will sit in gratitude.

A Note on Suffering

The perceived suffering on the cross was taken out of context at the time it happened. The watching crowd dreaded the notion that suffering may be a prerequisite to enlightenment. This belief caused some in the 'Church' that followed to become control freaks, declaring their position to be one of high spiritual office, important and necessary. The truth is that they were really trying to protect themselves from the suffering they feared they might be put through. At this time, a myth formed that has remained in the roots of the various Churches: 'He died for our sins so we don't have to suffer.'

Other factions, such as some of the followers of Jesus, were also very fearful of suffering. Did they all have to do what Jesus had done to enter the gates of heaven? Peter was a prime example. The answer is clear: none of us has to repeat what Jesus did. The cross and all that went with it were part of his journey. But we do have to run our own journey in whatever way it pans out, to set our own soul free and to reverse our own Split experience. Jesus did not and could not do it for us, but he did show us the way. The truth is: suffering need only come if it serves the highest good; it is not obligatory.

7
The Disciples

Over the years, I have met many, many people living now who also lived at the time of Jesus, and came across him somewhere or other in his short adult life. They seem to become drawn to me when their past life story is ready to unravel. I can always tell if someone has a connection to Jesus. There is a part of them that was touched by his presence over 2000 years ago that has remained with them, that is undeniable by them or me. It is a privilege when they allow me to feel into their story. I learn and they remember. They offer forgiveness and release the emotions they experienced, thus freeing themselves of trauma, and I grow in my knowledge and memory of all that happened at the time.

I will now try to relate what I can of a few of the disciples.

Andrew

I was visited by a beautiful lady, Bana. She had found me first when her husband was dying and we kept in contact over email. After he died, of course she wanted answers and to know why his death had happened the way it had and to know how he was faring on the other side.

Around the same time, I was also visited by a lady called Mimi who recognised for herself that her partner was from the soul group of Andrew. A third lady found me more recently. Her husband had died a few years before. It became clear that he was from the Andrew soul group. She recognised immediately the 'dilemma' I described in him and his kind, gentle nature.

Through various discussions with these ladies, I learned most of the following:

Bana, like Mimi, was a member of the soul group of Andrew's wife. As we spoke together, I felt her husband strongly around us and he told us he belonged to the soul group of Andrew. Through him, I learned that Andrew had met Jesus in the very early days of his teaching. Bana had resented the time that Andrew spent with Jesus and the influence that Jesus seemed to have on him, and therefore made association with him as difficult as she could. She was mostly angry that Andrew spent so much time away from her and their young family.

Mimi, on her visit to me, recalled a day when Andrew was having a very happy time, laughing and having fun with his friends, while fishing out on a lake. Just as they had finished their fishing for the day and were rowing into shore, he noticed a gathering of people standing lakeside. As the boat approached land, two of the fishermen got out and a man from the gathering said, 'Are any of you willing to take Jesus out in your boat? He would like to go out on the water for a while.'

Andrew was still sitting in the boat, housing the oars and collecting all the belongings together, as was his usual role. The other two fishermen showed no sign of wishing to go out on the lake again so Andrew, being of kind and selfless heart, said that he would take Jesus, despite the fact that he was tired and hungry. Jesus stepped into his boat and, as they rowed out into the centre of the lake, Andrew felt that there was something extraordinary about this man. Once in the centre of the lake, Jesus said to Andrew, 'I would like it very much if you would spend some time with me in the future and be part of what I am doing.' Andrew felt the pull of Jesus' light.

As I was tuning into the situation, I asked why Andrew had been chosen. I was shown that the Andrew soul group is the same one that had incarnated as Adam not long after the Split, whose remit at the time had been to help bring light back to the planet. Jesus had recognised the 'forgotten' light in Andrew and wanted to help him wake up. I was shown that the intention of Adam was still alive in Andrew, even though Adam had died feeling he had failed. (Adam, in his day, had failed to see that what he had set out to achieve was so much bigger than him and it could not be done in one lifetime. He had also failed to see he was a crucial stepping stone in today's success.) Jesus knew this and saw the potential in Andrew. His own light naturally pulled at the intention or spark within Andrew.

Andrew spent the next three years coming and going in Jesus' life. He could never completely let go of his fear and fully commit to service. When Jesus died, he sunk into a terrible doom and gloom, similar to that experienced at the time of Adam. As I stated this to Mimi, she told me that her partner was fast sinking into a similar experience in this life. I asked Bana's husband (in spirit) to see if he could go and help him.

Through Bana, I learned that after Jesus died, Andrew returned home a changed man. Bana felt she had lost her husband and she was very angry and sad. (She was going through similar emotions over the loss of her husband in this life.) I told her that Andrew had never fully realised who Jesus was when he was alive and that fact had made him very unsettled. He had felt a strong family duty to Bana and a strong pull to Jesus and had been very confused as to where his loyalties should lie.

A day or so after these revelations, Bana shared with me that she had visited Lesbos a few months previously, not long after her husband had died. She had gone there with his children for a holiday. While she was there, she had 'felt' an urge to walk past a small chapel which she didn't know was Andrew's tomb at the time. Nor did she consciously remember that she had any connection to Andrew at all. She spent quite some time mourning her husband at the tomb, quite innocent of the irony attached. She said that, at the time, she felt Andrew had died at sea and I felt strongly she was right. I could see it. I felt he had lost hope and allowed himself to drown.

Bana also told me that she felt strongly that Andrew had died before her in the past life, and after his death she had been angry with Jesus because Andrew had become such a changed man and she felt Jesus was somehow responsible for his death.

It is important to note here that Bana recognised all her emotions from the past life and asked for forgiveness from Jesus on her and her husband's behalf. She was able to let go of all the emotions related to the event on behalf of her soul group. Thus, she has set herself free and is allowing herself to serve as she could not before.

Further Insights from Two Incarnated Members of Andrew's Soul Group

A lady came to me some while after my conversations with Bana and Mimi and confirmed that she felt Andrew had drowned at sea. She had had a constant vision of being a fisherman with her feet in sandals, standing in water. She also remembered being at the crucifixion but standing at the back of the crowd, ready with a string of excuses should she be questioned.

A man found me at a similar time and I recognised him clearly as part of the Andrew soul group. Every cell in his body oozed the gentleness and light nature of the man. He told me that he was currently in a constant battle between his soul's pull to heal and his wife and children's activities. Plus, he had almost drowned in this life. He had been wondering why he could not follow his heart and felt he must not leave his wife and children in this life. When I explained to him that he had left them in the past life (when he drowned) and did not wish to repeat his actions this time around, this resonated deeply within him.

All five of these souls (two in spirit and three currently incarnate) from the 'Andrew' experience have much in common. They are all divided in their soul as to what route to follow—the inner or the outer! They all struggle to trust and accept the inner journey, just as Andrew did so long ago. However, the good news is that a few years on, two of these souls have finally let go of the trauma and are enlightening rapidly. The other three are slow to progress, are each torn apart by the dilemma within themselves and have little confidence.

Bartholomew

Some understanding of who Bartholomew the disciple had been was brought to me by a man called Dusty over a period of about four years. That the universe brought Dusty and I together in a very unusual but purposeful way was without doubt to both of us and it wasn't long before I started to remember his past life. I did not know at that time that my befriending of him, when he was in trouble in this life, would be an opportunity to give back to him something he, as Bartholomew, had given me at the time of Jesus. Ironically, too, Dusty had brought himself to live in my parish, which 'happened' to be the parish of the Church of St Bartholomew, and he had the humble job of tending many of the parish greens.

After a few weeks, I told Dusty that I thought he was connected to Bartholomew and he just said 'Oh' and did not question me about it. But, gradually, as his life mess got worse, we talked and talked more until the unravelling of his story became totally unavoidable.

To start with, it was only I that remembered Bartholomew, for he was very familiar to me. I had been a merchant travelling through Jerusalem at the time of Jesus and had been selling cloth of some sort. I was laying out my wares in the front room of a customer when Jesus walked past on his way to the crucifixion. I caught sight of him passing by, through a stone-framed window that looked out onto the street. He was surrounded by crowds, but I could still see the brilliant white light which shone both from within and around him. I knew he was resonating deeply with what my heart had been searching for. Leaving my wares where they lay, I dashed out of the house and started to follow the crowds, intent on finding out who this man was.

As the crucifixion took place, I stood watching as so many did, in complete dismay. This man was innocent! Surely everyone could see that? Why was he being crucified and why were so many people interested? Something extraordinary was going on here. I watched uneasily, feeling the sorrow and pain within me and within those around me. I asked myself: 'Who is this man?'

After the crucifixion, I was desperate to find out more. I questioned and questioned whoever I could, in an effort to understand what was going on. I was pointed in the direction of the disciples and eventually to Peter, who simply turned away from this annoying stranger (me) and told me that now was not the time: couldn't I see he was mourning his friend?

Eventually, Bartholomew appeared to take pity on me. He took me to one side and explained a little of who the man Jesus had been. He allowed me to stay near him in order to listen and learn a bit more. My wares were forgotten and never to be retrieved. I never even thought of them again. I only knew that something of a profound nature was unfolding here and I had to know what it was. I stuck to Bartholomew like glue.

This part of my past life came vividly back to me over a few weeks after meeting Dusty. His behaviour in this life triggered the memory and I began to realise that the Bartholomew I thought had been so very kind to me in the past life was not in fact all that he had appeared to be. Two thousand and more years ago, I looked up to him. After all, he was the only one who had befriended me, taken me under his wing and answered my questions with patience. As I recalled this gradually, I also remembered that I instinctively knew something was amiss with him. I saw his ego and stubborn side and yet he was the one who had seemed to be the most genuine. After all, hadn't the others turned their backs on me? There was a state of confusion within me.

***

Bartholomew was not a disciple in the ordinary sense. He was travelling around the area that Jesus was teaching in for the three years before Jesus' death, but he often did his own thing and was not following Jesus on a daily basis. When he was with Jesus, he respected him, listened to him and learned from him.

Bartholomew was not present at the crucifixion. He was out preaching and teaching nearby. He did not believe (or even want to believe) for one minute that Jesus would really die. He felt frustrated and angered by the other disciples. Why did they not trust as he did and go out preaching and spreading the word, as Jesus had told them to do? He saw their fear and belittled them for it.

After Jesus died, Bartholomew made himself even more visible as he felt he needed to continue the work that Jesus had been doing. While other disciples went underground, so to speak, he spoke out. He did not respect their need to mourn or indeed how they felt about his death. Rather, he judged them. The reason he befriended me (the merchant) was down to his frustration with the other disciples, and he wanted to show them up. It wasn't because he took pity on me at all!

However, Bartholomew sensed my doubt of him so he decided to take me along to the Ascension when he was made aware of it. He wanted to prove to me that he was the 'real deal' and knew what he was talking about. For quite some time after the Ascension, Bartholomew went about his business gaining many followers and spreading the word wherever he went. He would stand amongst the crowds, on some stone or other, to raise himself off the ground a little, and speak to the people, encouraging them to live in love and not fear.

One day, some soldiers went to Bartholomew's house to arrest him. They had been arresting anyone who had been seen to follow the teachings of Jesus. When they got to his house, he was not there. His wife greeted the soldiers and, as she was jealous of Bartholomew, of who he was, his popularity and what he did, she told the soldiers where to find him. They immediately went and found him and arrested him.

Dusty had met and partnered up with the same woman in this life. Things were not going well between them but she refused to leave him, insisting she loved him too much. However, once Dusty had got to grips with the past life situation that lay between them, he said to her, 'I forgive you.' Like magic, the following day she packed her belongings and left him. She had got what she needed and her soul knew his apology came from the right place.

Bartholomew was tried in a courtroom. He had never believed he would be arrested and taken to court because he was sure that the only reason Jesus was killed was because he had somehow failed in his faith. He never believed he himself would be taken. In the courtroom, he was relieved at the sight of a couple of very familiar faces standing by the dock. He considered them to be two of his closest friends and most trusted followers. His astonishment was absolute when they did not stand up for him and stood silently as the judge sentenced him to death. No one in the courtroom defended him. All to whom he had preached were silenced by fear. The shock, shame and disgrace he felt lay deep in his soul.

***

Heidi was a frequent follower of Bartholomew and was totally devoted to him. She lived and breathed every word he spoke. When he was captured and tried in court, she was there, amongst many of his followers and 'supposed' friends. Heidi was absolutely convinced that he would be exonerated and set free. He was the genuine article in her eyes and nothing could touch him. She went into a real state of shock when he was sentenced to death. She started to doubt herself and him, and told herself that he couldn't have been who she thought he was. In this life, she currently carries a huge anger towards him for what she came to believe in the past life had been a huge deception, for Bartholomew's death had left her without a reference point and she did not know how to continue with life.

I learned this through Heidi when she finally met Dusty again in this life. The relationship in this century was doomed from the start but it brought about the opportunity for them both to heal the past, teaching Heidi why her reference point was not Dusty and teaching Dusty that he owed her nothing, amongst many other things. His karmic debt was paid and he had the opportunity to forgive her for what she had done in the past life that had repeated in a different form in this life.

After four years of slowly unravelling the truth about Bartholomew, it came to a sudden conclusion when Dusty decided suddenly to move away. Through what happened next, I realised that while Bartholomew had tried to convince himself that he had no ego, he actually believed that Jesus had failed in his faith by dying on the cross. He concluded at the time that he was the only one left who would or could do the job that the universe required to be done and bring the light back to the planet. He rode roughshod over everyone's feelings and emotions, declaring (loudly in the past life and quietly in this one) that his way was the right one. He had completely missed the real reason Jesus had died on the cross. He tried to force his own ideas on the crowds.

When Bartholomew was finally captured and put to death, he became incredibly angry. Through association with Dusty, I saw that Bartholomew had suppressed that anger and become numb to all other tangible emotions, scared to show them in case they emerged in some way that he could not control. When the affair with Heidi occurred, he ran from me and from the truth, just as he had run from it at the time of Jesus. I told him I forgave him and sent him only unconditional love as I understood the total replay of the last life that was playing out in this one. I knew I had repaid any karmic debt I owed him, in gratitude for all that he had given me in the past life, whether he had done it for the right reasons or not.

To date, I have not been visited by anyone else from the Bartholomew soul group. However, the close association with Dusty provided all that was needed to start healing the past and point the soul group in a better direction for the future.

Peter

Peter is probably the best known of the disciples of Jesus and certainly his actions and decisions impacted on history in a hugely significant way after Jesus' death, due to the fact that the Church, as we know it today, was built around much that he initiated.

Approximately 50 per cent of the energy that was Peter is in the incarnated state of many different beings at this time and around 50 per cent of his energy is in spirit. The entire soul group has been struggling to heal due to the enormity of the story that has grown out of Peter's actions following the crucifixion. The ancient beings who watch over us therefore decided to send one of their own to earth in the shape of Geoff, to immerse him in the Peter story, and then in an incarnated state, to try and help heal the soul group and bring the truth through. It has taken many years to put the following together but on 14 December 2017 Peter's story was healed at its roots and I am going to try and convey how this came about.

I had been helping Geoff to unravel his past lives since July 2014. When he first came to see me, I very quickly recognised, amongst other things, that he was part of the Peter soul group. I was reminded, by tuning into Geoff, that Peter himself had chosen to take on the role of 'leader of the disciples', his ego making him feel responsible for Jesus' well-being and for the others around him. He was a strong character and somewhat liked to control his fellow disciples.

As Peter and many of Jesus' followers were making their way through Jerusalem one day, a sudden premonition flitted through Jesus' mind. As it quite shocked him to know that not even Peter would stand up for him in his hour of need, he blurted out in front of everyone, 'Peter! One day, you will deny that you have known me on three occasions and after the third time a cock will crow and you will remember what I have said.' Peter denied strongly that this would ever be the case and the matter was dropped.

When Judas had his outburst after the reputed 'Last Supper', a warning light went on in Peter. However, Jesus' calm response to it quelled his fears and he thought no more about it until Jesus was arrested. After the arrest, his anger and fear re-awoke in him and started to fester: 'Why had Judas told the authorities where Jesus could be found? The stupid man had caused Jesus to be arrested. If he had kept his mouth shut, none of this would have happened.'

This belief festered inside him as the week before the crucifixion went by. He was full of fear for his friend and full of increasing anger towards Judas who he chose to see as causing the situation. He remembered Jesus' words in the tavern (see page 221) but could not understand them. Why would anyone in their right mind put themselves in such danger? It must be Judas' fault.

When questioned by the authorities as to whether he had known Jesus, his turmoil was such that he finally said in anger, 'I tell you, I do not know this man!' A cock crowed in the distance. What Peter really meant was that he did not know how anyone could put himself into the position that Jesus had apparently volunteered to be in. In his desperate struggle to understand, he felt he did not know this man who he had walked the earth with for three years.

As Jesus Hung on the Cross...

Peter stood with a few of the other disciples to the right of the foot of the cross, as Jesus was dying, watching with horror like everyone else. He then saw a sword coming down from just behind but slightly above Jesus. The sword cut into Jesus' body below the left ribs and above the hip bone and the thrust went downwards from there into his body. Peter's instinctive reaction was that the Roman soldier did this to speed up Jesus' death. It was also what Peter wanted to believe because he couldn't handle the suffering anymore. But on looking at the soldier's face, he then realised it was full of anger. (The soldier turned out to be part of the Christ energy who had agreed to come and help and support this mission.) He did actually speed up Jesus' death, which was indeed a good thing, but he did it because his own guilt caused him to hate the crowds surrounding the cross and to hate his girlfriend who seemed so enamoured of this prisoner. The soldier was asking himself: 'Why are you all so emotional and why are so many of you interested in this man? He is a criminal. Can't you see we are getting rid of him so you will be safe?' The soldier was trying to make his own part in it right. He was unable to reach his blueprint for this life so he 'appeared' to be on the wrong side of the fence. He attacked Jesus in anger, being sore and confused in his heart.

After the sword went in, Peter could bear it no longer. He turned his back to the cross, his head hung low. A few of the other disciples were standing in a circle with him, their heads also bowed. Peter had fully believed that Jesus could overcome death and had expected him to come down from the cross and end the 'nonsense' at any moment. He had been waiting for that moment, wondering when it was going to happen, but getting increasingly worried that it wasn't. When the sword went into Jesus' side, glimmerings of the truth began to enter Peter's mind and he played with the possibility that Jesus was actually a man like them, not a god who could overcome anything. He felt at that moment that he had to turn away; he had to try and come to terms with these new thoughts.

Geoff and I asked for the Roman soldier to be forgiven for his rash and angry action, for his failure to understand why he was really there and for succumbing to his own weaknesses. We also asked for forgiveness for Peter, who turned his back on his dear friend in his hour of need.

There was a tremendous feeling of disbelief in the circle of disciples when Jesus was finally declared dead. Peter turned his head, seeing it for himself, but he couldn't move his body. Everything he had built his belief around had now become void. What was going on? Why had he died? Who was Jesus? What was he (Peter) to do now? If he wasn't the son of God, who was he? So many questions flooded his mind.

For the next few days, Peter kept a low profile, trying to figure out what had happened and to come to terms with this deeply shocking turn of events. It was during this time that Peter finally accepted that Jesus was an ordinary man, like himself. The truth hit him like a thunderclap. Until the sword had struck, he had been waiting and trusting that Jesus was extraordinary and would perform a miracle to save himself. When this hadn't happened, his whole world was thrown into turmoil. Peter was already turning inward for answers but his great difficulty was that he had already set himself up as a leader and people kept coming to him and asking him, 'Peter, what shall we do?'

Lost people everywhere were looking to him to provide answers. His ego began to respond. He abandoned his inward journey as he felt it was his duty to guide and lead others. He was somewhat lost himself and didn't realise his fear was to the fore, and therefore his reactions to every situation that followed were based in fear.

Peter began his mission of what he believed was 'following' in Jesus' footsteps. What very few have realised is that, at this point, Peter had not given himself the time needed to become fully self-realised and therefore his actions over the rest of that life came from the belief that he was now in charge and he had to carry on what Jesus had started. Hence, the 'Church' that was created around this mission was built from the perspective of an ego and not from the vantage point of being in harmony with unconditional love. In this state of ego, many things have come about which have proved to be very hard for those who know the truth, to come to terms with. One is the ego-based Churches that have been built all over the world which may never have come into being if Peter had not put Jesus on a pedestal, labelled him as special and wanted to immortalise him. Another is Peter pointing an accusing finger at Judas, in his angry, distraught state; sadly, here, the whole blame for Jesus' capture and subsequent demise had found a scapegoat. The finger-pointing came about because of Peter's own self-accusation, the self (denial) he could not come to terms with.

Peter was filled with muddled and anxious thoughts and questions:

- Did I let him down?
- Is there something I could have done differently?
- Why didn't I take him away and hide him?
- Why did I deny that I knew him?

- This is my fault.
- Why did Judas have to go and tell the authorities where they could find Jesus?

The scapegoated Judas has had to live ever since with the consequences of Peter's finger-pointing, and the strength that the story carries is very damaging to the whole soul group of Judas.

When Peter allowed himself to be persuaded that he must carry on where Jesus left off, he tried to hold everyone together out of his own strength. He overlooked his own life journey as he did so and his own spiritual development faltered. He never acknowledged his faltering mind to himself, and therefore never found the real truth that Jesus was trying to convey and teach. He died knowing something was wrong and that he was unworthy, asking to be crucified upside down.

One member of the soul group who visited me felt intense regret that Peter didn't stand by Jesus in the way he had needed to and therefore wasn't the friend he wished he had been. He felt devastated by the fact that he had turned his back on his friend while he hung on the cross, leaving him utterly alone.

A second man from the soul group came to visit me and, interestingly, carried the aspect of Peter's death heavily in his soul. He relived the upside-down crucifixion every day through playing out a sense of extreme unworthiness. He came to me at a late stage in his life, by which time he was carrying physical symptoms from the death. His left leg had been diagnosed with cellulitis which caused redness of skin, pain and swelling in the lower half of his leg. Looking at Geoff's leg, we discovered that both men had identical symptoms. On tuning in, I relived the agony of Peter's death where he was hung upside down in an uneven fashion, his left leg bearing much more weight than his right one. This also caused a crick in the right side of his neck as he hung uncomfortably in this lobsided fashion. When the man released the emotions that he carried from the soul of Peter and asked forgiveness for his part of the story, his leg became pain-free overnight.

Geoff's Story

Geoff and I realised we needed to focus on the extremely important point in the life of Peter just after Jesus died and before people kept coming up to him for help and guidance.

Peter was inwardly working things out at that moment. He was trying to understand how this wonderful friend of his was no more. But, instead of giving himself the time he needed to come to terms with it, to comprehend properly what had actually happened and what Jesus had actually come to show the world, he allowed his ego to feel it was indispensable and that he had to 'do' something. He turned away from his inward search and from that moment lived outwardly, caught up in the 'doing', from his own limited strength and perspectives only.

When Geoff realised this, he immediately went into a replay of the moment. He decided to go within and find the missing truth that Peter had neglected to do. These are some of the revelations he came up with:

- Jesus was not a leader. He just 'was'.
- People gathered around Jesus because of his truth, not because of what he did.
- Jesus' life was a way of being, not a set of behaviours to act out or follow.
- The Jesus way of 'being' is something that we can all emulate if we want to.
- Jesus died (physically) rather than compromise the truth in his heart.

Many, many times over the last few years, I have tripped Geoff up as he replayed the Peter pattern. There was a twist to Peter's truth which has come out in Geoff. Slowly, Geoff learned to live the truth of Jesus and slowly he has released the trappings of the past, asking forgiveness where necessary on behalf of the soul group and taking on all the aspects necessary in order to heal it.

At this point, life was taking Geoff on a universal training course. We didn't realise where he was going with it at the time or how it would end. Dreadful things were occurring but, with each occurrence, Geoff was getting stronger and stronger. He was learning not to compromise the truth.

14 December 2017 turned out to be 'D' Day. We did not know this as we set off at 4.00 a.m. for the International Dispute Resolution Centre, Fleet Street, London. (What better place could there be for the Peter story to be finally healed?!) We thought we were going to try and settle a five-year dispute that had been hanging over Geoff around an insurance settlement on his houses, office, business, belongings, and so on. A mediator was to be present, ready to mediate between Geoff, his son and a solicitor on one side and the insurance company's head of claims and board secretary, and their solicitor on the other. I myself was feeling I needed to be present to hold the light and ensure that the highest good should prevail in this very difficult situation.

As the powerful insurance representatives slowly knocked Geoff, his son and his solicitor down to a settlement that would offer them less than a tenth of the losses, the shock and disbelief on our side of the room was tangible. The power that the opposition assumed, to be able to withhold payment and ignore all the arguments in a perfectly genuine case, was ugly in the extreme. They knew they could outspend Geoff and, on that basis, they chose to refuse to see Geoff as a human being they had let down. The whole thing was incomprehensible to the average person.

Geoff and I walked away from the dispute centre at 6.30 p.m., shattered. At the last minute, they had asked Geoff to accept an offer that meant he could not pick up the pieces of his life's work in any shape or form, despite being innocent. He had been attacked from all sides, and even his son's preparedness to keep fighting became too much for him. And, despite the gruelling last five years, and the length and weariness of the day itself, in the final five minutes he managed to say to the opposing solicitor, despite knowing he might lose even the small morsel held out to him, that he would not sign on this deal today. He walked away from it, knowing he was not in a balanced place, trusting only in his intuition that he was doing the right thing. In that moment of truth, I saw the 'ancient soul' in him come to the fore for the first time.

It wasn't until the following morning that I understood the universe had been training Geoff for five years: training him to withstand the strength and bullying tactics of such people so that, against the odds, he would have the choice in that moment to hold his hand up to them all and hold the balance of power by saying, 'Wait, I need time to reflect; no deal today.' His courage was the reverse of the fear/ego that Peter showed at the time of the crucifixion. He had learned to trust his intuition more than fear it and, in doing so, had reversed the action taken by Peter from which today's Church was then created.

My heart filled with joy and relief. At last, he had done what he came from the ancient realms to do. At last, the foundation of the Church was undermined in its root. No money (an evil of our time) had tempted Geoff, no ego had taken hold—there was just a simple trust that the highest good would prevail, however grave the situation looked. It was a time of true hope for the future and a celebration for us all.

I have come across at least eight other members of the Peter soul group during the last 12 years. All of them carry the same twist. All of them are still playing out the fear story in differing forms and do not have the courage as yet to face their inner truth. However, Geoff and I know that light has now been brought into the soul of Peter and the blueprint for any of them to heal is there forever. The fear in the heart of the soul group has become lighter and Geoff's sacrifice has not been in vain.

**

A young man visited me who had a vivid memory of being with Peter on the night Jesus died. He described Peter as inconsolable watching him crying his heart out, feeling lost and frightened. But he also witnessed that the next morning brought a strong Peter emerging from his sleeping place, pretending all was well. This man was a member of the Peter soul group and he had brought this memory back into incarnation in order to help the soul group heal by remembering this truth.

Peter's Wife

Peter and his wife had known each other for many years before Peter met Jesus and they had a very harmonious relationship. After Peter met Jesus, it was to her as if her husband had become besotted with another man. She knew Jesus was a good man but she was very resentful of the influence he seemed to be having on her husband and therefore she became angry and jealous, pinning the changes that were happening on Jesus.

When Jesus was crucified, she was not present and did not help Peter afterwards to regain his equilibrium. Instead, she watched his ego take a hold as he tried to be everything to everyone in their hour of need.

When Peter himself died, she was present. She heard Peter's request to be hung upside down as he was not worthy to be crucified in the same way as Jesus had been. She was filled with pain, rage and sadness in that moment and blanked the situation out of her consciousness in order to cope. From that moment on, she turned her back on the inward journey that Jesus was teaching and, in future lifetimes, turned her back on all that the Church represented.

Thomas

As Thomas stood watching the crucifixion alongside the other disciples, he was unaware what the outcome of this terrible situation would be, but he was hoping against fading hope that Jesus would somehow come off the cross and show the crowds his power and that he was above such things as death. He was convinced that this was what ought to happen.

As Jesus deteriorated, he became more and more worried, but he was one of the few who opened up and called out to 'God' in that moment: 'Help! Help him. Please help him.' It was a pure, unconditional cry from the heart.

Many souls were watching the scene anxiously from above the cross, seeing that Jesus was sinking into doubt about what was happening to him but, at the same time, intuitively knowing that somehow what was going on was right. When Jesus cried out 'Why hast thou forsaken me?' and disappeared for a few seconds into total separation from his Source connection, the souls above him in spirit were petrified and waited extremely anxiously to see if he would or could recover his trust.

During Jesus' moment of separation, one of the souls hovering above Jesus, who was actually from the soul group of Jesus and whom I shall refer to as Bev, panicked and replayed her personal Split story. She saw the soul of Thomas opening up and asking for help, so dashed hurriedly into his body, deciding, as she had at the Split, that this was the way to help. This was both impetuous and an action full of fear, without reference to its Source connection, which therefore did not necessarily serve the highest good.

Thomas then became the embodiment of this soul as well as his own. He had knowledge within him for the first time that Jesus was attempting to reverse the Split, but he also retained his own personal beliefs which were endorsed as he moved amongst others. Therefore, he became a very mixed-up being. He did not know quite what to believe which is why he later became known as 'Doubting Thomas'.

He struggled for the next few weeks of his life, swinging from one belief to another in a crazy fashion. This went reasonably unnoticed as many were struggling with their own thoughts at this time. Thomas was responding to a very strong pull in his heart when he walked along to the place where Jesus was to ascend. As he turned the last corner, he could see Jesus ahead of him, surrounded by a strange glow of light shining outwardly from him. He could not take his eyes from the light and when he got close, he fell to his knees. He fully recognised that Jesus had indeed overcome the Split and he cried, 'My lord and my God!' The flame of truth lit within him for a short while.

As Thomas watched Jesus rise into the clouds, he felt very alone with his understanding. Everyone around him seemed like they were in a trance and on a different plane to him. After Jesus had disappeared, he fell from his high level of understanding and returned to his doubt and became an uncertain personality again.

Deep inside the Thomas soul group the truth of the Ascension is known. However, he has carried a long scream of anguish within his soul from that moment on, causing Bev, and possibly other aspects of his soul group, to malfunction ever since.

His scream was: 'I know who he is. He overcame his darkest fears. I witnessed it.' But there was no one to hear and no one that could hear. The world has put its own spin on what happened to Thomas during this time, and the grip it has on Thomas' reputation after 2000 years or so will be very hard to shift.

However, during the summer of 2019, Bev told me she was at last able to 'release her own conflict from the Split and live in the now', for herself and for the benefit of the Thomas soul group. At a later date, she asked to be forgiven for diving into the soul group of Thomas at the cross, thus causing all the doubt and conflict within him, and has asked for the influence of her energy to be removed so that all may heal. This can only happen because she saw the patterning from her roots at the Split, and knows now that to act without going within is done from a belief in separation, not oneness, and that she will never do it again.

Bev died a few months before I started to put this book together. We had almost all of the truths included in the writing before she died. However, as I re-read Bev's section, I became uncomfortable and aware that I was not happy with it. I asked Bev to help me. Immediately, I knew that the emphasis in certain parts needed to change. She guided me through a rewrite and her story has become so much richer and more accurate because of it. As I typed, 'I will never do it again' at the end, I could feel her energy endorsing this through me so tangible was it. She wanted us to know she has truly healed.

John

I have little knowledge of John except a snippet which has been brought to me from a member of his soul group who happened to be a young boy at the time of the crucifixion. He watched closely as Jesus was laid on the cross. He saw that Jesus was weak, thirsty and hungry as they roped his hands to the crossbar. He noticed that Jesus hardly winced as the nails were put into his wrists because his thoughts were concentrated on all other men who were put through this ordeal. Jesus was also feeling for the other men being crucified on either side of him and was full of sorrow at what man could do to man. As Jesus was lifted high in the air and his wrists took the weight, the young boy saw that Jesus experienced enormous pain.

Through this young boy, I saw the deep love that he had in his heart for Jesus and that he had known of his innocence at his death. As Jesus died, he surrendered himself to God, recognising that Jesus was the true light, the purest person he could ever encounter, and he wanted to be part of what Jesus was doing.

A few years after Jesus' death, the boy was old enough to try and share what he knew with some of the disciples. He tried to tell them of the real message of surrender that Jesus brought and to advise them on how they should 'be'. He was soon after arrested and killed.

I felt the quiet man who had come to see me was opening up to a long-lost secret to which he had been shut down since his death during that era, and we both knew he now had the chance to explore all that it could mean in the present.

Judas

Judas is one of the most complex of the disciples and, over the years, I must have come across at least 16 members or more from his soul group. Sadly, I have not recorded my conversations with the majority of them as they came in the early days of running the retreat. However, I have used the knowledge that I gained so often that it is very present in my mind.

The first encounter I had with a member of the soul group was through a lovely man, Alan, who came to stay with his wife. I saw immediately that he was from the soul group of Judas but was nervous about how I was going to put it over to him for two reasons. First, he had serious cancer and, second, I had never done it before. I took a deep breath and gently told Alan that I was seeing him at the Last Supper and who I thought he was. He took it well but I could see that he believed Judas carried the ultimate dark energy and the knowledge was making him squirm inside. I was astonished at his bravery as he admitted to knowing what I was seeing was correct. He didn't run, or pretend it wasn't true; he simply asked for forgiveness for anything he had done which had not served the highest good. Alan then went on to describe various events in his life that endorsed what I was seeing. To my amazement, he told me that he and his wife were off to Glastonbury the next day where there was an upper room which contained a lifelike layout of the Last Supper. They had booked to visit this a few weeks before, planning it to follow on after they had been with me! I can still remember how astonished we both felt. Alan's revelations gave us perfect confirmation of our findings and gave me the gift of not being afraid to speak my truth. I was able to help him heal somewhat from the emotions his body held from that time. Sadly, he died a few weeks later but his cancer was already quite advanced and I felt he had died in a better place than he would have done had we not spoken. I also felt that he had achieved all that he was able to in this life.

Various Judas souls then came thick and fast to stay at the retreat. It was as if the universe wanted me to fully understand who this man had been and I learned the following.

A well-meaning, pleasant lady came to stay who oozed Judas energy from every pore of her skin. When I told her what I was seeing, she said to me, 'That explains why I was cast as Judas in every junior school play I was ever part of.' She began to laugh and then so did I. This energy must have seeped into every teacher's awareness and they could cast her as nothing else!

A different woman, Yvonne, showed me the incredible love that Judas had for Jesus. I have not felt such a strong love for Jesus emanating from anyone before or since that compares with hers. I told her what I was seeing and she said, 'I know.' The passion in her heart was spilling out. However, Yvonne was very stuck in her story and could not cope with the knowledge I gave her. She went on to treat me and the rest of the residents at the retreat in a rather concerning way. She even persuaded a very gentle soul that she too was from the Judas soul group. This was principally because the knowledge she had received made her so uncomfortable that she was trying to make herself feel better and less alone. She was struggling to hear the truth in what I was revealing to her. It was very sad.

Through experiencing Yvonne's passionate love for Jesus, I started to ask questions of the universe and then other aspects of the Judas soul group came to the retreat. The following is a collection of what they shared with me, together with a clear memory I was given of the event.

At the Last Supper, most of the disciples and a few other souls were present. I had a vision of them in the upper room, tearing at meat with their bare hands, eating bread and drinking wine. They were all very jolly. Jesus sat quietly amongst them, not saying very much. After a while, he spoke to them in a quiet voice with words along these lines, 'This is the last time I shall eat with you. Soon I shall be arrested and taken for questioning. I'm not sure what will happen after that but I know things will not be the same for us again.' (Something in his soul was already feeling the nearness of his arrest, even though he had no personal knowledge.)

The attendees in the supper room came to a shocked silence. All present stopped their jollities just as they were, hands holding food in the air, mouths open, stunned by what Jesus had said. Jesus went on to explain a little more. Then he fell silent. Those in the room stared vacantly at each other, not really knowing what to make of it.

Judas stood up very suddenly, his face showing his fury. What Jesus was suggesting was surely impossible? He was the light. He was pure love. The idea that he could be arrested was inconceivable. He desperately wanted Jesus to end all the growing controversy around him and show the world who he really was. It didn't cross his mind that maybe there was a different path for Jesus to tread. He wanted only for his beloved friend to put all this unrest to bed forever so that they could get on with what he saw as the real job.

Judas shouted at them all, 'Are you just going to sit there and let our friend tell us these things? Are you all going to let this happen? Are you all going to sit there and say nothing?' He became so lost in anger that he turned his back on them and swiftly left the room, letting himself out through a backdoor and running down a flight of stone steps to the road.

His anger peaked. He wanted this whole game to stop. It was time for everyone to understand what he already knew about Jesus (that he was unconditional love). His mind erupted in desperation and screamed, 'Come on, man! Show them you are worth more than this!'

He stood for a minute and then took the road downhill to a fork, about 20 yards from where he had been standing. As he approached the fork, he saw two Roman soldiers chatting to each other. He was moving so fast that he nearly cannoned straight into them; one of the soldiers grabbed wildly at Judas and asked him if he knew where Jesus was or where they might find him in the future. Judas was in such a blind rage that he was acting from outside his body at that stage. He was desperately wanting Jesus to be wrong about it being their last supper together so he barked out in agitation, 'Oh, he is often to be found in the Garden of Gethsemane. You're bound to find him there at some point.'

One of the soldiers gripped Judas' arm even more tightly and asked for more information. The way in which he was being forced brought Judas out of his anger and back into his body somewhat. He pulled away from the soldiers as they pressed more questions upon him. Judas wanted to get away as quickly as he could but the soldiers thought to bribe some more information out of him and offered him money. Judas turned and strode off down the hill and the coins that were thrown at him hit his back and then the cobbles on the ground. Judas took no heed of this or of anything that the soldiers shouted after him. Never for one second did Judas believe he had put Jesus in any danger.

As these visions were given to me through various people, I knew I had seen the truth. I knew that all Judas had ever done was to love Jesus so much that, in a moment of unbearable hurt, he had acted indiscreetly. He was a man capable of great passion but, at the same time, he could totally lose the plot in blind rage.

An older man, possibly Judas' uncle but certainly someone who cared about Judas very much, had been standing on the other side of the wall to where the encounter with the Roman soldiers took place. He had been taking in the evening air outside the tavern in which the disciples had been gathered. As he heard Judas' upraised voice, he came to from his reverie and listened intently to what was being said. He heard the coins being thrown at Judas and heard Judas walk away. He then heard the soldiers muttering as they picked up the coins from the road. One of them said something like, 'We couldn't even bribe him with 30 pieces of pure silver.'

The uncle heard no more. He became lost in emotion. What had Judas done? Why had he exploded on the Roman soldiers? He had always warned Judas that one day his hot-headed temper would get him into trouble and his instinct told him that now was the time.

He contemplated what he should do for a while until he heard the rest of the disciples coming down the steps and into the basement of the tavern. He quickly went to find Peter and tell him what he had overheard. He felt Peter would be a good 'middle man' to speak with. Peter immediately said they should warn Jesus so the two of them approached Jesus and repeated the conversation that the uncle had overheard. Jesus was unperturbed and simply said to them, 'What will be will be. I am not afraid of what is to come and this outburst from Judas will not change anything. Come, let us not dwell further on this matter.' Jesus' very calm approach to what had happened served to dispel all the fear in Peter and some of the fear in the uncle, and the matter was dropped.

The next evening, Judas was to be seen striding along a path towards his friends who were indeed gathered in the Garden of Gethsemane. As quickly as his ill temper had come, it had gone. As he approached the group, he was ribbed good-humouredly for his outburst the previous evening. Jesus was standing quietly nearby, under the shade of a tree. Judas, also in fine humour, said casually, 'I ran into a couple of soldiers outside the Inn. They threw money at me! Thought they could buy me! Idiots.' Peter asked, 'Did you tell them anything?' Judas started at the question. Something inside him stirred. He mumbled something unintelligible under his breath as he fought for a lost memory.

Meanwhile, there was more general laughter and ribbing amongst the friends that were gathered. At that moment, Peter felt jealous of Judas and his straightforward nature. He felt that Judas was free to be himself as he himself had never felt free to be. Peter never felt he could love and live without stress, because of his own self-inflicted feeling of responsibility.

A few moments later, some soldiers were seen to be approaching the group. Judas' heart leapt in fear as a sudden thought occurred to him: 'Was this his doing?' Peter, in full responsibility mode, leapt forward to defend and yet ready to attack, with his sword raised high. Suddenly, Jesus loomed large amongst them, 'Be at peace.

There should be no blood shed here. I have to leave you now and find out what all this is about. Lay down your sword.' He held out his hands to the soldiers, looked directly at them and said, 'I am ready to come with you. No need for trouble here. Take me as I am.' Chains were put on him and he was dragged away, leaving the friends stunned into silence.

***

At the crucifixion, Judas stood at the back of the crowd, next to his uncle. His uncle was there in concern and in a very protective mode for Judas rather than for his love of Jesus. Judas himself was 100 per cent sure that Jesus would somehow come down from the cross and show the world who he really was. He had watched Jesus perform 'magic' ever since he had known him and nothing would have convinced him that the best magic of all was not about to come now. He waited and he waited and he waited. He sent a shaft of deep love to Jesus who was clearly in pain. He completely believed in him. His heart was calling: 'Come on, Master. Show them who you are!'

But, as time went on, he grew more and more concerned. He began to contemplate a world without Jesus. It was inconceivable and pointless to him. The pain in his heart was beyond measure. He began to contemplate that perhaps dark was stronger than light after all. He faced a real confusion and despair within himself. He had been on the cusp of total surrender to the light but, as Jesus died, the opportunity seemed to slip away.

After Jesus' death, Judas could not contemplate life carrying on as it had before. He believed the light in his life had gone out. His reason for living had gone and thus he felt there was only darkness left for him. He had been unable to receive the beautiful message that Jesus had sent him through an understanding shaft of love. Instead, he wondered: 'Was unconditional love a myth?' From this dark place, which had taken a hold on him, he felt like a snake. He took himself off and subconsciously punished the very thing he feared may have betrayed his friend—his voice. He threw the snake-like rope around his neck and hung himself. He could not face a life in the future without Jesus/the light.

The uncle watched in a worried manner as the 'lost and devastated' Judas turned and walked away from the cross, his head hung low. He knew better than to interfere with Judas at that moment and fully planned to speak with him later that evening. In his mind, he feared Judas had put Jesus in this position somewhat because of what he had overheard that night at the tavern. He feared for the safety of his nephew. What the uncle had failed to register was Jesus' true response to the situation at the time, more especially because he did not know Jesus very well. Rather, the uncle was thinking: 'You put your friend to the test. Now, look what has happened.'

Over the past 2000 years, the Judas soul group has reincarnated on earth in many differing forms, only to find that the betrayal of Jesus to the Roman soldiers had been pinned on him in a manner that held a grain of truth but was for the most part not the truth. It has been recorded over and over again in every language. In his heart, Judas knows this was never his intention. (This has been agreed with by every Judas soul who I speak to.) But the soul group has had to face a story that has been spread worldwide and contains this tricky twist, century after century after century. As the soul well knows, Judas lost his rag at the time, and the guilt he holds within him taps into that and takes hold. Suppressed anger then emerges and the soul becomes very unbalanced. I witnessed one Judas soul call out in agony: 'Why did you die? Why didn't you save yourself? You could have done. Why have you left me in my darkness to carry the can?'

The Judas soul group in a reincarnated form believes that the world has put everything on his shoulders and it is grossly unfair. It leaves many of the soul group deeply resentful and even asking themselves: 'Is it true? Am I perhaps guilty after all? If it is true, I can never be forgiven. If the whole world thinks this is true, then perhaps it is?'

This deep wound is impossible for most of the soul group to live with. It doesn't seem to matter what I say, I have not yet found a Judas who truly can let the stigma go and face the world in his/her truth. It doesn't matter how I express the unfairness of what happened, they do not seem to be able to hear me. But I know that one day one of them will hear the words sent to his soul by Jesus as he hung on the cross, and allow the dread from his core to be released. This will light the darkened space from which Judas functions and from that more light will grow.

'It's alright, Judas. Don't worry. Everything is alright.'

***

A young man came to me who believed the whole world was against him and it didn't matter what he did; he felt fingers were being pointed at him from every direction. He could not function properly in life and, at the age of 26, felt totally lost. He said no doctor or therapist wanted to listen to how he felt and he was constantly reliving being misunderstood greatly. I told him the true story of Judas and he was both relieved and awed. His prime emotions were fear, resentment, anger, judgement and being overwhelmed and he visibly lightened when I showed him that, if he managed to let go of those emotions with forgiveness and love to those who pointed at him in this life and the Judas life, he had the potential to set both himself and others in his soul group free.

The Mother of Judas

This quiet, elderly woman lived in the vicinity of Jerusalem and was exceedingly close to her son. She loved nothing better than to feed Judas and look after him when he popped in to see her, showering him with love and attention as much as she was allowed to. She lived alone and spent her time busying herself in her house and not going out much.

In later years, she loved to hear the stories that Judas had to tell her of this man Jesus who he loved and spent much time with. Judas used to invite her to come with him and meet Jesus for the day and, though her heart longed to, she could never pluck up the courage.

One day, Judas came to see her and was unusually glum. He didn't speak as she fussed around him. (Little did she know that it was the night before the crucifixion.) When she got up the following morning, Judas was nowhere to be seen. She did not know at that point that she would never see him again.

After Judas' death, his mother hid herself away from everyone, alienating herself in her shame, sorrow, pain, regret, humiliation, shock and even guilt. She did not dare to be seen, for the stories that were being bandied around did her son no credit. It was even said that his guilt was proven by the fact that he hung himself.

As I sat with a member of this dear lady's soul group, I could feel the love, truth and sincerity that oozed from her. She knew her son would never have betrayed Jesus for such as he was being accused. She knew her son loved Jesus with a passion that few had shown. She knew he was innocent of these charges but she had no proof, only the inner certainly in her heart. She suffered greatly, not just because she had lost her beloved son but also with the terrible lies that surrounded his death. In her hours of anguish, she called out to God: 'I would have given my life to save him. Why did they not take me instead?'

When I first saw this lady, I knew she had turned from the cross 2000 years ago in her despair and anger. She had pinned some blame on Jesus. After we spoke, she managed to turn back to the cross, apologise and face everything. Her testimony to this truth will be greatly needed if the world is ever to right the great wrong of those times.

At a later date, this same lady sat with me and I recalled her anguished cry: 'I would have given my life for him.' As this cry had so completely come from unconditional love and she had offered to give her life for his in such an unconditional way, the universe was able to use this energy to spark up the light Jesus had sent to Judas from the cross. We felt it infiltrate Judas' soul and in that moment we realised he carried a connection to the dinosaur age. His hot temper in the upper room and his subsequent actions then became explainable. His ability to only see the light of salvation through Jesus (outside of himself), instead of believing he could be forgiven in his own right, was explained. Through his mother's unconditional love, we were able to send that forgiveness into his soul, uprooting the belief that he could never be forgiven from the dinosaur connection, and reminding the soul of Judas that, before the dinosaur experience, he had known he was the light, and he now had a chance to reconnect with it. The woman in front of me suddenly knew her soul mission was complete. She had given her life for her son and now, at last, his healing could begin.

8
Memories of Others Who Saw the Crucifixion

Zina spoke to me about the recall she had of being a child watching Jesus walking the Via Dolorosa. She felt she had given him much-needed water. It is of course possible she is in the same soul group as Nisha (see 'The Water Girl' in Chapter 5).

I felt an urge to explain a little to Zina about Jesus and his journey, and when I told her he had sunk the energy of who he was into the ground at the foot of the cross, she did a double-take. She told me that as a child her eyes had been transfixed on the ground at the foot of the cross, just before he died.

I told her that what lay in the ground was the memory of what seemed like magic but, in reality, Jesus had only used his intuition and trusted his intuition, in all his doings. Zina had found me because she needed to remember why her eyes had been transfixed and to know that the only magic she needed was to trust her intuition.

The Story of Tay and Ray

I had known Tay and Ray for most of my life. It had always struck me as peculiar that husband and wife should look like brother and sister, and it was commented on by many others too. One of their children was the same age as one of mine; we parented in a similar way and, as such, got on very well. When the two children reached 16 and went their different ways, we only kept in touch sporadically and I hadn't thought much beyond it feeling right to keep in touch, see Tay occasionally, and note that there was a fond history there. It came as a shock when the following history awoke as I wrote the pages concerning the crucifixion.

I was passing near Tay's house on my way to somewhere else and I thought to call in and see her. Over a cup of tea, we reminisced, talked about grandchildren, as one does, and at one point she said to me, 'You've been on my mind for the last few weeks and I have so wanted to find time to come and see you. You are one of the few people with whom I feel that way.' I replied, 'Well, obviously I do too, because here I am!'

As I left the house, I had quite a headache and thought I had become dehydrated because of her heating and the cluttered energy in her house and farm. I was also puzzled as to why I kept in touch with her so specifically when we were not really of the same ilk. Over the remainder of that day, I could not shift the headache so went to bed thinking it would go as I slept. I awoke the next morning feeling very rough and the headache was still there. When I asked why it was there, I immediately remembered it had started at Tay's house. 'Was there a connection?' I asked myself.

I tuned into Tay for probably the first time in the years I had known her and immediately saw her as a Roman soldier. I was very puzzled as she did not behave as such at all in this life. I also felt the crack of Jesus' neck as the soldier had wrenched it to the right so unceremoniously. It took me a while to unravel that Ray (her husband) had been the soldier who had nailed Jesus' wrists to the cross. It had been his job to crucify criminals for many years and he had a horrible laugh in him as he nailed each one, almost like he was saying: 'You are getting your just deserts. Serves you right! We are well rid of you.'

Tay was in the same soul group as Ray and she had watched the goings on from spirit. When she watched Ray nail Jesus, she was horrified because she saw, for the first time ever, that Ray was saying this man was getting his just deserts and she could see Jesus was as innocent as the day is long. She suddenly saw the error of her whole soul group's ways and backed off the impending scene in a panic.

Tay has been paying her karmic debt for many lifetimes since and in this life had chosen to reincarnate with Ray in order to try and remember this event for herself, so that she could let it go and also to help Ray (if he was willing) and the rest of her soul group. Her need to keep in touch with me was driven by the blueprint in her soul, and my sense that I should maintain this unlikely friendship was in response to her need.

Geoff started to try and release the tight muscles in my neck and, as he did so, I experienced the deep shock, extreme fear and pain that Jesus felt when Ray shoved his head to the right so violently. The huge crack his neck made as it had happened all those centuries ago, came back to me just then. The pain was so severe that he hardly felt the nails go into his wrists and foot. It was a moment of real deepening in his consciousness that maybe he was actually going to be crucified and physically he was fast reaching the point of no return. I asked for the light in Jesus' heart to shine with forgiveness onto Ray and Tay from that place and I felt it shoot out to reach their hearts. Tay let it into hers and Ray was at least able to let it surround his.

I walked across the fields to try and let the emotions held in my neck release but I couldn't get any further until I remembered they had given birth to a further son in later years. I suddenly knew this son was also part of their soul group and had come for healing and to help them. He was still living with them and had become part of enabling them to stay on the farm. As I remembered this and asked for the pure light of forgiveness to reach him too, there was a sudden shift. I felt the forgiveness and light fly through their farm in a very uninhibited way, reaching through the house, their belongings, animals, fields, equipment and beyond. I knew the energy on their farm would never be the same again and their journey to the light would begin. My reason for staying in touch had been fulfilled and now it was up to them. I knew I would always be on call for them should they reach out.

A Friend of Mary's

A soul from the Czech Republic found me a number of years ago, named Mona. She was sceptical of me when she arrived at the farm and I could feel her hostility. However, four of us sat amicably enjoying a mug of tea around a table one sunny morning when she suddenly asked me, 'Why can I feel a shackle around my left ankle?' As I was feeling a little wary of her, I said, 'You tell me!'

Mona sat silently for a few moments and then launched into the following story with tears running constantly down her face and a huge degree of sadness emanating out of her as she spoke. The extreme depth of her emotions is something that neither I nor the others listening will ever forget, and also the truth of what she was saying was not to be doubted.

Mona described how she had been passing the time of day at Mary and Joseph's house when they were disturbed by the sudden and unexpected arrival of some soldiers. They forced their way in and proceeded to arrest everyone in the room, putting a shackle with a heavy chain attached, around their ankles. They were all forced into a cart of some sort and driven over miles and miles of bumpy track.

Long hours later, they were dumped at the foot of the cross and the chains were dug into the ground so they could not leave the site. In horror, they looked up and saw Jesus on the cross. Mona at this stage was talking very hesitantly, with great difficulty and between huge sobs as she relived the pain and shock. None of them had even known Jesus had been taken prisoner, let alone been hung on a cross as a criminal.

Jesus' Sister

One of the ladies who had accompanied Mona to the farm was sitting beside me quietly with tears running down her face. When I looked at her, she blurted out, 'I was there.' I asked her who she was. She (Suzy) was unable to reply at the time but at a later date she shared the following:

> I was a young girl of about 8 or 9 years of age. I believe I was Jesus' younger sister. The crucifixion came so suddenly upon us, like a storm from nowhere. I was dumped in front of the cross and left feeling useless, insignificant and small. My fear was unbounded as I believed that perhaps I was going to die too. Perhaps my whole family would be crucified like my brother. Why else would we have been brought here? I was terrified of the pain that might come to me. I felt bewildered, lost and so, so frightened.

As time passed, Suzy allowed herself to think that perhaps she was not going to die and that it was just about watching Jesus die. This brought a fresh set of thoughts to the fore. She panicked:

> What can I possibly do? I wanted to shout at all the adults around me and tell them they were making a huge mistake but no words would come out. I sat on the ground hugging my knees, searching for protection. I couldn't bear what was going on. I couldn't watch him suffer like that. I wanted to be anywhere but where I was. All my emotions were racing round inside me. I stuffed them away, deep down into my core. I held my head low. I could not watch my beloved brother.

This youngster did not realise that most of the 'adults' she was surrounded by were expecting Jesus to perform a miracle. They had watched him perform what they perceived to be miracles for a few years and could not believe that he wouldn't jump off the cross in some fashion and show the authorities who had the real power. The young girl had no conception of this as she suffered in front of the cross. Instead, she felt immense anger that they did nothing to save him.

Suzy later unearthed a deep recollection of the moment that Jesus passed the point of no return on the cross. Her inner knowing at that point, knowing he was not going to come back to her, is etched in her heart.

Suzy has held her emotions stuffed deep inside her since that day. She has been gradually letting out the pain over a period of years since Mona spoke with us and this is allowing the numbing within to thaw. Her progress accelerated enormously the day that she acknowledged she was actually angry with herself. She had finally allowed herself to face the fact that she herself could have done something for Jesus and that she was no better than anyone else.

* * *

Another member of the soul group whom I met, remembered taking her anger a little further. She described herself as feeling she wanted to throw stones at everyone around her and her hand was anxiously raking the soil around her in readiness. She felt full of guilt, helplessness and aloneness.

Yet another soul who had also stuffed the event deep down inside gave further insight into this little girl. Through tuning into her, I discovered that she had a huge problem discerning between light and dark energies. This was rooted in the fact that every adult who collected around the cross seemed dark to her because they were allowing Jesus to be crucified. It is currently dawning on her that she actually believes herself to be dark because she too stood helplessly at the cross.

Interestingly, both these women have chosen partners who are of a darker nature. One of them indeed is from the soul group of Barabbas and fully believes he is above the law! The women have done this to highlight the dark/light confusion within their souls, with their dark partners pointing them back to their own light. When fully healed, these two ladies offer an opportunity for their partners to recognise they have been forgiven and to begin their own healing journey.

Another member of the soul group, Gida, came to me and was so scared of facing this trauma within her that she ducked and dived when around me, trying to avoid remembering the pain. It was only when her soul started to dim quite seriously that she finally allowed us to see what was hidden there.

This is what Gida unearthed:

> After he died, I felt so lost and alone. I tried to please my mother, Mary, to connect with her and have her love and attention. However, I felt she pushed me aside and I was insignificant. I felt I was not enough for her and never would be. Jesus seemed to have been everything to her. I just wanted my mum and her love and the grief and heartache were so heavy within. In this life, I felt I was always treading on eggshells around my mother so as not to do something wrong and get told off. I felt I must please her and feel her love. This caused me to grow up carrying huge anxiety and constant tension. I feel frustration (which is anger) but I am aiming it at her as an adult and have yet to own the anger in myself.

Gida was revealing her pain very slowly, as was Suzy. It seems that the young child's memory within her was so deeply damaged by the crucifixion and the seeming loss of her mother afterwards that her suppressed emotions are struggling to emerge. It is only with a lot of love, care and understanding that they are slowly allowing a release.

However, as they both gradually understood the full reason why Jesus died and that it was all about reversing the Split, they were able to accept that what they had watched was not the disaster they had thought at the time but truly an amazing occasion. Both their journeys took a massive leap forward and both began healing deeply, searching for the soul within them that existed before it all happened. Gida had a huge release whenever the song 'Ave Maria' came to her. She was then able to say, 'Mother, welcome back into my life.'

It is also interesting to note that Gida, later on her healing journey, became aware that in front of the cross she had totally blocked out the moment that Jesus had overcome the shadow and trusted again. She carried clearly the memory of his sinking into fear, and at the time believed he had died in that state. By allowing herself to reconnect to what actually happened in a personal way, she then freed up her ability to surrender.

Yet another soul visited me some time after Gida and Suzy. She was experiencing much of the above but also an intense fear of suffering, feeling almost as if it had been her body on the cross. As she replayed her emotions at the foot of the cross, she felt a huge fear that nothing would ever be the same again. She felt let down by 'God'.

She sometimes feels overwhelmed by and frightened of the deep grief she carries from those times. This fear of a repeat has resulted in her having a huge fear of being left alone in any lifetime since.

Mary's Second Son

A man named Poga came to see me in his later years. He had spent much of his life searching for his truth and never realised he had been born to a member of the Virgin Mary soul group, even though his mother's birth name was Mary Joseph! Together, we uncovered the following.

The second son had been born to Mary around two or three years after Jesus. His father, Joseph, was his natural dad and there was nothing exceptional about his conception. Growing up was fun and normal. When Jesus went to the temple at the age of 12, his life changed a little. Suddenly, Poga became 'as' the eldest son and his role in the family was therefore different. He didn't notice anything really uncomfortable until Jesus returned home on visits, at which time he felt rather pushed into the background.

Poga described feeling similar to how the son had felt in the parable of the prodigal son. Poga saw himself staying with his family while the prodigal son went on his travels. When the prodigal son (in his case Jesus) returned home and got all the attention, he became resentful, angry and jealous of Jesus' popularity and experienced a deep feeling of not being enough. When Jesus was not around, he regained his balance again.

In this lifetime, Poga had left home at the age of 15 to join a Christian brotherhood, leaving a bereft mother. His inner motive was to try and heal his restless spirit by becoming as much like Jesus as he could, although he was not conscious of it at the time. In later life, he attracted young people around him who were searching for something deeper in their own lives.

As we chatted, the way this life had unfolded began to make sense to him, and he realised he had been trying to find Jesus in himself all the time. He then saw that he did not need to be 'as' Jesus to be acceptable as his role had been a different one. He had been Mary's anchor all through her troubles and had helped hold her stable in her hour of need. This realisation brought him balance and healing.

I later had the following statements from him:

'I have stopped drinking after 40 years of having a few glasses of wine with every evening meal.'

'I have renewed my relationship with Jesus and remembered that when he said, "I am the light of the world" he was telling his followers, "And so are you".'

'The kingdom of Heaven is that part of us which resonates with the fullness of "being".'

Caiaphas

After Jesus died, some of his followers were being punished or even put to death for showing signs that could potentially cause the authorities further trouble. Caiaphas himself was getting more and more exasperated with 'how long this business was carrying on'. There were a few Roman soldiers who worked in and around the building in which Caiaphas had his offices. He blew his top when he overheard one of them talking about Jesus as he walked along a corridor. He could do nothing about a Roman soldier who was seemingly advocating the innocence of this man under his nose, and he was furious that this 'thing' could not be put to bed. It seemed to him that he had to endure the legacy that Jesus had left at every turn. He cried inwardly: 'When will I be free of it all?' As his irritation peaked, he ordered the Roman soldier out of his sight, saying that he did not want heretics such as him around.

The Roman authorities turned a blind eye to the unlawful dismissal of one of their men as they considered Caiaphas to be a bit of a 'case'. They had witnessed his unbalanced cruelty and hatred to men who followed Jesus, so the soldier was ordered to return to Rome. Later, the soldier connected with Peter and eventually became converted as a follower. The soldier knew of Peter's death and was saddened by it so he kept his interest to himself after that. He met with the converted in secret places and learned to follow his heart.

Andi's Dream

Andi lived near Jerusalem at the time of Jesus. He had a dream one night that he was in a large crowd of people who were all angry, disruptive sorts and they were all calling out, 'Crucify him! Crucify him!' He looked up and saw a young man being held high above the crowds, looking forlorn and sad.

He didn't think much more about the dream until, one day, his two daughters brought a friend home with them for supper. As the man entered the house, the girls' father went pale with shock as the man looked exactly like the one he had seen in his dream.

'What did this mean?' he asked himself and very quickly became overcome with emotion and withdrew from the room, shutting the door. He put his ear to the door and could hear the young man having wonderful conversations with his daughters; he longed to join in but his fear got the better of him. This young man was alive and well. Why had he had that dream? Did it mean he would be crucified one day? Was it up to him to do anything? His internal questions and thoughts came thick and fast as he sat pondering on his own. His own lack of self-worth kept him silent and fed his own fear that he should not be part of the conversations or ever go near his daughters' friend.

The young man, Jesus, came to supper a few times after that. Each time, Andi hid in the next room, tapping into his unworthiness and not trusting he would be wanted in their presence. When Andi witnessed Jesus' crucifixion from amongst the crowds and saw his daughters' distress, he was beside himself with regret. Why had he not done something when he had the dream? Maybe he could have prevented this disaster? It did not seem to him that he could tell anyone about his position and what had happened so he buried it all deep in his soul, trying to carry on normally with his life. The deep sadness that was his lay stuck in his system and dormant until the day in this life when Andi allowed himself to remember what had happened and had healed from the Split enough to be able to forgive himself and know that the real truth was that he could have done nothing about it anyway.

Andi is a member of the soul group of Jesus. He had the premonition because his soul saw in advance which way an important member of his soul group was heading. If he had been more evolved, he could have asked for the highest good to come for this soul, instead of just burying it away. The reason we have premonitions is so that we can hand the situation over to a higher power and ask that the highest good be achieved. It is the universal way of gaining the energy to help or steer an impending situation. It only happens when help/energy is needed on the other side.

Theo's Denial

I had known Theo for a number of years and she had slowly been awakening to who she really was. She had known Jesus as a teenager. He had visited her family home just outside Jerusalem several times and she grew to absolutely adore him. On one visit, she remembered she had washed his feet.

Theo was not present at the crucifixion but when she heard of his death the following day, she dropped everything and ran towards the place where it was supposed to have taken place. Her intention was to ascertain whether the news was really true. Her whole body could not believe that it could be so. As she ran, she was filled with growing panic.

As she neared her destination, some Roman soldiers caught and stopped her. They asked her if she had known Jesus and, in her fear of these men, she denied that she had known him. They turned her around and told her to return whence she had come.

Theo was devastated. She ran away, feeling horror, shame and guilt that she had denied knowing the man she so loved. In her anguish and anger, her legs shaking, she fell to the ground and began pulling at the sand beneath her hand. Her heart cried out, 'You don't know what you have done.'

This agonising moment had remained hidden away in Theo's heart for over 2000 years, but in this life she has at last allowed herself to remember it, after many years of creeping closer and closer to the pain. It remains for her to forgive herself and to let go of the pain and emotions she has tucked deep inside. Only in that way will she become free to be who she really is.

Freddie's Reluctance

A young man who I have known for quite a few years now, Freddie, had known he needed to come to the retreat for some weeks but, on each approach, had then decided the journey he had to make was too difficult. One day, he found himself on a bus which took him within 14 miles of the retreat when he thought he had got on a bus to somewhere completely different! He took the hint and came to see me.

As we sat together, Freddie remembered he had stood amongst the crowd watching Jesus die. But he could not take the memory any further and was reluctant to let me go into it either. However, the universe was clearly not going to let this opportunity go by. When he suddenly left without saying thank you or goodbye to me and leaving no note, I went into a state of shock and felt sick because I had trusted him with a document that I did not wish to leave my premises.

After I released my own shock, the state of sickness remained within me so I realised it was not mine. On tuning into it, this is what was given to me. It was self-talk that had lain deep within his soul since standing at the crucifixion and had been crippling the young man:

> It should be me on the cross and he should be where I am. I am the bad one. This is all the wrong way round for he is the good one. I am the one who sleeps with many women and he is the one who takes care of many women. I mess about and don't take life seriously. He is the one who bravely takes every hit that comes towards him on the shoulder.

I felt his immense guilt. I was shown that he had agreed to come and help the soul group affect the highest outcome during Jesus' lifetime. He felt he had let Jesus down. He told himself: 'I've pranked about and now failed to do the very thing I came to do. How can I ever put this right?'

After Jesus died, Freddie had set about finding his truth but, to this day, has always got stuck on this moment at the crucifixion, because he believed he could not be forgiven and was so ashamed. However, he had reached a point in this life when he knew he had to face it so his soul found this way to remind him of his inner conversation.

Five minutes after these revelations were completed, I found an answer-phone message from Freddie, explaining why he had gone so quickly, apologising and telling me that the document was safely hidden in a drawer in the bedroom he had used. So I had been right to trust Freddie after all!

Esme's Infatuation

Esme carries the memory of being a young woman who knew Jesus in the years before he died and was often to be found among the crowds that surrounded him. She lived near Jerusalem and had become besotted with a young Roman soldier who was posted there. She felt he was a wonderful, amazing man who held an assurance about him that she lacked. It was this, coupled with his strength as a person, that had drawn her towards him. He, in turn, was flattered by her attention.

She had never spoken of Jesus and her love and respect for him because she somehow felt her Roman wouldn't want to hear it. However, on the morning of the crucifixion, she learned that he was to be part of the Roman 'team' that were to guard the cross while the crucifixion took place and ensure that there was no trouble. For the first time since they met, Esme found the courage to speak up for Jesus. She tried to tell him that Jesus was no criminal and that he was being wrongly put to death. She knew she risked losing her potential beau but she felt compelled to do it. The soldier was extremely angry to be questioned about his role and shouted her down in no uncertain terms.

Later that day, Esme stood amongst the crowds at the cross in frozen horror. She had previously felt sure that Jesus would perform a miracle and somehow jump off the cross. She waited and waited. Her thoughts wandered: 'Here is a really good man being treated like a criminal ... I can't bear this injustice ... When is he going to save himself?'

Suddenly, Esme felt she must do something about the situation. She eased forwards through the crowds towards her soldier friend. He turned round as she approached and caught sight of her pale, stricken face. He had already been getting more and more agitated by the growing crowds. He had been in the process of asking himself: 'Why do they care so much? Why have so many people come to watch such an everyday occurrence? What was so special about this man?'

As he caught sight of Esme, it all became too much for him. He turned away from her, raised his spear and thrust it into the side of Jesus. He wanted to get the whole thing over with quickly and get out of this awful situation. Esme, watching this terrible act, felt responsible for it and felt an unreasonable guilt that she had somehow allowed it to happen. The memory of the thrust of the spear for her contained, and has contained ever since, that moment of horror and she was unable to forgive herself. She turned from the scene in agony. She could not bear the double whammy. Not only was Jesus dying unjustly, but the man she loved had made his suffering so much worse.

She ran as far away from the scene as she could, knowing this was the last time she would ever see her 'love'. In her following lives, Esme's heart had always questioned what was written in the Bible because she had no knowledge of it for herself. Now, she is rebalancing her connection to it all, reconnecting with her own truth and allowing forgiveness into her heart. She knows Jesus has already forgiven her.

Miriam's Vision

A lady once visited me who carried a very unusual part of this fine jigsaw. The lady's name was Miriam and as a teenager she had adored Jesus. She used to love his infrequent visits to her parents' house. One night, she had a vivid dream of a brilliant white light in the shape of a cross and she woke up feeling that Jesus was being crucified. She ran to her parents who were both asleep and they comforted her, reassuring her that no one would want to kill an innocent man and that only criminals were crucified. After that, they managed to calm Miriam down and no more was said about it.

When later on Miriam heard of Jesus' death, she felt mortified and blamed herself. She asked herself in her agony: 'Why didn't I do anything? Perhaps I could have saved him? I was warned in a dream. I knew.' Miriam embarked on the long journey to Jerusalem to find out the truth of what had happened. She saw Nathaniel in a marketplace and rushed over to speak with him. She told him of the vision she had experienced.

Nathaniel was feeling lost and angry with life at that moment. He turned angrily to Miriam and said, 'Why didn't you come and tell us? Maybe we could have done something to save him.' Miriam was desperately shocked and fell to her knees in self-anguish. Nathaniel was confirming all that she had thought about herself already.

Miriam has blocked herself from her inner light ever since. She had been attracting more and more darkness into her life as she sunk lower and lower into her own lack of self-worth. This was the universe's way of trying to help her remember the pain and self-blame she carried in her core from that time. Now, having remembered her connection to Jesus, she has a chance to heal.

***

The father of Miriam came to visit me some years later. At that time, he had been jealous of his daughter's connection to Jesus when he came to the house and had wondered what this man had that he as a father had not. He pretended to be busy about his business while Jesus was there but had half an ear to what was being said.

After his daughter disappeared, he followed her to Jerusalem and found her on the outskirts of the town in a terrible mess. He picked her up, hugged her and tried to reassure her that Jesus could not have been the wonderful man she had thought he was as only criminals were crucified. He tried to console her but really he was consoling himself with his words.

This man spent the next 2000 years in various lifetimes trying to unravel who Jesus had really been. Now he has the chance to face his denial of Jesus and release the guilt, jealousy and fear he has been harbouring within him, thus enabling his soul to be free to love this man.

Ellie's Unexplained Pains

I had a visit from a 15-year-old girl named Ellie and it was clear from the start what a pure soul she had. However, she was complaining of aches and pains all over her body which had begun nine years before I met her and had escalated in the last ten months.

It became clear that the following memory was trying to surface in her consciousness. She had been a young teenager who adored Jesus. She lived for his visits to her village and hoped against hope when she heard that he was coming, that he would come and stay with her family, which sometimes he did.

One day, she was out by the central village well drawing water, which was where the village tended to congregate when Jesus was around. She was just drawing up her water when she felt a sudden feeling of tiredness. Her body began to ache and she felt very unwell. She made her way back home and lay down for the rest of the day and the following morning she felt much better.

A few weeks or months later, the village heard that Jesus had been crucified. Ellie did not equate the two events at the time and went into utter dismay, disbelief, sorrow and guilt when she heard the news of Jesus' death. Why had someone not saved him? Why hadn't she saved him? How could such a wonderful man be crucified? How could this have happened? She was full of unanswered questions and anger with herself and others.

When I told Ellie she had been feeling his pain by the well on the day of the crucifixion, she knew it to be true. She had been used as a clear and empty vessel to channel some of his pain as he suffered so much on the cross. So, while she had been chastising herself for not helping him, she could now see that she had helped him in the highest possible way. Her body had been trying to help her heal and to remember so that she could let go of the guilt and other emotions that were still locked inside her. What a beautiful and truly amazing young woman she was!

Hannah's Spark of Light

There was a girl called Hannah, aged around 4–5 years old, who used to love playing around the feet of Jesus while he was teaching. Her parents loved listening to him so she found herself in his company quite often. Being in his presence was very special to her for she became calm and happy. She didn't need to look at or speak with him but learned to communicate with him on an energetic level.

One day, Hannah found herself standing in the middle of a large crowd, with her parents standing either side of her. The mood of the crowd was sombre and she could just see the top half of Jesus in the distance. He had his arms outstretched and he looked very sad. The day seemed endless to her and she felt very tired. She eventually sat down at the feet of her parents, picking up the waves of sadness, darkness and heavy energy of everyone around her. How long would she have to sit here? When could they go home? She did not like to bother her parents but in her heart she cried out: 'Help me. Please someone, take me out of this place and come and look after me!'

Her father bent down and picked her up with his left arm. No words passed between them. She snuggled into his shoulder and he caressed her gently. From her newly elevated position, Hannah looked round to see Jesus. He looked very different. He was even paler than before and his head hung very low. She knew he was dying. She tearfully pushed her head back into her father's shoulder and started to communicate with Jesus as she did whenever she was playing around him. She knew in her heart that he was doing something that would help the world. She could not have voiced it, of course, but her little soul reached out to him and she gave her life into service at that moment. Every bone in her body knew she wanted to carry on where he had left off, to be as he had been, and immediately a strong light sparked within her heart.

Hannah was one of only a handful of souls on that day that recognised at some level what was really going on. However, the gift she received became buried because she grew up in a world that didn't resonate with it. Her communications with Jesus almost felt like a lost foreign language. The lady that she is now in this life had at last remembered what happened that day, and has chosen to reignite her promise and allow her spark to become a shining light.

After Jesus died, he saw just a handful of similar lights that sparked up from the crowd in the deepening dusk. It gave him hope that he had not gone through everything in vain as he transitioned from the earthly realm into spirit.

A Pharisee

A man named Taylor came to see me who I suspected had been around at the time of the crucifixion. However, it took me a few chats and visits before I heard the word Pharisee distinctly in my ear. What was a Pharisee? I had no idea.

I bravely told him I was seeing him at the crucifixion. He was startled as the thought had not crossed his conscious mind. However, I relayed to him that he had been a Jew who worked in a temple at the time. As he had heard more and more about Jesus, he became annoyed. He wondered who this young upstart was who could come preaching in his neighbourhood. When questioned, he fed his concerns to the authorities, stressing his indignation and disbelief.

Taylor decided to watch the crucifixion, partly to satisfy himself that this young upstart had been duly punished and partly to reassure himself that he was right. He had not expected to see a haggard and tired yet innocent man hanging before him. He felt uneasy. His discomfort grew as he watched the death unfold. Jesus' presence left a permanent mark on him. As he left the scene, he was full of doubt. During the following weeks, he discreetly began to search for answers. One day, he approached a group of Jesus' followers who were sitting quietly together. He felt their peace and he was jealous. He heard beautiful music coming from a lute being played from within the group. Suddenly, he was overcome with dread that he could never be part of what they were part of. Hadn't he given evidence against Jesus? He felt himself to be a sinner. A dark shadow began to grow within him and his lack of self-worth took hold. He shut down to it all and never again turned towards Jesus' followers or searched for the truth of what he had witnessed.

As Taylor felt the truth of my words, he understood himself as never before. He understood why he had taken a darkened passage in every life that followed and had struggled to keep himself out of deep depression in this life. He had come to me at a time when he was ready to face all that had happened and to find out if he could be forgiven. He was ready to be answerable for what he had done and to follow his truth. He had had dreams of the crucifixion ten years beforehand but the dreams came in a way that he did not understand at the time. After I had spoken with him, he knew his higher self had been trying to wake him up.

A Selection of Memories from Roman Soldiers

Cory

Cory came to see me a very long time ago, before I was recording any of the histories that were coming my way. She (as a female in this life) oozed Roman soldier energy, and I knew she had been someone who had been present at the crucifixion, whose job it had been to control the crowds. I was given the opportunity to tell her what I was seeing.

A few years later, Cory came to stay again. As she walked through the door, I immediately saw the same Roman soldier energy. I felt troubled for her because I knew this meant she had not dealt with it. However, very good news emerged when she admitted she had gone into deep shock over what we had discussed three years before, but was now ready to hear the whole story, ask forgiveness for her part in it and release it. The following is what we remembered together.

Cory had pretended not to be interested in Jesus as he and other legionnaires ate their supper round a campfire, the night after the crucifixion. However, he had to acknowledge that there had been an unusually large crowd present. He quietly noted several facts as they all chatted away but he did not admit he was part of putting an innocent man to death. The truth was that he felt he was just doing his job. However, the incident changed his life forever because he then began searching for the truth in a quiet way that did not draw attention to himself. (The shock Cory had gone into a few years before was because she had been rumbled unexpectedly.)

Amah

As Jesus was being questioned by Caiaphas on the day before the crucifixion, there were two Roman soldiers present, one standing to the right of Caiaphas and one to the left. The one to the left, Amah, shared his story with me.

Amah stood listening vaguely to the conversation going on between Caiaphas and Jesus. He came to suddenly, as the conversation ended with an angry outburst from Caiaphas where he found he was being instructed to take the prisoner back to his cell. He and his colleague marched Jesus away, down a passage and into a courtyard, intending to cross it. Jesus mentioned he was thirsty so the soldiers took him to the well that was in the centre of the yard. As Jesus leant over the well to lift some water, Amah took his whip out and began to thrash Jesus. After all, he thought, he has been condemned to death so I will have a little fun and give him a bit more of what he deserves. Even then, Amah inwardly knew that Jesus was innocent and his decision to whip him came from his own jealousy in not having power of his own.

Later the next day, as Jesus was being nailed to the cross, Amah was present. He gave the command for Jesus to be lifted into an upright position. As Jesus was lifted, Amah caught his eye and he immediately felt forgiveness flowing from Jesus through his heart. In that moment, something changed deeply inside him and he felt terrible. He felt he should fall to his knees and ask for forgiveness but he didn't because he felt the pressure too keenly of being a Roman soldier. He numbly carried on his duties in containing the crowd but inside he was shaken to the core.

As soon as he was able to, Amah requested permission to return to Rome. Once there, he relinquished his uniform and decided to return to Jerusalem to look for answers to the question that was plaguing him: 'Who was this man?' Amah wanted his wife and children to come with him but they were quite concerned for his mental well-being and elected to remain in Rome. Amah knew he would have to leave them, knowing he might never see them again. This was a sacrifice he was willing to make as he knew that to find the truth was more important. As he left Rome, he walked down the main street with his arms spread out wide to each side of him, asking for change to come to Rome.

Amah searched amongst the followers of Jesus for the truth. He never dared tell them what he himself had done for fear of being removed from their presence. Therefore, a feeling of guilt, sadness, unworthiness and a slight twist to his character became embedded in his heart. Now, in the 21st century, Amah has the opportunity to unearth his own truth, ask for forgiveness and let the emotions release from his heart.

Raphael

Raphael had joined the Roman army believing he would be serving the 'righteous'. He believed the Romans held the ascendency on the planet and that they would conquer the world so that the 'correct' way of living could be upheld. When he witnessed the conversation that took place between Jesus and Caiaphas, he was mentally floored. Here was Caiaphas declaring Jesus to be innocent, yet asking Jesus to tell lies to save his own skin. Raphael was astounded when the 'innocent' man refused to lie and was then condemned to death.

The guard was a simple man with simple values. In this moment of the interview, it felt like a fuse blew in his brain. He mechanically took Jesus back to his cell, desperate to talk to him and yet terrified of doing so. All night, he pondered what had happened, feeling more and more uncomfortable. What should he do? He fell ill the next morning, totally unable to get out of his bed. Later that day, word was brought to him that Jesus was dead. A huge feeling of guilt, anger, sadness and fear took over in Raphael and he became very unbalanced and lost. From that day on, he did not understand what was right and what was wrong and spent the next 2000 years floundering, unable to distinguish the difference.

When I asked Raphael to replay the moment that he stood in front of Caiaphas and Jesus and then asked what he would do if he was witness to it now, he said unhesitatingly, 'I would stand behind the truth which lay in Jesus.' The guard was now able to set himself free by asking forgiveness for what he had done, releasing all the emotional turmoil he had been carrying and being able to trust that his heart would guide him as to right and wrong in all future matters.

Chuck

A friend of mine from the soul group of Jesus had been healing herself for many years when she suddenly felt drawn to ask me about her husband and how he fitted into her personal picture. She was puzzled that she hadn't asked before but it soon became clear to us that he had not completed his karmic debt until very recently.

Her husband, Chuck had been a Roman soldier who had been called up as an extra pair of hands to help keep the peace during the crucifixion because the authorities were afraid that the crowds were so big that they would not be able to control them. Chuck therefore arrived on the scene with others and was given the task of keeping the crowds away from the immediate area of the cross. After a while, he began to wonder why there was so much fuss around this particular criminal. Other criminals didn't seem to be attracting the same amount of interest. He turned round and looked at Jesus' face. As he did so, he let out a huge gasp. This was the face of the man who had saved his daughter's life many years ago, long before Jesus' recorded mission began. Chuck could not mistake this face. It was etched in his memory and his daughter adored this man. Chuck himself was utterly beholden to this man. He turned away, absolutely horrified. He went through the motions of containing the crowd. His mind was racing: 'How could this have happened? What was he doing hanging from the cross? Why had he been labelled a criminal?'

Questions were pouring through Chuck's mind in an uncontrollable fashion. A few minutes later, he looked up at Jesus again, half wanting to see that he had made a mistake, for surely this couldn't be the same man? In that moment, he knew he was too late to help him, for he was breathing his last breaths.

Chuck continued with his job but he was weak at the knees. He wanted to run, to escape, to have time to think, all of which were denied him. He was at the point of collapse. How could he ever face his daughter again? I believe he never recovered from the shock and took his own life not long afterwards.

As I tuned into Chuck in my friend's presence on this particular day, I knew he was in the same position again. Everything in his life had come to a head and he was internally reliving the emotions that he had experienced after Jesus' death. I could see that various events in his life that my friend had relayed to me, had brought the opportunity to pay his perceived karmic debt, which he had undoubtedly done, and we managed to reignite the forgiveness Jesus sent to him on the day it all happened. As we surrounded him with forgiveness, we sent with it the prayer that he will face himself very soon. His wife would be able to help because she now understood his difficult behaviours and could love him unconditionally.

Antony

A man who came to speak with me on only one occasion had held a position in the Roman army stationed in Jerusalem 2000 years before, that saw him responsible for which soldiers were deployed where, on a daily basis. One day, he, Antony, was told that he needed to get extra soldiers ready for a crucifixion that was to take place the next day. He was angry. He didn't like the slight that the order seemed to present. Did his men not guard these events on a regular basis? Was someone saying he didn't do a good job? Besides, he had other places these men needed to be. In his anger, he became petulant and gave orders for every last man he had under his command to be present at the following day's crucifixion.

A little way through the next day, Antony began to wonder what the fuss was all about. His office was unusually quiet so he went out on horseback and watched the crowds from a distance as they made their way up the hill outside of the town. He could see no problems so went back to his office a little calmer in his mind.

A while later, he felt an enormous need to go out and check the situation again. This time, the prisoners were hanging from their crosses in the distance but there was still no sign of a problem. However, Antony was surprised at the number of onlookers around. He felt an unease within him but reminded himself that he was following the law to the letter and there was nothing to fear. He turned and left the scene.

The next morning, Antony asked around to see if the 'Nazarene' had been properly dealt with. The answer from one of the soldiers came, 'Yes, boss. He's dead and buried. We may have to move his burial site to avoid any trouble but all is in hand.' The officer thought no more about it other than that he had done his job, but he retained the feeling of unease within him. In this life, he has always been in touch with this mysterious sense of unease and has put law and order above his intuition (to make himself right). He has now realised that to live free of the unease, he must listen to his intuition first, whatever the cost or outcome.

Ed

One Roman soldier, Ed, was a seeker of the truth and had been for many lifetimes. He 'happened' to be one of the soldiers who was escorting Jesus up the Via Dolorosa to the cross. When he first caught sight of Jesus through the crowds, he saw a man who was bent over, carrying the heavy wood on his back. He immediately saw in his aura the innocence and light that were coming off him and more especially his resigned and forgiving nature as he trod the path to his death. There wasn't an ounce of malice in him. He wasn't cursing or blaming or declaring his innocence to himself; he just 'was'.

The shock of seeing this man out of the blue, who epitomised everything he had been looking for in his own life, hit Ed like a punch in the chest. He gasped for air as he hurried along, trying to keep pace with Jesus and understand what he was seeing. Why was this man being crucified? What had he done? Who was he? Questions like this crowded his mind.

Still gasping for air, Ed reached the top of the hill where Jesus was standing, waiting to be nailed on the cross. He had a desperate inner knowing that he could not watch this crucifixion. He was physically a big strong man but at this moment he felt so weak. He kept his eyes lowered, fixated safely on his own feet. As his panic grew, he turned away from what was going on and suggested to the commander of the Roman soldiers that he should go and prepare the grave. As this was not something that had been done, the commander agreed.

As Ed trod the path to the tomb, he felt terrible. He asked himself many questions: Why could he not stand up for this man? Why didn't he do something? Why did he not speak up for him? He hid behind the weight of his duty as a Roman soldier and persuaded himself he could not do anything. His mind was racing and he was very uncomfortable.

Ed had been avoiding looking at this impact or punch in the chest that he had held for so long because he felt such a coward not to have done anything and was therefore very angry with himself. Sheer fear of being crucified alongside the innocent man had driven him in the opposite direction in this man's hour of need. In later lives, this turning away from the truth was played out many times as Ed chose situations where he could kid himself he was on the right path, but they were in fact situations that led him to the opposite. He took on such roles as high priest and leading Druid and as such caused much pain amongst his fellows. Only now, at this time of the Second Coming, is he ready to unveil and face his cowardice with heartfelt regret and sorrow.

Kenny and Glen

I have met two members from the soul group of the Roman commander who oversaw the crucifixion of Jesus. Both are young men in their 30s—Kenny hails from California and Glen from Birmingham, UK. This Roman commander sat astride a large bay horse as the crucifixion took place. He was carrying a long whip in his right hand which he flicked ceaselessly on both sides of him as he held the reins with his left hand. He was circling the cross, intent on keeping the large crowds at bay to ensure the law was upheld.

Kenny remembered feeling a strange energy on one of the occasions that he rode past Jesus' face. He continued on his way but kept asking himself: 'Who is this man? Why are there so many crowds round him? Are we crucifying an innocent man? Is there something special about this man?'

He rode on in his circle, his mind questioning and his whip cracking. He was about to go past Jesus' face again when he found he couldn't. He stopped, feeling so unsettled. He turned his back to the cross and, as he contemplated, a soldier came running up to him and cried, 'He is dead.' The commander said gruffly, 'Take him down and sort him out.' Kenny turned his horse and rode back to his quarters.

Glen had a very different story to tell. He initially insisted to me that he was the reincarnation of Jesus. He could remember the crucifixion, had constant visions of it and in his mind there was no argument to be had. He *knew* he was Jesus. However, I knew this was not true and I told him that the vision he kept having was one of 'seeing' the crucifixion rather than 'being' it, and that he needed to face the unhealed horror of those last moments. Because he did not want to face the fact that he had allowed Jesus to be killed, and he absolutely knew he would not do that in this life, Glen's fear convinced him that he *was* the reincarnated Christ. The young man withdrew from me and what I was trying to convey to him and broke down in tears. It was clear we could not speak to each other any further that day.

Approximately four years later, Glen found me again. This time he was ready to face what he had done and his courage was second to none. He now knows who he was, has faced it all and asked for forgiveness. His honesty and bravery will not only help the rest of his soul group but also those of us who are struggling to face our own truth, and I have great gratitude and respect for him.

Stephen

A charming, helpful man named Stephen kept popping into my life who seemed to be very familiar to me. I learned over time that he had been a centurion posted in Jerusalem around the time of Jesus' arrest. He had heard increasing rumours of a man who might become a threat to the authorities for he had become very popular with the crowds. The centurion longed to get his hands on this man but it seemed to him that Jesus kept slipping through his fingers. As a power-loving, inflexible and self-important man who liked to control everything around him, he was not happy with this situation.

When Jesus was arrested, Stephen's first comment was, 'We've got you now. You can't slip out of this one.' He had seen Jesus as a disturber of the peace and stated that he was glad to have got the better of him. Jesus was fully aware of this centurion who popped up in the crowds that surrounded him every now and then. He was not fazed by his presence as he was fully aware of where true power lies. He looked at the centurion with forgiveness and kindness.

This man behaved exactly the same in this life. He had to be right, he had to have the last word and he liked to control in the same way. The difference in 2000 years is that he is now searching for the truth, but again cannot quite see what has been presented under his nose. But, as he keeps presenting himself, I have asked the universe to help him remember his past life and to help him face himself.

Lucius

This Roman soldier has not been to see me himself. However, I know of him through two members of Jesus' sister's soul group who have visited me independently. This is the memory they describe.

Lucius was standing very close to the little girl as Jesus was being crucified. He had been one of the guards who had fetched the family from their home and deposited them at the foot of the cross. He had handled them roughly, as criminals, and shackled them by their left foot. He had decided for himself not to shackle the little sister as she was so tiny and young. He had instead placed himself near her to keep an eye on her as he felt he should carry out his orders responsibly. In this manner, he found himself surveying what was going on in a more intimate way and discovered to his horror that the little girl knew her brother was innocent. He then took more interest in the crowd and realised just how many also thought Jesus was innocent. He felt uncomfortable and uneasy. Who was this man? He wanted to get away but he felt he must stay and watch this girl. His soul has been rejecting Jesus ever since through his possible feelings of guilt at the time.

The women who brought this memory forward were able to describe this Roman soldier's feelings because one had chosen to marry a member of Lucius' soul group in this life, and the other had chosen him as her brother. Both therefore had a very dedicated approach to helping this Roman soldier be forgiven and find his truth.

10
Joseph

Joseph came to earth as a supportive soul who had volunteered to help achieve the highest outcome for the Jesus soul group on its quest to heal the Split. He had already agreed to support Mary, as her husband, should she take on the role that was offered to her. His support never wavered through all that happened at the birth and the first few years of Jesus' life, and it continued long after he died.

As Joseph arrived at the cross with his family, shackled and shaken, he saw Jesus suffering such as no father could have wished for. His innocent son was hanging from a cross between two criminals. That in itself was bad enough for he dearly loved this son, who he had taken on as his own, and when he saw what was happening his role became very hard indeed. His wife collapsed in grief, his other children needed his support and there was pain and confusion wherever he looked. He felt, as head of the family, responsible for what was going on. He felt he should have stopped it all long ago and not allowed this to happen. He felt devastated, angry, confused, resentful and totally overwhelmed.

One deeply sincere member of the Joseph soul group told me that he had heard Jesus call out, 'Father, why hast thou forsaken me?' Instead of realising the words were meant for a heavenly father, he took them to mean himself. It was how he was feeling, and therefore his interpretation was understandable. However, this same soul went on to remember that Joseph followed his inner instructions to the letter. To achieve this, he buried his own emotions deeply and set about supporting his family as he had promised. He was the ultimate rock. If he had not adhered to his inner instruction in the way he did, he might well have gone to the rescue of his son and in that way scuppered the whole mission. In every incarnation since, through all that has been relayed down the centuries, this soul group has felt unacknowledged and real anger has been suppressed within.

One soul, Vim, remembers that he held resentment, judgement and anger because Jesus was not his son and he felt the role had been foisted upon him in an unfair way. He had forgotten his soul contract. When I reminded Vim of it, he was able to release his anger and resentment and manage to rebalance.

This is what Vim wrote down for us:

> The Joseph soul group has never been honestly acknowledged throughout history. The commitment that had been taken on was huge and self-sacrificing. He had brought up Jesus as his own son in blind faith that it was God's will that he support Mary through the birth of Jesus. As part of this agreement, he also had to take on board the accepting of the loss of this child on the cross, for wrongs he had not committed. He had to stand by and witness the death and had no choice but to hold all his emotions in as he watched Mary crumble in front of his eyes. He had to support Mary through the rest of her life while trying to keep Jesus' siblings in balance, and his utter dedication to the role caused him to put his own needs into the background, thereby taking all his pain to the grave. The resentment within him has grown through every lifetime since, because there was never an acknowledgement of his own sacrifice.

After understanding where all these emotions were coming from, Vim then wrote the following:

> All is well. Joseph, you have been validated and recognised for what you helped to achieve all those centuries ago. It is now possible to heal and let go of the deep wounding within. No longer do you have to hide the pain and responsibility for the secrets of old. You are free, you are pure, you can return to the oneness.

A few years later, I shared Vim's writings with another member of the soul group of Joseph while in a meeting of around 20 other souls. Joe was married in this life to a member of the Mary soul group but was struggling to acknowledge who he was. In this meeting, I was telling everyone about some of the understandings that were coming to me around the life of Jesus when I suddenly felt an urge to share the Joseph findings. I read out what Vim had written and felt myself sliding out of my body.

From this altered place of awareness, I found myself looking Joe straight in the eyes and apologising for everything. I knew Jesus had watched Joseph from spirit and felt very anguished that he had not been able to speak with his earthly father before he died. Jesus watched as his father suppressed all his emotions in order to keep going. His courage was immense. On Jesus' behalf, I found myself speaking with a huge depth of emotion, expressing deep gratitude to him for all he had done for the family and apologising for leaving him in such a mess. Everyone present, including myself, was hugely moved by the very profound place this acknowledgement was coming from. Without a doubt, Joe allowed a huge shift in his energy in that moment, which would go on to aid his healing in the future. What is more, I was able to release the sorrow and guilt for all that Jesus had not completed concerning his father, for the soul group of Jesus.

***

While these two souls, Vim and Joe, could not be more different in character, they share certain qualities:

- Both are able to love at a deeply committed level.
- Their dedication to duty cannot be questioned.
- They were both left with an almost insurmountable barrier to feeling the pain held from that time.
- The switch 'back on' button inside them is so deeply hidden that it is very difficult to find.

While I believe this soul is as yet unhealed, I think that, as the soul group of Mary heals itself, it will give those who hold the memory of what happened to Joseph permission to start facing themselves.

11
Mary

Some Background

As a young girl growing up, Mary was shy, a loner; she felt different to others but was confident in her own space. One particular member of the soul group, Anna, remembers the energy that used to flow through Mary's hands. She recalls holding a butterfly with torn wings in the palms of her hands, allowing the healing flow to run through its body and watching it fly happily away.

Anna felt that God was an integral part of Mary's existence as a child. She lived only from her inner connection and her desire to serve was very deep-rooted. She felt Mary had a very good connection with her mother but not much at all with her father.

***

Mary had held herself strongly together since the moment of Jesus' birth, until the moments before his death. Through thick and thin, she had trusted her intuition and smiled. What I know of her very early experience is recorded in Chapter 1, while snippets are mentioned throughout the book and another important section is recorded in Chapter 12.

Watching Jesus grow up, Mary had a telepathic bond with him that was never referred to but was utilised by both of them. She had a longing for him to stay small and *hers* in order to keep him safe. One woman remembers a moment just before Jesus went into Jerusalem when he said to her, 'I feel it will soon be time for me to go, but I will always be a part of you and you will always be a part of me. There is no separation. It will always be like this.'

Later, from Mary's enforced position at the foot of the cross, she became aware of the familiar dark shadow that she had first experienced around Jesus when she was carrying him in her womb. She felt disempowered and terrorised. The shadow appeared to have control and she had a fear that her son was consumed by it and she couldn't help him. Her own heart felt void and that somehow all was lost. She persuaded herself that she had failed in her duties and responsibilities. For a few seconds, she felt a distinct separation between mother and son and, while Jesus quickly regained his trust, she fell into deeper despair with the added fear that her own soul had separated from Source.

As Jesus died, the pain and loss were too great for her to bear out of her own strength. She started to crack and a silent agonised scream filled her body: 'How can this be right?' Her separation from her truth was complete. She asked herself: 'Why did I ever agree to have him? Did I even do the right thing? Maybe I misheard what was being asked of me? How could it be right to have given birth to him when something like this was going to happen to him? Did I make it all up?'

All the doubts in her came to the fore and her anguish hit its most extreme. She feared she herself would be taken; such was her disconnection to the mission in her soul. She felt herself to be a failure and a fraud. As the anguish peaked, Mary lost herself mentally and was thereafter unable to grieve properly for her son, which meant she never fully recovered her sanity before her own death.

From the Mary Weekend

It became clear that all the Marys had brought all the sorrow, guilt, anger, injustice, pain, helplessness and her belief of her own responsibility for it all, back into this life. One woman had felt all this life that she manifested people's deaths when she came into contact with them, such was the unhealed part of her soul and the belief she had done wrong by giving birth to Jesus in the first place. Others got totally stuck on the helplessness side of things and could not face going within to the painful memory that was attached to that state of being.

Many of the soul group resonated with the scream inside them and have lived with it stuck in their heart. It is a strong feeling among the members of the Mary soul group that Mary never recovered her equilibrium after the death of Jesus. Some have 'lost the plot' in this life and others have been very near it. As each member of the soul group recognises the truth that her separation from Jesus 'had to happen' in order to bring about the reversal of the Split, they have been able to let the scream dissolve, forgive themselves and recognise that the role Mary played had an equal importance to that of Jesus. Nothing could have happened the way it did without her sacrifice.

The grief within the soul group of Mary seems to be held in several different ways. Of course, the main bulk is the loss, as described above. However, several souls describe a grief at the loss of Mary herself as she had been. Another describes a grief at the loss of how much she was loved at the time, believing herself ever since to be beyond redemption. A third describes the supposed loss of her connection to Source and the conviction that she didn't deserve to be reconnected. One particular soul felt she had failed miserably in what she saw as her responsibilities and had closed off her heart ever since. These grievances are deeply held in the soul, until the bearers face themselves and allow the truth through.

Anger was expressed by one member of the soul group in the following way: 'Is God having a day off? Why didn't He do something? My son was too young to die. He had so much more to give.' This person felt Mary went into complete denial of what she had been told before his birth. She continually thought something would happen to prevent his actual death until it happened.

An unexpected root

The climax to Mary's story came to my attention in a very unexpected fashion. A lady I had known for some years who had been feeling her Mary life stronger and more passionately than most, had a final revelation which enabled her to let go of her entire Mary lifetime and at last feel the joy of living without the pain she had carried for so long. As part of this process, she went into an altered state of awareness from which I saw the anger she had for Jesus. I was so surprised. I had never ever suspected that Mary had been angry with Jesus after he died. The lady concerned became outwardly angry with me very suddenly. When I tried to send her unconditional love and forgiveness, I could only approach her soul through the open portal of love that lay between Mary and Jesus. However, to my surprise, thick, yellow poison poured out all over me from this portal and engulfed me before I could do anything. I knew it represented the previously hidden anger she held for Jesus. I asked for all the anger to be released and dissipated immediately. I waited while it oozed out and until it was all gone.

I knew then that this lady had completely healed herself from the Mary memory and I didn't know if this had ever been done before by anyone else. However, a huge sense of peace came over Geoff and me, and we knew that this unexpected healing was gifted to the rest of the soul group forever. Since then, two others from the soul group have released their anger towards Jesus with very positive results.

12
After the Death of Jesus

I have a friend, Pop, who gives off a strong Buddhist energy which I feel every time I see him. He had been trying to release his blocks for a few years and to understand why he had steeped himself in Buddhist teachings, amongst other things. He had never mentioned to me that he had a brotherly affection for Jesus until recently.

One day, Pop showed me a very small lump on his head and I asked him why he thought it had come up. He didn't know so I went closer and had a look at it. As I bent over him, I saw a cross in the middle of the round swelling. The whole thing looked rather like a screw head. I thought it was odd so I put my glasses on to take a better look at it but there was no cross to be seen. I took my glasses off again and there was the cross.

We both knew there was something significant in what was happening so we agreed to delve into it the following day. During the next 24 hours, Pop spent as much time as he could clearing the energetic mist that surrounded him. When I saw him again, his memory of his association with the cross was ready to be made conscious.

Pop was a Jew who manned his own street stall on a main throughway in Jerusalem at the time that Jesus was going through his last weeks. He used to see Jesus and his friends approaching and hoped against hope that Jesus would one day stop at his stall and wish to purchase something. He used to fantasise that when Jesus asked to purchase some goods, he would humbly bow in front of him and simply say, 'No payment needed; it is a pleasure to give it to you.'

When Jesus never even seemed to notice him, his inner sense of low self-esteem grew larger and larger. At the crucifixion, when it was clear that Jesus had died, Pop eventually managed to overcome his fears and found the courage to ask the Roman soldiers if he could take the body down from the cross, sort him out and bury him. He felt a massive inner push that he should be the one to do this. He felt it was the very least he could do. As the Romans did not really want to do it themselves, they agreed. The Romans watched as Pop took the nails out of Jesus and extricated him from the cross. Pop wound Jesus' body in a cloth and put him over his shoulder. He carried him across the rough terrain to where the Romans dictated he was to be buried. The Roman soldiers surrounded him for protection as he did so and many of Jesus' friends and family followed.

Pop lay the body in the back of a tomb which was built on rocky terrain on a bit of a gradient. He had difficulty holding his balance on the small stones. He hammered some wood into place to stop the body rolling off the ledge and then he and some others rolled a large heavy stone uphill to seal the tomb. When this was done, Pop had the strong feeling that his job was done. He knew Roman soldiers were going to guard the tomb so he wasn't worried about leaving it. He did not wish to stay on the site any longer so he turned and headed home with a heavy heart.

The next hours were spent at his home, trying to come to terms with all that had happened and the enormity of what he had done. It had not been a pleasant task. As he sat in solitude, there was a sudden, heavy and insistent knocking on his door. As he opened it, an agitated man hurriedly informed him that 'the body had gone'. Pop went hot and cold all at once. The shock was enormous. His mind jumbled with many questions:

- Where has he gone?
- Who took him?
- What has happened to him?
- Why did I leave him?
- I can't have finished my job properly, can I?

As he left his property and walked the streets, he discovered that stories around the town were rife. Some said Jesus' body had been stolen. Others said the Roman soldiers had taken it. A further story was that Jesus had risen from the dead. It was wondered whether the disciples had taken him, and so on.

Reluctantly, Pop felt he had to go and see the tomb for himself. He knew how hard it would be for anyone to roll that stone away from the entrance. Why, it had taken many men to put it there in the first place. When he stood in front of the empty tomb, he was filled with shock, guilt and anger at himself, together with shame, pain and fear. It all felt like a stone in his heart. Pop's overriding thought was that even after Jesus' death, he had failed him. In that moment, he built a wall around himself, feeling he could never now be worthy enough to approach any followers of Jesus or his kind again.

Pop ran from the weight he carried at the time and has hidden himself away (partly in the Buddhist tradition) ever since. The wall he had built around him was first loosened three years before I spoke with him and when he felt it, he let out copious amounts of anger. Since then, he has been getting closer to his truth and now he is attempting to face it and release the emotions locked within.

***

Mary, totally overwhelmed after the crucifixion, as were many, had been hanging around aimlessly near the tomb. At one point, she overheard two Roman soldiers talking to each other. One said, 'I don't like this. There are too many people around that could cause yet more disturbance and trouble for us. I don't know why this man should be creating such a stir but I suggest we take his body and bury it somewhere safe when no one is looking.'

Mary immediately resolved not to let her son's body out of her sight. She was inwardly terrified she would lose the only part of him she felt she had left. Soon after that, the Roman soldiers made moves to disperse the crowds that were hanging around. Mary enlisted the help of a friend named 'Kit', and the two of them hid themselves in a nearby bush. They waited silently until late into the night but soon realised they could not survive much longer without help, food and water. It was decided that Kit should go back to Jerusalem to fetch Peter. She left via a path (path A) that led away from the tomb so that the Roman soldier standing on guard could not see her. Mary, keeping watch on her own, realised she had no need to be frightened of the guard and she crept forward towards the tomb. In the dark, she knelt in front of the huge stone that sealed the entrance to the tomb, fell to her knees and wept.

The Roman Guard

(Through the eyes of one of the Marys who has partnered him in this life.)

The guard that stood on duty by the tomb of Jesus was bored and cold that dark night. He was wondering why he even had to be there for he felt it was pointless. When the guard saw Mary come out from behind the bush, he felt surprised but realised quickly she posed no threat to him or the body he was protecting. He guessed she might be the dead man's mother. He watched her for some time and, as he had nothing else to do, he became heavily invested in what she was going through. He began to view the whole situation differently. This body that he was guarding had belonged to a man who had a mother who clearly adored him. Criminal or not, he had been dearly loved. This brought him to reconsider the crowds who had watched the crucifixion: 'Why were so many people affected by the death of this man? Who was he?' As his soul searched for answers and he watched Mary kneeling before the tomb, his heart began to melt and he began to change.

As the new day dawned, Mary heard footsteps coming along path A from Jerusalem. It was two Roman soldiers but she did not look up as they stopped, one each side of her. The guard at this point had come to a confused place in his heart where he was unsure whose side he was on. He felt torn. He watched silently as the two soldiers gently drew Mary back from her kneeling place and rolled the stone away from the tomb. Mary was surprised when she saw a light shine out from inside the tomb and thought someone must have left a lit candle beside Jesus' body. She and the guard watched as the two Roman soldiers entered the tomb and one of them brought Jesus' body out, carrying it over his left shoulder. The two soldiers made to leave down a different path (path B) to the one they had arrived on and the guard, lured by his fear and habitual duty, stepped down from his position and went to leave with them. As they left, he felt compelled to turn round and warn Mary. He said quietly, 'For your own sake, don't follow us.'

Unacknowledged by the guard, a deep change set in that day. He began to feel inner stirrings in himself which later became divisions that he could not handle. In some of his soul group, it has come out as narcissism.

The Mary soul group member (who brought this memory to our consciousness) and I felt deep gratitude to this man. He had allowed Mary to grieve on her own for a long period through that precious night without interfering. This was very special and could not have happened if he had followed his orders to the letter. We asked for his soul to be forgiven for his earlier part in the goings on and for him to have help to come to a place of understanding of who he was for himself, so that he could set himself free from the divisions within him.

The following passage is a personal testimony written by a different member of the guard's soul group. He refers to himself as a Roman legionnaire:

> As I stand outside the tomb of the man they call Jesus Christ, my heart and thoughts are heavy and uncomfortable within me. As a Roman legionnaire, I have witnessed so many crucifixions and thought nothing of them. This time it is different. The overwhelming sense of innocence of this man has touched me deeper than anything else in life. I can see the injustice of my so-called 'authority', the authority that I allow to govern me.
>
> I know that if I speak out now it could mean my death and I do not have this man's courage and heart to take that on. The

least I can do is to allow the mother to be as close to her son as circumstances permit. Without speech, I assist her grieving and allow her presence to go unhindered as my fellow legionnaires join me. I assert my authority over them to desist from any harm, mockery or disdain they might have shown her. I stand in my authority as a Roman legionnaire but that which I uphold is no longer the Roman Empire. I stand unseen as a witness to the true light and its divine truth. I know my life will never be the same again. I determine to find a way to uphold the truth and prevent further injustice, whether openly or by stealth. I know that a time will come when I no longer have to hide any knowledge of truth, a time when I can allow my tears to be seen and not be fearful of the consequences.

20.10.16—Today I know that I share the Christ energy. I have rediscovered that which I have been searching for. I now know why I have not found it in the Church or my established rituals of faith. I now see through the pretence of authority as I did so long ago as a Roman legionnaire. I now know that what I had thought to be true is a fabrication; it is derived from fear alone and not of the true Christ energy. I have asked and received forgiveness for the error of my ways. I have allowed myself to be misguided and I forgive those who set out to misguide me.

Today I am freed of that authority and I can allow the Christ energy within me to shine and resonate out from me, as we all can when we allow ourselves to remove the pretence. I can now step into enlightenment and grow...

Back at the Tomb

A few minutes after the three Roman soldiers had departed, Mary heard more footsteps approaching her from footpath A. It turned out to be Peter, Andrew and her friend Kit. She quickly told them what had happened so Peter and Kit hastened to follow the soldiers down path B, while it was decided that Andrew should remain with Mary at the tomb. Peter and Kit caught sight of the soldiers fairly quickly and followed them at a safe distance. They could see one of the soldiers carrying Jesus' body over his shoulder, which was obviously slowing his progress, so they took great care to remain under cover. Soon, they became aware of a man approaching the soldiers from the other direction. When the man came abreast of the soldiers, they all stopped and had what looked like a discussion. From the distance, Peter and Kit watched as Jesus' body was handed over to this man and he, now carrying the body, took a path to his right, which led back to Jerusalem. Peter and Kit got taken by surprise when the soldiers turned around and started to retrace their steps towards them. They had no time to hide so they pretended to be drunk. They pushed and shoved at each other playfully, crossing the path from left to right and back again, and eventually falling and rolling together into a ditch at the side of the road. The soldiers were very suspicious as they approached but when the two rolled into a dirty ditch and lay there without moving, they decided the pair posed no danger and they continued on their way, passing Mary, Andrew and the tomb, and then taking a further path that led back to their camp.

As soon as the soldiers were out of sight, Peter and Kit crawled out of the ditch and quickly made their way to the path on which they had last seen the stranger carrying Jesus' body. They turned towards Jerusalem, knowing they were a long way behind this man and fearing they had little chance of finding the body again. They searched the outskirts of Jerusalem for many hours. At last, feeling exhausted, desperate and unhappy, they stopped in a roadway, wondering what to do. As they did so, they heard the sound of someone chiselling some stone. They looked at each other and, without saying a word, crossed the road and walked cautiously behind the house from which the chiselling sounds came. Sure enough, as they rounded the corner of the house, they saw a man working hard, with a small pile of stones scattered around him. Furthermore, they saw beyond the man, a body clothed in white, lying in a large opening in the grassy bank. The man looked up and immediately fear crossed his face. Peter strode forward and assured the man they were friends of Jesus and that no one knew they were there. Peter managed to calm the man down until he eventually allowed them to see the body closely and help him to prepare it for a decent burial. Kit remembers distinctly how remarkable it was that the body had not decayed in any way. They sat Jesus up and pulled slithers of wood out of his back and arms. They then took the rest of the thorns out of his forehead and hair and washed his face and body. (As Kit was remembering all this, tears were rolling down her face while she relived the terrible pain and stress of the moment.) The man had already changed the dirty old sheet that Jesus had been wrapped in for a clean, white tunic.

When the three of them were satisfied that Jesus' body was prepared as they felt was his due, Peter spoke with the man. He conveyed to him that Jesus' mother should be allowed to see her son before they closed the tomb. The man became fearful again and refused permission. However, Peter spoke in a gentle, persuasive manner with him and finally he gave in. Peter ran back to the original tomb as fast as he could, to fetch Mary and bring her to her son's body.

Meanwhile, back at the tomb, Mary and Andrew were waiting anxiously. Mary peered into the empty tomb, telling Andrew she had seen what she presumed was candlelight coming from the entrance. However, when she got inside she saw no candle had been left, and she concluded that the light she had seen must have been emanating from around her son.

Shortly after this, Mary and Andrew heard a whole lot of footsteps and quite a commotion coming from the direction of path A. She and Andrew sat in front of the tomb to wait. It turned out to be a few disciples, Mary Magdalene and a few other interested parties. The Virgin Mary pointed at the tomb and simply said, 'He's gone.'

She felt she could not say more because if she told them where Peter and Kit had gone, they would all rush after them and she might lose Jesus' body forever. It was at this moment that Mary Magdalene, who had really not wanted to believe that Jesus was dead, began the rumour of Jesus' resurrection that has lasted for over 2000 years. (This is further explained in Chapter 15.) The Virgin Mary, in her fear and desire to protect her son's body, did not dispute it.

From the Mary Weekend

As the Marys together felt into the moment outside the tomb, they all agreed to having experienced the feeling of how Mary nearly passed out and everything then became too much for her.

One of the Marys walked with me not long after and told me that she relives the desperate fear and feeling of guilt that Mary experienced at that moment, regularly. Her journey in this life is to release the guilt and fear for the soul group, understanding now that Mary was completely overcome with emotion and should be forgiven for keeping the truth to herself and allowing a false story to rise from the situation.

A second Mary told me she felt like she lived in a bottleneck. She was afraid to move forward into 'service' but, for the same reason, felt she couldn't go backwards in case she was asked to do a similar service to the one she performed at the time of Jesus. Either way, she was terrified of being asked to suffer in the same way again. I pointed out to her that she would never have to do the same again but that true service meant that she must be prepared to do whatever was asked of her, no strings attached. I also said that the only reason she suffered so much was because, after Jesus died, she tried to continue out of her own strength instead of keeping attuned to the Source within. If she had stayed attuned, she would not have suffered nearly so much. She managed to let go of her fears a few hours later.

A third Mary was having problems with her heart. At the time, she was living with her daughter who was a part of the soul group belonging to Jesus' little sister. This daughter kept prompting her just by 'being'. As this third Mary unveiled the truth within her struggling heart, she realised she had already let go of the grief around Jesus' death but had not released the pain of losing herself, Mary, after his death. In that loss, she was only vaguely aware of the rest of her family and certainly in no fit state to see that she was making their path so much harder. As she came to realise what she had done, she asked forgiveness for all the pain she had caused to friends and family both then and since. As forgiveness came, the knowledge of how much she was loved by them all came back to her and she remembered she was loved as much as Jesus. She recognised that their sacrifice, though they had different outcomes, had been of equal importance.

**

Upon reaching Mary and Andrew at the tomb, Peter had to explain to Andrew that he could not accompany him and Mary as he had made a promise to a man that must be kept. So, leaving Andrew behind, he and Mary made their way back along path B to the house where Jesus' body lay.

Mary, Peter, Kit and the man wept together for a while before closing the tomb and putting stones and grass roots in the gap that had been dug out of the bank. They cleverly made it look as if it had never been dug out. Then the four of them swore each other to secrecy, knowing that if anyone else ever found out then there was a high chance his body would be tampered with. The four of them went to their death with this secret in their hearts.

More from the Mary Weekend

One of the Marys was having a bout of depression. Upon looking into it, she felt Mary had gone off alone for a while after sealing

Jesus in the second tomb. She strove to put the thoughts of Jesus and what he had been through out of her mind but in doing so went a little bit crazy. Many of the Marys agreed with this and a few had been along that road in this life.

Another Mary confided that she resonated with Mary's entire journey but in particular had felt like she held a massive secret all her life. As she now understood the secret, she felt able to let the feeling go.

After Jesus' death, Mary had asked herself: 'Why did this happen?' and on the cross Jesus had asked himself: 'Why was this happening?' What is clear to us now is that Mary and Jesus made the same sacrifice but it played out in a very different way for each of them. Mary said, 'Thy will be done' at Jesus' conception and her life was one of unconditional love. Jesus said, 'Thy will be done' on the cross, and his life too was one of unconditional love.

***

A few centuries later, a member of Mary's soul group was drawn to live at the very house connected to the tomb that Jesus had been buried in the second time. As she randomly pulled a stone out of the bank one day, a light like the one she had seen shine out from the first tomb, shone out at her. She sensed immediately that she must investigate further and, as she pulled out further stones, she found Jesus' bones and the white tunic they had put him in as they prepared him for his burial. In her heart, she knew exactly what she had found.

13
The Ascension

The following memory was gifted to me one night, many years ago now, as I lay lightly asleep in bed. I became 'as Jesus' once more and experienced the following as he had, not long after he died.

Over the days following his death, Jesus watched all his loved ones closely from spirit. He saw they were lost and frightened. He was desperate to convey to them that he was still around and they could talk to him. They simply didn't know how. He decided to come close to earth and found he was able to use the body of one of his followers to incarnate himself for a short while. From the borrowed body, he began to teach and reassure those who were nearby. He then left the body and watched again. Over the next few weeks, he borrowed a body several times in several different places, trying to encourage everyone and reassure them he had not left them.

Then, one day, he realised he had overdone his appearances and they were all beginning to ask each other if they knew where Jesus was going to pop up next. They all wanted to see him and were impatient to know where he might be found. No one wanted to miss the opportunity to see him. Jesus set out to rectify his mistake. He put into the hearts of all who were asking for him: 'If you want to find me, I will be in such and such a place at such and such a time. Come and find me there.'

Of course, that is exactly what they wanted to hear so they all made their way to this place, early one morning. As they approached the designated spot, they could see a clear, bright, see-through, gold shape ahead of them which looked a little like a doorway with rounded upper corners and which came to a point at the top. Jesus' energy was within a light body, inside the gold shape. (The shape is the same as found in many doorways in churches today.)

As each of his 'friends' approached, Jesus laid forgiveness at their feet, knowing they were not in the right state of mind to receive it there and then, but leaving it for them to pick up when they were ready. Then he spoke to each of them in their hearts: 'I am going to leave you now. If you want to find me, look within your hearts.' He then let them watch him rise up slowly into the clouds and disappear from their sight.

His plan worked. The disciples, followers, friends, family and all those who had been searching for him stopped looking for another incarnated appearance and began to look inside themselves for his teaching.

14

John the Baptist and his Mother, Elizabeth

I have pieced the story of Elizabeth together from three different people. I have given two of them labels, one being Fay and the other being Bay.

Elizabeth knew she would have a child long before she actually became pregnant, even though she was traditionally beyond child-bearing age. When she first held her son in her arms, she intuitively knew she would lose him one day. She was, in that moment, filled with dread and fear. In order to overcome her fears, she later convinced herself that it would be her cousin Mary's child who would die. Her own son would be OK. After all, why would she have a son so late in life if only to lose him? She did not wish to believe this could be possible.

Fay imparted the following to me: she (Fay) was a friend of a woman in this life who was from the soul group of Elizabeth. They had known each other since before their children were born and virtually brought them up together after they were born. Over the years, Fay had often found herself in places where she noticed there were pictures of John the Baptist, such as on TV or in a stately home or museum. One big house had a picture of a scene where Salome demanded John's head on a plate. She had asked herself at the time: 'Why would you put that up in your house?' From this, Fay always had the idea that John's death had been a party trick.

When I told her who I thought she had been 2000 years ago, she talked of this with me and took herself back into her life at the time of being a friend of Elizabeth. She found it hard to believe the rumours circulating that John had had his head cut off so she decided to go and see for herself if what was being said was true. She travelled a long distance to where the truth could be discovered and was really frightened of going back to Elizabeth when she found he had indeed died. Fay was filled with shock, a sense of injustice, a feeling of failure, helplessness and a hatred of Salome.

In this life, her soul had been trying to get her back in touch with these deep emotions which is why she had kept coming across the pictures everywhere. She didn't realise, until the moment I talked with her, that she needed to forgive Salome, let go of the hatred and release her own emotions at the same time.

When Bay came to see me, instantaneously we both felt she was from Elizabeth's soul group. She held emotions from the following aspect of Elizabeth's life. Having lived a life of denial, Elizabeth could not understand why the two boys, Jesus and John, had differing outcomes to their lives. John had given his life to the cause and so had Jesus. Why, therefore, did Jesus have all the recognition and John none? As she saw it, John was known for being beheaded and Jesus was the seeming 'saviour'.

Bay carried this jealousy in her soul. She needed to understand that John had chosen *out of his own strength* to put himself in this position, took the risks and was arrested and beheaded for it. Jesus was *intuitively guided* to put himself in this position and he chose to listen and go ahead with it. When Bay understood the difference, she was able to let go of her jealousy, anger, sorrow and shame that her son had been taken for a 'party trick'.

John the Baptist

When John was a small baby, he was taken to the temple to be anointed. He was handed to an elderly rabbi who held him cradled in his arms. The rabbi had anointed many babies before but, as he held John close to his body, he was immediately strangely affected by him. This baby seemed somehow wiser than him and he exuded a peaceful, loving, gentle energy. The rabbi was shaken and puzzled by what he was feeling. How could this be possible? How could a baby be wiser than he?

He managed to anoint the baby John but felt uneasy all the way through the ceremony until he handed the infant back. For the rest of his life, he recalled what had happened but could find no answer. On every occasion, he had to speak before people he felt to be inadequate and shallow. He knew there was more ... but how to find it?

When this same rabbi came and spoke with me, I revealed his past life and that the baby he had held was John the Baptist. I was able to tell him that the answer he was looking for was in his heart and that he should have the courage to look for his own inner truth and learn to trust it. This poor man had only ever believed he lived from others' wisdom and the teaching he had been indoctrinated in, and his lack of self-worth has prevented him going into his heart. Now that he has been reconnected with the memory of holding John in his arms and of how that felt, he has an opportunity to change and follow his own intuition.

John and Jesus both had specific jobs to accomplish. John's was to help prepare the region for the coming of Jesus and this role was established before he was born. The two saw each other fairly regularly as children. They had an unspoken kinship but John, despite being the older one, always felt the lesser of the two. At the age of 12, Jesus moved out of John's life for a long time and John grew up using what he termed as his 'limited' gifts. He had a following but always referred to someone who was greater than him.

When John saw Jesus coming towards him at the river's edge, he was busy helping people forgive themselves for their past misdemeanours and encouraging them to turn over a new leaf. He used water as symbolism for washing away their past. (It's interesting to note that the soul who shared this information with me described Roman soldiers coming to be baptised by John.)

When Jesus drew close enough, John said to him, 'You don't need this!' But Jesus replied along these lines, 'I am the same as everyone else and I wish to be part of what you are doing.' Jesus then bathed in the water alongside others and, as he came out, John saw a massive light around him. John then knew this was the time for Jesus to start his ministry and he announced to everyone, 'This is the one I've been talking about.' After that, many followed and listened to Jesus but also many stayed with John.

* * *

Years later, when John found himself imprisoned alongside others, his beheading came as a complete shock to him. He was, at that time, a being on earth who was one of the closest to understanding what Jesus came to do. The darker forces recognised John could be a future danger and used Salome to bring about the death of the one whom they feared.

One evening, he was suddenly removed from his cell, taken out into a courtyard and… It all happened so quickly. He found himself looking down at his own body from spirit in complete shock. He saw his body being kicked around by soldiers like a football. He was hardly aware that his head was not attached. Then he watched his body being wrapped up and put with other bodies.

A lady, Pam, came to see me who was partnered in this life with a man who she recognised as being the soldier who cut off John's head. On tuning in to her partner, we felt his anguish as he realised there was something wrong about what he had done. His eyes had met John's just before he brought down the axe and he became aware of John's innocence. Afterwards, he could not come to terms with what had happened and has been trying ever since to find forgiveness. Shortly after Pam remembered her past life as part of John's soul group, she experienced a blood clot at the back of her head which gave her a stroke. She knew it was related to her past life memory and, at that point, her partner of many years took off without a word and left her. He had not been able to cope with the energy she was emanating and the reminder it produced. Five years later, Pam is now ready to understand and forgive him for what he did so that they can both move on.

Words from Jesus in Spirit to John

'I am so sorry, my friend, that I was unable to be there for you. You did so much for me and I am so grateful. I am so sorry that it ended in the way it did for you. Let go of the anger that is festering in you. Be at peace, my friend. All will be well.' (This was a promise received by a soul from the John the Baptist group as he called for help in his anguish. The frustration in this soul was coming to a head at this time.)

John understood Jesus as very few did at the time. He was someone to whom Jesus was most grateful. While the removal of his head was indeed symbolic, he did not deserve this. While history has put a different slant on the story of John, he was in fact a true carrier of the light. He surrendered to the light as totally as he could at the time. After his death, he felt unrecognised, unseen and disbelieved. The anger became trapped inside him and it has been bubbling underneath ever since. The main question within him was: 'Why was I not heard?'

***

Tammy came to see me because she thought her third eye was damaged; it was painful and it stopped her functioning properly. She also told me she thought she was from the soul group of John the Baptist. On tuning in, I saw she was indeed from the John soul group and had been watching the crucifixion from spirit. I saw her above Jesus as he hung on the cross and when I started to describe his point of doubt, she suddenly said to me, 'It all felt so pointless. Why was it happening? What was it all about?'

The energy she was giving off in that moment was like a replication of what I had known when I had gone into the Jesus experience. I was astonished. I then realised Tammy had got stuck in that moment. Above the cross, she had felt remorse, guilt, fear, anger and failure and had never seen beyond it. Those emotions had got stuck in her third eye because she got lost in feeling she had failed Jesus and that, because of her, he had been killed.

When Tammy understood that all that had happened had been a resounding success, she began the process of clearing her third eye; first forgiving herself and others, and then releasing the stuck emotions from within it.

A different soul, Max, describes John's anger as he watched the crucifixion from spirit. Through Max's eyes, we were shown a jealous man who saw that Jesus at his death was revered, recognised and loved by a massive crowd of people, whereas John went to his death in a prison environment, with no recognition and indeed being ridiculed when his head was presented on a plate at the dinner. Given that he believed before they were born that they would begin their journey as equals, this was very difficult for him to stomach. On reincarnating since, his belief has always been confirmed by the fact that Jesus has been remembered everywhere and he himself has had comparatively little recognition. I have found with several members of John's soul group that they have got stuck on this, together with some of Tammy's story, and it has yet to be fully overcome.

15
Gabriel

The energy that makes up the Gabriel soul group does not incarnate as often on earth as others but resides mostly in the outer echelons of earth where there is little to disturb it. As Jesus was born into troubled times on this planet, energy from the Gabriel soul group drew closer to earth to help redress the balance. It felt a push to bring the joyous news to earth by presenting itself to any soul who was open enough to receive the knowledge. Its actions helped to ensure that the moment of Jesus' birth was duly celebrated and did not go unnoticed.

Gabriel souls tend to keep themselves well hidden. As they have not incarnated very often, they still feel a deep over-responsibility for earth's livelihood. One such soul described her unhealed feelings within as follows:

- I have broad shoulders; I can take anything.
- I am a balancer.
- I feel responsible for everyone.
- I am in touch with my inner wisdom.
- I struggle to accept the limitations of my body.
- I have an importance.
- I have an agenda to fulfil.
- When a shift is happening on earth, I am present.

The souls I have met who stem from Gabriel seem to stubbornly hold on to their egoic importance, which is of great sadness as there is so much more they could give to the world at this time.

At the crucifixion, one particular Gabriel soul told me he felt he had misread what was actually happening, decided the soul group had not called on Source enough for help and became too embroiled in what was going on. This action has led to much imbalance within the soul group today.

16
Mary Magdalene

That Mary Magdalene loved Jesus with all her heart, there can be no doubt. Was she a prostitute? Probably not, as we know prostitutes today. But it is inwardly felt she slept around in her search for a 'love' that she believed lay outside of herself. Members of her soul group tend to be more comfortable around men and not comfortable with the feminine within. Therefore, today's version of the soul group unfortunately believes she holds or comes from a strong male energy field.

On the very first occasion Mary Magdalene saw Jesus, she felt deep excitement as she felt his presence pass about one foot away from her and, in that moment, she knew she had to follow him and be as close to him as she possibly could. Her life totally changed. Before she met him, she had always felt in control of her emotions; after she met him, she felt she had lost control. She followed him along with the disciples because of her deep need to be near him, giving him all the attention she could.

I have met a large number of souls from this soul group and there are many common denominators between them, the most common being a confusion or twist in their character. Angie aptly puts this into two sentences for us, 'The confusion within Mary Magdalene lies in the difference between unconditional love and passion. She mistook the unconditional love she received from Jesus for a personal love for herself.'

What follows is an attempt to understand this confusion or twist by some of those who have come to see me. At one point, five from the soul group met together for a weekend and, over that time, thrashed out how they felt, how they remembered the lifetime and awoke the truth in each other, finding common denominators and therefore harmony between them.

Angie's Account

Angie is one of the five souls who met in an attempt to heal themselves and help their soul group. The following words are hers.

In order to unveil the confusion in my heart, I have had to face the discomfort and embarrassment of how I have acted in the past. Not only do I carry the memory of the Mary Magdalene story because it is in my energy field, but I have always wanted to be 'the special one'. I have lived, yearning to be in a space where I am held by someone else, blocking out the rest of the world as if nothing else exists and thus pursuing a fantasy land.

This is my recall of Mary's life: I was a young girl looking constantly outside myself for a love that I felt would complete me. I was attracting men who appeared full of light and, when I was with them, I would feel light too and that I could do or be anything I wanted. It was an addictive feeling that made me feel strong and full of life. When those men were gone, I couldn't grasp that light fully in me anymore and I became lost and enveloped in a deep sadness. I therefore went searching for more light, believing it came from outside me.

In Jesus, I found the strongest light I had ever known. When I was with him, it seemed as if the whole world sang. I clung to him, desperately wanting him to love me more than anyone else. When I was not in his presence, I seemed to lose any feeling of light. Therefore, I wanted to be 'the one', to be special, to be his muse. The longing for his love made me look for ways to make him want me. When Jesus died, it felt like the chance to become light had been taken away from me. I felt cheated.

Letting the dream go was hard because it felt so good, but I acknowledged it was a trap. However, one day in this life, as I was relaxing in my sitting room, I suddenly realised that this story was so much bigger than just me and Jesus. I also acknowledged that to desire to be loved by Jesus, above all else, was not pure love, and to possess that for myself would be harmful to others and would also deprive others.

I had to let go of the need for Jesus to love me more than anyone else. His love is boundless and can heal us all. It can never be harnessed to one person for it is the Christ consciousness. What I was hanging on to was limiting me and therefore the world. I finally accepted that the myth I had created could only ever fall short because it was built on conditional, not unconditional, love.

All my lifetimes, I had always looked for my light in others, never able to accept that the light was already within my own heart. I had lived like a moth to a flame, unable to let the myth go. But Jesus knew that all of us deserve love equally—that no one is more deserving than anyone else. Until each member of Mary Magdalene's soul group lets go of these needs and disbeliefs, she will only ever be 'playing the part' of one who loves unconditionally, all the while having a very subtle personal motivation to be seen, to be loved, to feel worthy of love and/or to feel special.

Thank you, Angie. What you have so bravely shared here is a massive opportunity for others from the soul group who are reading this to face and heal themselves.

***

The following was written by a lady, Gail, who visited me regularly for a few years. I have chosen to include this piece, which was written in anger before Gail understood *why* she felt this way and was able to heal herself. Her words express the opposite extreme that lies within this soul group, and this unhealed area is clearly driving the unhealthy actions of other members of her soul group who still carry this inner misery.

There was only one person I was interested in and who I wanted to spend time with. Jesus brought out my passion, wisdom, love, and made me feel connected to myself. When I was not in his presence,

I felt a deep sense of isolation and felt unable to live fully. He made me feel dependent, needy and as if my happiness was tied to his existence. The rejection of my advances in any context felt like he was deliberately causing my suffering.

My isolation and anger were at the forefront of my emotions. Had I not helped him? Had I not softened him? Yet he rejected me. I had given up friends and family to be with him. It was a lonely, lonely road. I was the only woman in a sea of men, and my needs were unmet. I followed him blindly and yet he rejected me. I could not see or feel his love, only separation. I felt like a pawn in his plan.

He refused to show the world the beauty of the divine coupling with a woman. Why did he not take me as his and show the world that women are necessary and to be respected? He could have shown that we women matter, that we have value and that together we can be divine. His rejection of me has had deep consequences for he has angered and offended me.

Why did he ask me to follow him and then proceed to take away everything I had? His death left me devastated and my soul has not recovered. I do not understand why he did this to me; why he made me suffer, why he left me or why he did not save himself to be with me. I have ached for him. I have wanted him to connect me with God and to elevate me to the divine. Anger has eaten me up and the frustration of it all has sapped my strength. Clarity, wisdom and love were only present in me when he was with me.

She recalls the following yearning in her heart after Jesus' death:

I do not know who I am without you.

I am not whole without you.

I am incapable without you.

I am lonely, frightened and exhausted without you.

I am only half of me without you.

I cannot live without you.

Gail and I had a further conversation a few months after she wrote the above. Gail felt Mary Magdalene and Jesus never made love. She feels that a huge part of Mary's problem is that she does not want to accept this. I explained to her that a fully self-realised soul cannot love one above another for it knows everything and everyone is equal. Thus it was with Jesus.

Mary Magdalene's Soul on the Road to Healing

A lady who I could describe as half-awake to all of the above, who does not run away from her connection to the soul group but chooses to remain trapped by the twist, experiences the following:

> I live in the anguish of my unrequited love.
> I am so bad.
> I can never live happily again.
> I must punish myself.

This woman, Beth, has punished herself by filling her body with pain until she cannot walk comfortably or function normally. It is difficult for her to find rest.

***

What follows are some further thoughts Beth's soul conveyed to me in my sleep while spending a few nights at the retreat:

> He died ... I didn't. (*He was the good one and she was imperfect, so she believed.*)
> He suffered ... I didn't. (*Guilt*)
> He took the blame ... I didn't.
> It should have been me ... He is innocent.
> I must now bear his pain alone.
> I must suffer.
> I feel ugly.
> I should not be happy or enjoy myself.
> I am so angry. (*at myself*)
> The pain and hurt ... They are unbearable.

These thoughts gave this particular aspect of Mary Magdalene no rest. Beth told me that these expressions continually repeat in this life.

**

Further thoughts, taken from the five souls who met together but containing much input from others too, are those that tend to dog each aspect of the soul until acceptance and release occur, as collated below.

With reference to the need to feel special when Jesus was alive, it was felt that in this century it had become an addiction, more prominent in some than others but always present in some form or another. Mary Magdalene believed she needed to be special to Jesus. There was a desire to *make* him love her. She would fantasise that the acts of kindness and consideration he showed her were because he loved her as much as she loved him. She felt in awe of him and yet also experienced extreme excitement when he was near her.

Mary Magdalene wanted to tend to Jesus' every need, as a woman. It had to be her. Her need for the proverbial fairy story to be true was, and still is, in many parts of her soul group, absolute. One lady described her life as being one long search for a man who lived up to who she felt Jesus had been to her, and of course no one had been good enough. This lady now knows that the relationship she is looking for is already deep in her own heart.

In the courtroom at the end of his life, Mary Magdalene knew that the moment the wonderful message 'We believe in you' was sent through her, she was in a state of pure unconditional love. As she connected with Jesus' misery and pain, the aligned part of her heart reached out to him. (It was less clear whether she knew how healing her message was in that moment.)

However, she later persuaded herself that she was cheated, as putting herself on the line in that way was seemingly not reciprocated. She had wanted a reward for 'being with him every step of the way'. Her inner anger over this is still an unhealed trait. As Jesus died, Mary Magdalene felt she had been abandoned, rejected and even forgotten by her love. A deep sorrow and numbness crept over her as the inner turmoil became too much for her to bear. She felt her association to Jesus was deeper and more painful than anyone else's because she had loved him more. She experienced deep anger that she had not been enough reason for him to stay. She found it impossible to accept that she had not got what she wanted from the relationship.

She anguished: 'Why am I not enough reason for him to stay? Why does he not stop this charade and save himself? Why does he allow the authorities to treat him in such a brutal way?' She could not grasp that Jesus' love was unconditional while hers was conditional. His death seemed to be such an injustice and one that she had not prepared herself for.

One woman agonised over the following:

> When Jesus died I felt like my heart had been stolen out of me and so I could no longer be my true self. Part of me believes Jesus left because of me, because I did something wrong, because I couldn't accept that he couldn't be with me. I cannot feel angry at Jesus because I love him but all this now creates a twist to help me avoid the shame, unworthiness and anger within me.

When one understands the deep unbalanced anguish that lies in the members of Mary Magdalene's soul group and the turmoil that has lain in Mary Magdalene's heart since the crucifixion, it is no wonder that the unhealed soul is struggling to face or unearth the truth in the 21st century. But, most sadly of all, in front of the tomb, these imbalances caused Mary Magdalene to initiate the story that Jesus had risen from the dead.

As she stood looking into the empty tomb that morning, she was unbelievably shocked and horrified. But, as a woman so deeply in love is always more open, she very quickly became aware of a swift visitation by Jesus' soul. She felt his presence a few feet from her and saw him with her inner eye. As she wanted him to be alive more than anything else in the world at that moment, and in subconsciously needing to relieve the pain, she burst unwittingly into her own fantasy and called out, 'He is alive. He is risen from the dead!'

In that moment, she created a myth that her 'love' had been returned to her. She fantasised that she would be able to experience his wonderful presence once more. Her balance felt restored and was further confirmed when he 'appeared' to others in the following days.

Fabrication

One lady told me that, for certain members of the soul group, in not accepting the physical death of Jesus, they were able to keep the fantasy alive. They didn't want to let the fantasy die; they don't want to even now—the grip is still tight.

A further reflection from another member of the soul group came thus:

> Mary Magdalene felt like a slighted woman after Jesus died. The situation couldn't be truthfully resolved and she was angry about being left in that position. She created and has subsequently created so many lies about herself and Jesus in order to justify her position and make herself feel better about herself.

It is true to say that countless stories have since been related by various souls who have not faced the part of themselves that mourns or even accepts his death. Many accounts have appeared in book form and it is interesting to note that the authors of these stories do not relate the same details. Some details are so laughably different that the mistruths behind them all are now beginning to become apparent. There are souls who are still so strongly resonating with the pain that they try to persuade others that she and Jesus were equals and that she must now be the one they turn to.

The Truth

As the five souls who had gathered to share the truth of Mary Magdalene's story that lay within them, brought their meeting to a close, I suddenly felt an urge to share the moments I had experienced when the two separate individuals caused me to bring up the uncontrollable deep grief of Jesus from within my core. (See Chapter 5 on the Jewish priest and the record keeper.) As I did so, the incredibly deep pain the soul group of Jesus carried became alive in front of them. I heard myself saying, *The myth of Jesus' resurrection that Mary Magdalene created was taken up by others at the tomb in their hours of pain and has now become the supposed truth throughout the world. Mother Mary also did nothing to dispute what Mary Magdalene had said at the time in her fear that her beloved son's body would be found. Between them they caused a myth that went on to be misleading and the truth of his real mission became blurred and tainted.*

There was a short pause. I took a deep breath, 'The pain and deep sadness of all the "supposed" friends, who turned their back on him, is beyond words.' As my words, which in that moment held the tangible energy of the pain, sank in around the room; there was a completely stunned silence.

After a while, one lady said, in a state of shock, 'So the very man we loved so much and wanted to protect has been sorely let down by us.' Another said, 'We are not special. He chose everyone.' A third said, 'We betrayed Jesus and he was the source of hope.'

In the silence, the ugliness of all they had held onto within the soul group was realised. Each of the five souls experienced deep healing and for them the fight was over. It became a moment of extreme joy and relief. It was a moment that held both sadness and joy in the same expression. It was a turning point in history.

These souls were now free to relive the moment in front of the tomb, knowing that, were it to happen today, they would not have created such a myth. Safe in this knowledge, they could therefore ask for forgiveness and release the fear, sadness, remorse, feeling of betrayal, vulnerability, shame, guilt, regret and anger that had lain inside them for so long. This is true of all members of the soul group who wish to make amends for the damage done.

***

Various members of the soul group have stated feeling the following about Mary as she lived on, 'I believe Mary Magdalene lived an uneventful life after he died with bitter, helpless, unresolved feelings swirling round inside her.' Another said Mary had felt she must carry on the work, for she had a duty for which she was now responsible. Several said they felt strongly that Mary, in her delusion, had always felt that, had he lived, they would have been man and wife.

A Final Word from Angie

Angie came to see me on this occasion as she wanted to understand the connection she had with her husband in this life. It transpired that he had been a Roman soldier in the year Jesus was crucified and had met Mary Magdalene soon after Jesus had died. He had fallen deeply in love with her and, while he knew nothing of Jesus' death before he met her, he soon learned about Jesus from this woman who he adored. The more he learned, the more he told himself he could never be forgiven for being a Roman soldier and part of a force that had put Jesus, this obviously innocent man, to death. The pain in him grew and was made greater by the fact that he could not win his woman. This aspect of Mary agreed to meet him in this life in order to help him heal. As soon as she remembered the agreement they had made between them before they had incarnated in this lifetime, she forgave him and asked for healing to be sent into the crack in his soul that was badly damaged. After this was sent, she felt enormous relief and as if her duty towards him was now complete. It has yet to be seen whether he will pick up her gift in this life.

Another lady also connected with an aspect of the Roman soldier in this life. Their agreement before they incarnated was that they would meet, fall in love and replay the lack of attention Mary gave the Roman soldier in her blind love for Jesus, while he would help her burst the bubble of the longing for the fairy story she held within her to be true. This has successfully been done.

***

In incarnations in following centuries, the Mary Magdalene soul has found it difficult to distinguish between the truth and the long-held twist. Sometimes I have seen that, when someone approaches their truth, the soul throws up a smoke screen, as Mary did at the tomb. I met a lady who was in spirit at the time of Jesus. When I shared with her what I knew, her 'twist' dropped away with no difficulty as her heart recognised what she had witnessed from spirit. She found it more difficult to let go of 'needing to be special' and finding the 'man in her life that would make her whole', but I suspect she will let go in due course as her heart is true.

In the last few decades particularly, some parts of the soul group who represent the incarnated side have created many different variations of the truth that it wished had been, such as:

> Jesus didn't really die.
> He went into a deep sleep and later woke from it.
> Someone swapped another body with his, either on the cross or afterwards.
> Jesus lived in hiding for the rest of his life and had children with Mary. They lived here, there and everywhere...
> So and so feels s/he is the son or daughter of Mary and Jesus.
> And so on...

The troubled soul has an inner knowing that the time of reckoning is approaching and it seems to have been throwing as much dust into the world's eyes as it can muster. When I first came across these fabrications, I was very honest with myself and began by wondering if there was something massive that I had missed in my understanding. I perused one of the texts three times and on the third time through, the universe woke me to the flaws in what was written and I reconnected with the truth. At that point, the deep pain within the Jesus soul group became active in me. It has increased slowly over time until it came finally to a head a few years ago. Some of the pain Jesus suffered because the truth about his real journey has not been truthfully represented became very deep in me, and was released through me as follows.

As I experienced the above, the universe built a further series of circumstances around me that caused me to feel the pain of all the misunderstandings that Jesus experienced, at its harshest. I could also feel pain, not just in the Mary Magdalene soul group, but in all those other beings who had been present. The pain seemed to be present in everyone and everything. It was in the land, in the buildings, in the ether … I asked how it could ever possibly be overcome or released. As I admitted to the strength of the pain in Jesus and forgave all who had misrepresented him, the pain started to slowly melt away. I lay still, knowing I could do nothing. I was simply a vessel that was being used to pass the emotions through, in order to release them. As the pain diminished, I felt my soul being drawn (at a snail's pace) from the tomb, above Jerusalem to where it had been after Jesus' death. It was during the dark of night and the stars and a new moon were out. I saw little lights shining amongst the houses and I could just discern some rooftops peeping out from the shadows. I saw Jerusalem exactly as Jesus had seen it from spirit. I then felt that the painful energy had released from the soul group. At the same time, I felt the energy driven primarily by fear, created all those years ago, release from Jerusalem and dissipate. I knew in that moment that the old town of Jerusalem would fundamentally never be the same again.

The new Jerusalem is here. It is in our hearts. As we relinquish the hold our own fears from the Split have woven into our fabric, and that we replayed at the time of Jesus, we bring the gift of enlightenment ever closer to our core.

Jerusalem Hymn

And did those feet in ancient time
Walk upon England's mountain green?
And was the holy Lamb of God
On England's pleasant pastures seen?
And did the countenance divine
Shine forth upon our clouded hills?
And was Jerusalem builded here
Among those dark satanic mills?
Bring me my bow of burning gold!
Bring me my arrows of desire!
Bring me my spear! O clouds, unfold!
Bring me my chariot of fire!
I will not cease from mental fight,
Nor shall my sword sleep in my hand,
Till we have built Jerusalem
In England's green and pleasant land.
[William Blake, 1804]

17
Who am I?

Over the years, I have come to know that I was also a part of the soul group of Jesus that incarnated at the time he did. I believe I may have been Egyptian, and at the time of Jesus' arrest I was a merchant travelling through Jerusalem, who sold cloth. Some of my story has been written under the Bartholomew section, which you will have already read, so I will only repeat a little of it here to reset the context.

I was in the downstairs room of a house one day, with all my cloth spread out in front of a customer, when I glanced up and saw a huge number of people going past the window. As I caught a glimpse of Jesus carrying the cross, I saw his inner light and it resonated with something deep within my heart. I left the pieces of cloth exactly where they were and ran out of the shop door. I looked up the street to the left where I had seen Jesus pass. He was out of sight due to the crowds surrounding him. I followed the crowds, feeling driven to know who this man was. That he was the light there was not a doubt, but why was he being crucified?

As the crowds reached the outskirts of Jerusalem, I had caught up with Jesus and I followed him up to the place where he was to be crucified. I had no eyes at all for the two criminals beside him who were also to be crucified. I watched at a distance while the preparations took place and then saw him being hoisted up on the cross. I wanted to ask someone who this man was, but I knew no one and there were so many Roman soldiers around that I felt hesitant.

I stood in the middle of the crowds. Jesus was high in the air where we could all see him. He was wrapped in a dirty old sheet-like thing which was a rusty, muddy reddish-brown. His long, wavy hair was very dirty and of a mid-brown colour, hanging below his shoulders. His face was gaunt and thin, covered in blood and mud. His head hung to his right with his face pointing downwards.

I picked up the thoughts of those around me as they raced through the crowd. Questions and comments arose, such as:

> This is beyond comprehension. Why would anyone do this to themselves?
> How can this be right?
> I don't understand why you have got yourself into this mess.
> Are you going to get yourself out of the mess?
> You could have avoided all this.

Such thoughts in some part help us to understand why no one jumped to Jesus' aid. Many thought he had brought this on himself to teach us something and were expecting him to put it right. I myself did not know what to think, other than my whole soul was shouting at me that there was a huge mystery here and this man in front of me was innocent.

After Jesus died, I was questioned like many others, 'Did you know this man?' I said, 'No.' But my heart said the opposite. Somehow, though I didn't actively know him, I did know him! I recognised him and felt a deep kinship with him. He felt like family. It was at this point I felt driven to start asking questions to try and find out who Jesus had been.

When Bartholomew took me under his wing, I was so grateful. I had no inkling that he was doing it for his own reasons and not particularly to help me. When he felt in his heart that he should go along to the Ascension, he asked if I would like to go too. Of course I was keen to go, knowing nothing of the 'inner invitations' that Jesus sent out from spirit.

As we approached the place where Jesus had taken a light body, there were already a number of people gathered. I recognised some of the people I had questioned and who had spurned me, so I kept a low profile. Everyone was quiet, standing in front of 'Jesus' in what seemed to me like awe. He cast his gaze slowly over us all.

When Jesus' attention came to me, of course I had no history with him from that life. But he recognised that as I had stood at the cross I was a soul who selflessly gave my life into service, just after he died, so he left in front of me the gift of discernment. He knew I would pick it up one day, when the time was right.

***

Twenty or more years ago, I was coming down the staircase in my house when I heard the word 'discernment' in my head. I went outside my house and thought about this word. I did not know exactly what it meant so I went back inside and looked it up in the dictionary. As I came to understand the word, I wondered why I had heard it. I was soon to learn because from that day onwards, I had the most amazing ability to discern truth from fiction. This gift has been well used, as thousands today can testify to. It seems I was always destined to incarnate during the Second Coming, in order to discern the truth for us all, as best I can.

Today, as my work on this topic comes into its final stages, I know that my yearning to do something for 'the true Church' has been granted. I had always thought I would maybe help at a Sunday school or do a reading, and from there might be able to bring a little light to the people I made contact with. I never dreamed I would be asked to be part of something like this. I now understand why all the doors were closed to me when I attempted to 'fit in' with the Church as it stood. There had always been a greater hope or divine plan that I would evolve enough to be used on a much larger scale. However, I know I have quite a way to journey as yet and that thought is exciting.

Through all Jesus' experiences in the last week of his life, he was slowly being broken down until he reached the isolated space from which the Split could be reversed. When he was in the courtroom, outside energy gave what he needed to recover, for the words 'We believe in you' brought him back on track. However, as he hung on the cross, and he hit his deepest fear (born of the ego) once more, no outside influence would pull him back. On this occasion, he did it by himself. He, *alone and isolated*, let go of his fear and trusted within once more. If we are to fully heal from the Split, we have to be able to do the same. When I went through the experience on the cross, I called for help from outside. Geoff came and put his hands on me and I recovered. If I had gone within and asked for that help, it would have come. I pray that I and many others will find the courage, the presence of mind and the trust that he found, long ago, in order to fully heal ourselves.

This book is a platform from which the truth of who Jesus was and what he did can grow. Others will crack open their own truth as they read, and more and more mistruths will become revealed and released. I rejoice that this is just the beginning, but from this platform I pray that the maximum healing be achieved in the future.

More than this, let this be the beginning of finding the truth of other great teachers such as Buddha, Mohammed, Ramakrishna and others. Like Jesus, they were not perfect, but they brought the truth through in the best way they could at the time. They were never supposed to be emulated and religions were not meant to be built on them; these men were simply incarnated empty vessels of truth with a job to do. Many came before them and many came and are coming after them.

18

Jesus at Work in the 21st Century

The following are first-hand accounts of some extraordinary present-day stories.

Nicha's Encounter with Jesus

I am aware that I have always had a problem with self-worth. For as long as I can remember, I didn't value myself. I felt I was my parents' daughter, my friends' friend, my husband's wife, my children's mother, and so on. As such, I wasn't important and therefore I have always spent my life trying to do my best to please other people, rather than being true to myself.

A few years ago, I was in hospital, in isolation with an acute type of leukaemia, and I had been given only a 20% chance of survival. In my enforced, isolated position, I had to face myself in my roots for the very first time. I had been given weeks to live and I knew if I didn't work very hard and very quickly to see why I found myself dying, it would soon be curtains for me. I was talking to a friend on the phone who mentioned that when Jesus addressed a crowd of people, he held his hands out to everyone, not just those that were 'worthy', and that was when my experience began…

As my soul accepted I was actually equal to everyone, my lack of self-worth started to ebb away. I experienced myself sitting on the floor, in the front row of a crowd of people, listening to Jesus talk. I saw him come and extend his hands out to me and help me to my feet. He took me in his arms and hugged me and said: 'Welcome home, my darling daughter.'

Then he turned to the crowd with his arm around my shoulders as if to show how pleased he was to have me back. I felt like the prodigal son. In that moment, I didn't recognise the girl as myself standing with him, although I knew that she was me, but I saw her standing upright and proud, and it felt like he'd given the girl the gift of self-worth. It was an amazing experience and one that will live with me forever.

A month or two later, I was in the bathroom and caught a glimpse of myself in the mirror and it was only then that I suddenly recognised the girl as myself—me with self-worth! That, too, was a very profound moment for me.

For a long time, I hardly mentioned my story to anyone as it felt like I was boasting because Jesus had singled me out from the crowd. It is only now, quite a while later, that I can see the bigger picture...

Yes, it was 'me' who, on that occasion, he had singled out, so why me? Well, firstly, I had been asking him for help! And it was me because I represented millions and millions of others who are also lacking in self-worth. It was me because I was dying and one of the many reasons I was dying was because of my lack of self-worth, which, in turn, meant that I wasn't able to live my life being totally true to myself. Having this amazing experience enabled me to see that, although *I* hadn't felt worthy, Jesus thought differently. Even though I had gone my own way and tried to live out of my own strength, as soon as I asked for help he welcomed me back with open arms and proudly showed everyone how pleased he was to see me again. And I know, for sure, that this was the first major step on my road to recovery.

Today, several years later, I am fit and well, with blood clean and clear enough for anyone to be proud of. That Jesus will forever be central to my life goes without saying...

Jodi's Remembered Story: An example of how revealing the past can heal the present

I was around 10 years old and I can remember being taken to the synagogue every Saturday. I thought this was just a playground where I could see my friends and didn't take any notice of what was being taught by the priests. One day, I found myself at the event that we now call the feeding of the 5000. As I watched what happened, I was amazed and started to open my eyes to this magical man called Jesus.

When I grew older, I used to stand on a box above the crowds and talk in public about how amazing Jesus was. One day, as I reached for my box, an inner voice told me I should stay at home. I ignored the 'inner voice', picked up the box and stepped outside in my usual way. That very day, I was arrested and put in a cold, dismal, white stone building that constituted the town jail. I felt utterly miserable, that I was a very bad person and I had let my family down. I had been singled out to be killed by the authorities who later surrounded me and stoned me to death. I hung my head in shame as the stones were hurled at me; some were hurled from the very father and mother I had chosen to come back to in this life. I had chosen them in order to remember what had happened in the past so I could forgive them, and to help me remember who I had been and what I had done.

In this life, here and now in the 21st century, I have carried deep fear and humiliation from this event and now I have at last been able to forgive the perpetrators of the past and release the emotions of terror, betrayal etc. I now feel so much better about myself and my life, for this memory has answered so many questions that I had stored away, and had rendered me unable to understand why I was the way I was.

Having forgiven all those who played a part in killing me, I can truly start walking my walk from a clear intuition on every occasion and not from the guilt, humiliation and shame that had been mine.

Today's Jesus, by Louisa

In the autumn of 2019, I asked the universe if I could walk the earth as Jesus would have done had he been born now. Little did I know at the time what a huge request this would turn out to be. Nor did I fully understand that I had carried the emotional impact of what he had experienced on the cross for the whole of this life. It had caused me to malfunction and held me prisoner since birth. As I slowly came to grips with this enormous fact, I was able to understand my life so much better and let the imbalance drift out and away from my body.

This is how my request played out. I was almost immediately started on a very difficult journey which caused me to let go of whatever shadows were left that I needed to release before walking the earth as a modern-day Jesus would have done. Various issues were coming up daily.

In January 2020, I was approaching the biggest issue I still had to resolve but I failed to completely understand what was being asked of me at the first attempt so my journey was put on hold for a recovery period. I did not know at this point that I had only released a quarter of the story. In April/May 2020, I was led through the remainder of the journey and it was one of the hardest things I have ever done. It caused me to have a breakdown of sorts; I had to be broken down in order for me to stop fighting it, and it was not fun.

I was at this time being hit broadside from every direction by someone I am very close to (I mention this from a different angle in Chapter 6). I was fine if I could see an accusation coming but when I didn't see it coming, which was happening increasingly often, I eventually became so fearful that, suddenly, a simple text out of the blue accusing me of something she believed I had done, which was completely untrue in my own eyes, started a process which caused me to become so unbalanced that I contemplated taking my life to greater or lesser degrees in the following few weeks. Eventually, I had the guts to tune into the fear that this friend brought up in me. I was taken back to the week before the crucifixion when Jesus was shocked that the crowds that had loved him one day had turned on him the next. He hadn't imagined such a thing could be possible. My close friend had been standing in the centre of the crowd in front of Pilate at that time, shouting, 'Crucify him! Crucify him!' What I was experiencing now through this person was a replay of that same experience. Understanding this was of great healing importance for both of us.

Then the universe caused me to re-experience hanging on the cross as Jesus had, once more. I felt the 'Why is this happening?' run through me again. It was the same 'Why is this happening?' that ran through all of us at the time of the Split. It suddenly dawned on me that I, as a member of the soul group of Jesus, had to *own* the emotions I was feeling as if the whole event was mine. It was only by owning it that the words 'Father, forgive them, for they know not what they do' could resonate through me with their full meaning. As I gave in to this, I found I was truly 'owning' my Split experience in a deeper way and the 'Why was this happening?' was able to leave me forever.

Following my breakdown, I was shown that, at the time of the crucifixion, most people got fixated on the suffering of Jesus on the cross. A lot of people became afraid that suffering was a prerequisite to becoming enlightened. Some then became power freaks in order to try to avoid such suffering. Later, many became part of the hierarchy within the Churches or other religious denominations, dressing themselves richly, holding power over the public in huge places of worship and dictating do's and don't's to the masses. This made them feel safer and they deluded themselves that they were on the 'path'. Others grasped the truth of what had happened and didn't run from it. But, sadly, they believed they needed to suffer to become enlightened because it was what they had witnessed, and they therefore attracted suffering in many different ways; many even ended up being crucified. The disciple Peter was a prime example.

I was then asked to release the false belief that we have to suffer, from the soul group of Jesus, and to replace it with the truth that it is only if it serves the highest good that we may have to suffer, but otherwise we can go about our business in joy, for it is joy we are seeking through the process of life. I then asked for any unnecessary suffering from now or in previous centuries to be removed from the incarnated and those in spirit in its own time. I felt an urge to ask for all the crucifixes in the world to let go of the suffering energy they emit, so that they could begin to represent joy and the hope that the crucifixion was always meant to bring. I asked forgiveness for all those who had 'hidden' in priests' clothing and caused so much suffering in others by doing so.

I came to know eventually that I had come through the biggest and last major experience when I heard the most surprising words one morning:

> You remember you asked to walk the earth as Jesus would have done today? Well, today you have become a portal for exactly that. There is a 50p piece size hole that runs from the ancient beings through you to the incarnate world that will last for the rest of your lifetime. Sometimes the hole will be bigger than at other times and the size will be measured by us, depending on what is needed at the time. Sometimes the light that comes through will be seen and turned away from. It will be too bright for the recipient. Sometimes the recipient will lap it up and want more and more. So it was with Jesus. And so it will be with you.

I was astonished. I did not know that all that I had been going through from January to May was linked to my request from the previous autumn. Suddenly, everything became clear for me and I understood why I had had to give up so much. Nothing but nothing can be taken through the eye of the needle, so when I made the request to walk the earth as a 21st century Jesus might do, it was a signal for the universe to strip me of the entire ego that was left. I was in shock for a long time. Not only had the stripping left me in a massive state of transition but the enormity of it was astounding. When we ask for things, we don't always realise the enormity of what we are asking. It seems so easy from the other side and so do-able. But I do know that these questions are only popped in our minds when we are ready—and I was clearly fully ready.

Not long after this, I had a vision of my body on the cross beginning to shrink until it eventually became a skeleton. I watched in awe as the skeleton slowly dropped off the cross and a modern, varnished, wooden cross stood in the place of the old one. It was completely empty, with no sign of a body or a crucifixion having taken place. I looked at the ground. The ashes of the skeleton were there but so intermingled with the ground that they were almost imperceptible. This could only mean one thing: I had at last let go of the majority of Jesus' pain with just a few tiny dregs (ashes) to be uncovered in due course.

Ever since this happened, I have been privileged to witness more and more people *fully own* their own Split experience. As they courageously face the truth and own their part in it, the negative energy is able to drop away and dissipate, leaving their body free and healed. The healing that takes place is forever and can never be undone.

Afterword

I have referred to many different soul groups in these writings, mainly as a form of identification to make things easier to understand. But, as my son once asked me, 'Aren't we all part of the same soul group?' I replied, 'Of course we are. We are all Source.'

However, the journeys we have all been on since last being unified have split us up into billions of different experiences, each of which have to be identified and healed, both in the collective and as individuals.

The soul group of Jesus was born from the golden lions, those lions that retained their connection to Source for longer than any other part of creation after the Split. Before the Split, there was no such soul group for there was no conscious individuality. The golden lions have been at the forefront of bringing light back to the planet ever since the great battle when they were wiped out of the incarnated state by the white lions. They have returned and returned, through Adam, Noah, Joseph and many other beings, until they finally succeeded through Jesus, at which time there was enormous celebration. This hierarchy of the watching Source energy, once fully healed on earth, has held firm since that day, growing slowly, getting a stronger foothold as the centuries have gone by.

That we will all become 'as' Jesus is inevitable over time, Jesus being the context in which we overcome the vulnerability of the Split, recognising the world outside of us as part of ourselves, rather than the enemy. As we let the divine in us come to the fore and allow the terrors to fall away, we shall at last experience heaven on earth.

***

Have you ever watched the films *Lion King 1* and *Lion King 2*? Our true lion story is told here in true Disney fashion, *Lion King 1* depicting the Split and *Lion King 2* depicting the healing of the Split. It's worth watching them again with your heart open to the beautiful messages that run all the way through them.

As Kiara professes right at the end of the second film, thus preventing further bloodshed:

> Daddy, this has to stop! A wise king once told me: We are One. I didn't understand him then. But now I do. Them! Us! Look at them. They *are* us. What differences do you see?

***

After the white lion, Deryk, attacked me, the golden lion, in this life and I almost died (see my book *From Chrysalis to Butterfly* for the full story), I spent many years recovering, forgiving and healing what Kiara had understood in her final message.

One day, I was doing housework and I had a strong pull to drive into town. It felt daft. I was halfway through cleaning the house! Why did I need to go now? I had very little shopping to do and I was busy. The pull to go was overwhelming.

I dropped the hoover right where it was and drove to town. I parked and walked along a little street towards the centre. Coming towards me, just as I crossed the road, was Deryk in his little blue car. Given that Deryk had moved house and now lived far away from me, this was quite extraordinary. He pulled his car up right beside me, not in the first instance realising I was there.

As we recognised each other, we were both startled to say the least. He wound down his window and asked how I was. I asked after him. I stood for a few minutes, chatting through his window and then I walked on.

It was with total amazement that I knew I had 100% healed. I had not experienced the slightest ripple of fear of him. Rather, I felt a complete love for him flow through me. Our battle was totally over. We were one.

A while later, I took him out for a meal and told him everything I knew. He understood it and he apologised, thus bringing the golden and white lion energy between us completely into harmony.

***

It's amazing just how many times white and golden lions partner up in this day and age. But the truth is, as Kiara intimates, we all know in our hearts that it is time for us to put our differences away and become as one.

Glossary

Dinosaur energy—the very first energy that experienced life on the surface of earth in the form of dinosaurs.

Lions—these animals represent souls which retained their Source connection at the Split.

Portal—an opening formed between inner and outer earth.

Second Coming—the energy that is returning to earth right now within many thousands of souls, that is ready to remember and heal its experience at the time of Jesus.

Soul group—a way to describe souls who have lived through the same experience (see page 114 for a fuller explanation).

Split—the moment that our experience on earth became individual as opposed to collective (see memoryreturned.com for an interview carried out by Gail Thackeray with Louisa which helps with the understanding of the Split).

Sun—the energy that entered the first set of planets after the Big Bang.

Swamped—the second experiment that took place after Sun failed to fully integrate.

'Watching' Source—energy that did not experience either the Sun experiment or the Swamped experiment but simply watched, took stock and learned what to do next.

Further Resources

Other Titles by the Author

Delves, A. (2008) *From Chrysalis to Butterfly*. London: AuthorHouse.

Delves, A. (2011) *A Memory Returned: Healing in its Deepest Form*. London: AuthorHouse.

Films Cited

Walt Disney (1994) *The Lion King* (D. Hahn, prod.). Los Angeles, CA: Walt Disney Pictures.

Walt Disney (1998) *The Lion King II: Simba's Pride* (J. Roussel, prod.). Los Angeles, CA: Walt Disney Pictures.

Useful Websites

See https://cotswoldhealingretreat.co.uk for further information about the author's healing retreats.

See https://auroragatherings.com if you are interested in getting involved with a local group in your area.

See https://memoryreturned.com for an interview carried out by Gail Thackeray with Louisa which helps with the understanding of the Split.

Books to challenge  *your perception of reality*

A message from Clairview

We are an independent publishing company with a focus on cutting-edge, non-fiction books. Our innovative list covers current affairs and politics, health, the arts, history, science and spirituality. But regardless of subject, our books have a common link: they all question conventional thinking, dogmas and received wisdom.

Despite being a small company, our list features some big names, such as Booker Prize winner Ben Okri, literary giant Gore Vidal, world leader Mikhail Gorbachev, modern artist Joseph Beuys and natural childbirth pioneer Michel Odent.

So, check out our full catalogue online at
www.clairviewbooks.com
and join our emailing list for news on new titles.

office@clairviewbooks.com

CLAIRVIEW